Women, Myth, and the
Feminine Principle

Women, Myth, and the Feminine Principle

Bettina L. Knapp

State University
of
New York Press

Published by
State University of New York Press

© 1998 State University of New York

Printed in the United States of America

For information, address the State University of New York Press,
State University Plaza, Albany, NY 12246

Production by Bernadine Dawes • Marketing by Nancy Farrell

Library of Congress Cataloging-in-Publication Data

Knapp, Bettina Liebowitz, 1926–
      Women, myth, and the feminine principle / Bettina L. Knapp.
         p.   cm.
      Includes bibliographical references and index.
      ISBN 0-7914-3527-X (hardcover : alk. paper). — ISBN 0-7914-3528-8
(pbk. : alk. paper).
      1. Women—Mythology. 2. Women and religion. 3. Women in
literature. I. Title.
   EL325.F4K54   1997
   291.1'3'082—dc21   97-26324
                                                                CIP

1 2 3 4 5 6 7 8 9 10

To my students,

from whom I have learned

so fruitfully,

at Hunter College and at

The Graduate Center of the

City University of New York

CONTENTS

ACKNOWLEDGMENTS

I would like to express my gratitude to the librarians at Hunter College—Norman Clarius and Suzanne Siegel. Their unstinting help in locating rare texts for me was invaluable.

INTRODUCTION

Like *Women in Myth,* the present volume focuses on the role played by the feminine principle in specific religious texts, epic poems, theater pieces, and tales narrating sacred events in which deities and supernatural or extraordinary beings move through their difficult celestial and earthly trajectories. Whereas the preceding volume dealt with ancient texts, the present one concentrates on myths that either sprang up independently or were reworked by writers during the common era. Both volumes follow the same format: each chapter is divided into two sections, the first comprising ectypal (or historical and social) overviews and the second consisting of archetypal analyses of the myth's psychological, philosophical, and metaphysical aspects.

My historical, archetypal, and hermeneutic approach to myths drawn from texts of various lands and centuries involves a *quest.* In that I am dealing for the most part with imponderables, the intellectual and sense-provoking journeys undertaken in my explications lead to other—frequently unknown—frontiers of the mind/sense complex. The excitement these trajectories may generate in the reader will, hopefully, become part of a learning experience.

Metaphors, symbols, and images of all kinds are crucial to the approaches in this book. The archetypal image as it appears in myths is considered "a living system of reactions and aptitudes that determine the individual's life in invisible ways." Archetypal images burgeon and breathe within what C. G. Jung termed the collective unconscious—the deepest strata of an individual's subliminal spheres (Jung 1969, par. 339). Arising spontaneously in certain kinds of writings—for our purposes, in myths—archetypal images may be seen "as autonomous elements of the unconscious psyche" (1959, par. 451). Jung adds that archetypes may be considered the fundamental elements "of the conscious mind, hidden in the depths of the psyche. . . . They are systems of readiness for action, and at the same time *images and emotions*. They are inherited with the brain structure—indeed they are its psychic aspects" (1964, par. 118; modified by Jacobi 1959, 38).

Jung further suggests that the archetype is

> an image in its own right . . . a *dynamism* which makes itself felt in the numinosity and fascinating power of the archetypal image. The realization and assimilation of instinct never take place . . . by absorption into the instinctual sphere, but only through integration of the image which signifies and at the same time evokes the instinct, although in a form quite different from the one we meet on the biological level. . . . It [instinct] has two aspects . . . it is experienced as a physiological dynamism, while on the other hand its multitudinous forms enter into consciousness as images and groups of images, where they develop numinous effects which offer, or appear to offer, the strictest possible contrast to instinct physiologically regarded. . . . Psychologically...the archetype as an image of instinct is a spiritual goal toward which the whole nature of man strives. (Jung 1969, paras. 414, 415)

In that the role of the female principle—or female consciousness—is emphasized in the myths under scrutiny in *Women, Myth, and the Feminine Principle*, the secrets divulged during the course of its reading will, it is hoped, broaden and enrich the reader's understanding as well as yield clues to the solution of the problems exposed. The aim of this book is to attempt to adapt myths to modern sensibility. Today's thinking persons may be encouraged to ponder—if need be to *reconsider*—their own frames of reference: ideations, religious beliefs, and pulsating emotions bound into their own lives.

Myths generally attempt to bring order to disorder, to render comprehensible that which is incomprehensible, or to regulate what lies beyond one's control. By their very richness and depth, they may be interpreted in as many ways as there individuals or societies that project upon them. In the words of the ethnologist Claude Lévi-Strauss:

> Apart from the fact that the science of myths is still in its infancy, so that its practitioners must consider themselves fortunate to obtain even a few tentative, preliminary results, we can already be certain that the ultimate state will never be attained, since were it theoretically possible, the fact still remains that there does not exist, nor ever will exist, any community or

group of communities whose mythology and ethnography ... can be known in their entirety. The ambition to achieve such knowledge is meaningless, since we are dealing with a perpetually shifting reality, perpetually exposed to the attacks of a past that destroys it and of a future that changes it. For every instance recorded in written form, there are obviously many others unknown to us; and we are only too pleased with the samples and scraps at our disposal. (Lévi-Strauss 1990, 3)

In my inquiry into the psyches, lifestyles, and ethos of the feminine protagonists constellating the myths explored in *Women, Myth, and the Feminine Principle*, I ask readers, as they had been invited to do in *Women in Myth*, to make *connections* between the texts under scrutiny and between the meanings derived from them. Both positive and negative reactions will certainly be aroused by the linking of connotations.

The meditations induced by specific chapters may not only lead some readers to discover new interests but may also shed a different light on their own lives and behavioral patterns. Others may feel destabilized by ideas that are incompatible with the social, religious, and political codes to which they adhere. New and unfamiliar postulations may irritate, disrupt, and raise doubts, or they may encourage a reshaping or rethinking of one's spiritual, intellectual, and emotional canons.

The world of myth holds enchantment and excitement in store for those who quest. Its allure has been described by the psychologist James Hillman:

Myths do not tell us how. They simply give the invisible background which starts us imagining, questioning, going deeper. The very act of questioning is a step away from practical life, deviating from its highroad of continuity, seeing it from another perspective. But—could this shift of perspective happen if there were not some other place, some other hidden ground to stand on, a mythical place that gives another vantage point, thereby placing us in two ontological positions at once, ourselves divided and yet conflict contained, ourselves already metaphors? As metaphors speak with inverted commas, giving a new double interiority, an echo, to a plain word, so when we begin to mythologize our plain lives they gain another dimension. We are more distanced because we are more richly involved. (Hillman 1975, 158)

Myths are generally believed to have been written by men, and perhaps that is the reason the portrayal and understanding of women in the mythical texts is sometimes rudimentary and distorted. "Gender is not a given. It is a culturally constructed notion" (Reis 1991, 26). Indeed, as Sylvia Brinton Perera has so aptly noted:

> The patriarchal ego of both men and women, to earn its instinct-disciplin-ing, striving, progressive, and heroic stance, has fled from the full-scale awe of the goddess. Or it has tried to slay her, or at least to dismember and thus depotentiate her. But it is towards her—and especially towards her cultur-ally repressed aspects, those chthonic and chaotic, ineluctable depths—that the new individuating, yin-yang balanced ego must return to find its ma-trix and the embodied and flexible strength to be active and vulnerable, to stand its own ground and still to be empathetically related to others. (Perera 1981, 7)

Women, Myth, and the Feminine Principle, like the first volume, has at-tempted to remain objective in its approach to questions of gender and sex in societies marked by deprecation, repression, and enslavement of women. But not only men must be considered responsible for the perpetuation of injustices toward women throughout the centuries. Mothers-in-law and fre-quently mothers themselves share culpability for the lot of their daughters or their sons' wives. Readers will be gratified to learn of the resourcefulness of some women who, thanks to their innate intelligence, sensitivity, insight, and willpower, were able to circumvent strictures and assert themselves be-yond expectations. Their unwillingness to sink into a morass of physical and spiritual subjugation inspired some to carve out a niche for themselves in the private and/or public domain. These women well understood that a great part of life is *striving*.

An archetypal analysis—or deconstruction—of the seven myths con-tained in *Women, Myth, and the Feminine Principle* may also serve to help contemporary women living in so-called advanced societies. Those who yearn to *see* may glean new insights and alternative directions for themselves by drawing upon and responding to the riches embedded in these myths. Many women seeking fulfillment in today's world try to juggle career, home, husband, and children in some tenable fashion, hoping to do justice to all of them. Others, although preferring to remain at home, are thrust into the workplace for financial reasons. The light shed by certain mythical protago-nists in their strivings to cope with unpleasant—and even pleasant—situa-tions may suggest to the reader ways of blending elements that seemingly are disparate and antithetical to one's set course in life.

Because "nature and culture" are forever intertwined, wrote the an-thropologist Edgar Morin, "human nature is the key to a culture and the key to our nature is in the culture." To familiarize oneself with different cultures, particularly when these concern women, serves to expand one's knowledge not only of the psyche but of the behavioral patterns of individuals and their interactions within the collective (Morin 1973, 19).

Dealing with the death/life experience—death being one aspect of life—is perhaps the single most important aspect of myth. The imminence of death frequently triggers dreams in both women and men, and because these dreams cannot be manipulated, they are considered "the voice within us." It is this voice that we hear and study in myths (Franz 1972, vii).

The notion of death may even be that crucial factor which gave impetus to the birth of religions. The Dalai Lama conveys his intuitions on the subject as follows:

> As a Buddhist, I view death as a normal process, a reality that I accept will occur as long as I remain in this earthly existence. Knowing that I cannot escape it, I see no point in worrying about it. I tend to think of death as being like changing your clothes when they are old and worn out, rather than as some final end. Yet death is unpredictable. We do not know when or how it will take place. So it is only sensible to take certain precautions before it actually happens. . . .
>
> The actual point of death is also when the most profound and beneficial inner experiences can come about. Through repeated acquaintance with the process of death in meditation, an accomplished meditator can use his or her actual death to gain great spiritual realization. This is why experienced practitioners engage in meditative practices as they pass away. An indication of their attainment is that often their bodies do not begin to decay until long after they are clinically dead. (Dalai Lama 1992, ix)

As metaphorically expressed in many myths, death is realized in the concept of rebirth and resurrection and in the parallel concept of maternity in its fertilizing aspect. Appellations such as Mother Earth, Mother Nature, and Motherland attest to this kind of alignment or analogy via the circular notion of perpetual creativity and demise. Similar connections may be drawn by means of visualizations as well. Water images, for example—oceans, lakes, ponds, and streams—are identified not only with the rich and nurturing female principle or consciousness but with the psyche: the personal and the collective unconscious, sometimes referred to as an inner ocean. Blendings or fusions of these factors frequently catalyze what has grown stagnant or arid within a personality, an ethos, or a creative work. A further example is offered by cave figurations, cavities in the earth, cellars, and underground regions, which have been equated with both uterine spheres and subliminal worlds. These dark and frequently humid places inspire fear in some, but are understood by others as reservoirs of untold fertility—passageways to unknown worlds.

Astounding discoveries about both outer space and the inner dimensions of the human brain and psyche increase today's scientific and spiritual complexities and add to the need for continuous modification of our concepts and theories. The awesome immensities of the Void, the Abyss, and the Infinite were intuited in Tibetan, Hindu, Guatemalan, Celtic, Germanic, Greek, and Kabbalistic myths, setting the stage for dialogue and the birth of inquiry. In Eliade's thoughtful words:

> Not to be excluded [in our time] is the attraction [people] feel for the activities of the Unconscious; for the interest aroused by myths and symbols; for the admiration of the exotic, the primitive, the archaic; for encounters with "Others"; with all the ambivalent feelings these imply. Not to be excluded as well, is the thought that one day all of this may be considered a new type of religiosity. (Eliade 1962, 15)

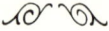

The choice of the specific myths explored in *Women, Myth, and the Feminine Principle* was purely subjective. The opening chapter concerning the "divine feminine" in Tibet's *Gesar of Ling* probes one of the most fascinating myths of all time, and perhaps one of the least known. Especially intriguing is the Tibetan hero Gesar's seemingly continuous dependency on the feminine principle for guidance. He experienced her in a variety of capacities: as an iconization of the Great Mother, known to Tibetans as Dölma, a symbol of compassion; as a *dakini*, a celestial inspirational force whose mission was to integrate the powers released into the psyche during meditation; as a *tulku*, the visualization of a "mental formation" or a manifestation of supreme reality in the form of an ordinary woman (or man) or a reincarnation of a dead master. The concretization of feminine figures answered a profound psychological need in Gesar, and by extension, in the Tibetan culture as well.

Chapter 2 deals with a Sanskrit drama, *Sakuntala* by Kalidasa, and centers on a myth embedded in a dramatic ritual. It focuses on a love sequence experienced first on an earthly plane and concluding in the supernal realm of blissful understanding and detachment. During the heroine Sakuntala's earthly trajectory, the obstacles set in her path are instrumental in her evolution from the stage of passive, unconscious, and withdrawn archetypal Maiden to that of the conscious, decisive, strong spiritual Mother—possessor of an adamantine essence. As catalyst for her own as well as her husband's psychological and spiritual evolution, she functions within the parameters of the ultrapatriarchal Hindu society of the time. Thus her progression from bondage to independence and functionality is that much more astounding.

Chapter 3 moves to Europe, to the Middle High German *Nibelungenlied*—exploring a poetic courtly mythical romance not to be confused with Wagner's version of the myth. Beyond the artistry in the depiction of Siegfried—the courageous and perhaps not so courageous hero—are the intriguing and highly complex personalities of the two heroines: Kriemhild and Brunhild. The former is Siegfried's beautiful wife; the latter, her brother Gunther's spouse. To explore the psyches of these two archetypal figures is to enter the realm of sun and shadow, the light regions of consciousness and the deep interiors of primal darkness.

Unlike Genesis in the Judeo-Christian tradition, which emphasizes the primacy of the male God, the Quiché Mayas' *Popol Vuh* presents a wholly different account of the inception of the world, as explicated in chapter 4. The *Popol Vuh* (Council book) introduces a primordial couple—"mother-father"—as active participants in the creation of humankind. Differing also from the biblical creation myth is the Quiché Mayas' belief that "divine women exist from the beginning, while human women, rather than being derived from men, are created separately, and they are never made to carry "the stigmas that God inflicts upon Eve" (Tedlock 1986, 80).

Racine's *Phaedra*, explored in chapter 5, was based on Euripides' *Hippolytus* and refashioned by the seventeenth-century French dramatist. Racine projected his own gnawing religious conflicts onto the mythical heroine. Questions of guilt, remorse, anguish, and fatality/predestination, as observed in such images as forests, the hunt, the labyrinth, the Minotaur, and an interplay of sun/shadow forces, are fleshed out in terms of the Phaedra/Racine complex.

Chapter 6 concentrates on Yeats's *Deirdre*, an Irish/Celtic feminist and heroine; it turns toward a period in Ireland's mythic past when life overflowed with fabulous and heroic happenings. By reactualizing for his audiences great historical, philosophical, religious, and psychological truths, Yeats succeeded in integrating bygone days into a present reality. As both a personal and impersonal or transcendental power, Deirdre has become one of Ireland's national heroines. Her inner strength and fortitude are so haunting, the poetry of her words so mesmerizing, her courage in the face of death so astounding, that she gives the impression of having stepped out of another sphere.

I. B. Singer's "Yentl the Yeshivah Boy," explored in chapter 7, is a dramatization of the events confronting a young girl from an orthodox Polish Jewish family as she attempts to break out of an ultrapatriarchal society toward the end of the nineteenth or in the early twentieth century. The struggle waged by Singer's protagonist, Yentl, reaches mythic proportions. Her peregrinations are all the more moving because of her need to remain *true* to her nature. Although she brings sorrow upon herself and those she loves in her desire to circumvent rigid spiritual and social conditions, the crux of the tale lies in her determination and perseverance in pursuing her quest.

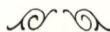

Great myths add to the luster and depth of visionaries' words and powerful works of literature; exploration of them will encourage us, as Jung wrote, "to dream the dream onwards and give it a modern dress" (Jung 1968, par. 271).

1 The Divine Feminine
in Tibet's *Gesar of Ling*

The mere mention of the "Land of the Snows," an appellation of Tibet, evokes a sense of mystery. The dramatic and indescribable beauty of the region, surrounded as it is by the Himalaya chain of mountains and glaciers, with its deep ravines and valleys, brilliant blue lakes, and desolate and solitary plains and grasslands, remains impressed in the psyches of those who have come to visit this region. Tibet's multiple colorations and ever altering hues, ranging from pale or somber blues to gray-blacks, light and shimmering lavenders, or emerald greens, depending upon the intensity of the rays cast by the sun and moon, add to its magic and luster.

Natural frontiers, high altitudes, and seemingly endless stretches of land account for Tibet's past and present isolation from the world. Even after China's invasion of the region in 1950 and the Dalai Lama's exodus in 1959, foreigners have gained little knowledge of Tibet's history, religious ideations, and written texts. Understandably it remains a land of wonderment and magic—a Shangri-la—for most people.

In contrast to other cultures, religious rather than profane literature predominates in Tibet. Fictional works, such as novels, were virtually unknown until recent times. Not that imagination had been suppressed. Quite to the contrary, writes Alexandra David-Neel, this faculty was allowed "the fullest possible scope, and the fantastic element flourishes in so exuberant and candid a fashion in their writings, that its equal is only to be found in our fairy tales" (David-Neel 1981, 13–14). What distinguishes Tibetan fantasy and wonderment from that of other lands is the manner in which events were and are depicted. In *Gesar of Ling*, for example, they "were held to have happened, the heroes of the tales to have really lived, and the stories themselves to be authentic from beginning to end" (2).

Like other myths, *Gesar of Ling* supplied an empirical need: had not a

1

solar hero sprung into action, ideological disaster would have struck many Tibetans. Not only had the "true Religion" of the time declined toward superstition, but rival groups from foreign lands as well as within Tibet itself attempted to downgrade its "purity." A strong leader, therefore, had to come into being to combat religious persecution and spiritual contamination. Motifs of Tibet's autochthonous and imported religions—Bön, Shamanism, Lamaism, and Buddhism—are, then, implicit in the epic's every word.

Even more distressing were the ever-present health problems among Tibetans due to all types of disease, including plagues. Gesar of Ling—defender of the "true religion," avenger of evil, ejector of foreign invaders, restorer of order and justice, transformer of arid into fertile lands—also came to be known as the annihilator of dreaded sicknesses. He accomplished his missions thanks to the help of a historical figure who, in time, was divinized: Padma Sambhava (755–97 C.E.), one of the founders of Tantric Buddhism.

Inherent in *Gesar of Ling* is the principle of warriorship: the realization of self-dignity through the exertion of power over oneself. So important was warriorship to the ancient Tibetans that continuous *wakefulness*, or *awareness* of one's thoughts, speech, and actions, was stressed, and difficult, frequently harrowing physical and psychological rites of passage were required. Thus could strength of mind and human potential—one's individual resources—be developed. The practitioner would be able to step beyond the terrestrial realm, overcoming fear of death. An acolyte was made to look fearlessly, directly, and openly *at* or *into* her- or himself. The very power it took to meet such a challenge could, under specific circumstances, liberate the person from the pain of samsara, the cycle of rebirths.

Gesar met the above requirements of warriorship. He faced problems with "unwavering wakefulness" and with profound understanding of their ramifications. He called upon feminine divinities and semidivinities to enlighten him in his ordeals. Always present when needed, the feminine principle appeared to him in a ray of light—as visitation or apparition—in dreams, or in daylight hours near trees, on mountains, in rooms, or elsewhere. He saw these manifestations, heard them, related to them through projection.

To project, psychologically, is to thrust or throw forward ideas or impulses that belong to some extent to the subject. It is a "process whereby an unconscious quality of one's own is perceived and reacted to in an outer object" (Edinger 1978, 147–50). Each time divine apparitions presented themselves to Gesar he was, in effect, drawing on his own sustenance, on his own reserves. The energy inhering in his being succeeded in motivating him to rectify an evil by overcoming whatever obstacles had been set in his path.

What is of extreme interest to us is Gesar's close relationship to the feminine principle and perhaps continuous dependency on her for guidance. He experienced her as an iconization of the Great Mother (known to Tibetans as Dölma and also referred to by her Hindu name, Tara), a symbol of compassion; as a *dakini*, a celestial inspirational force whose mission was to integrate the powers released into the psyche during meditation; and as a *tulku*, the visualization of a "mental formation" or a manifestation of supreme reality in the form of woman (or man) or as a reincarnation of a dead master. Generally the concretization of feminine figures answered a profound psychological need not only in the individual bringing them to mind but, by extension, in the culture as well (David-Neel 1931, 147).

Ectypal Analysis

The ancient Tibetans were nomads. Although some natives built houses and even cities to protect themselves from the treacherous icy snows and other climatic rigors of their wild highlands, most felt the urge to move on and set up their tents in new grazing ground. Animal sacrifices (sheep, dogs, monkeys) were offered yearly; and oblations (horses, oxen, asses, and even men) every three years. Because Tibetans could neither read nor write, they recorded important information by notching pieces of wood and by knotting cords. A written language and literature came into being only in the seventh century, with the introduction of Buddhism into Tibet.

Tibet was first mentioned in Chinese texts during the reign of Emperor Shun, in 2255 B.C.E. Herodotus, seemingly, was the earliest Western historian to write about this remote area of the world (Shen and Liu 1953, 3). Documents dating to the sixth century C.E. describe it as a conglomerate of independent feudal states in the process of centralization. Its ultracomplex autochthonous Bön religion underwent radical transformation due to the inroads of a form of Mahayana Buddhism known as Lamaism or Tibetan Buddhism.

The Bön Religion

Bön was an animist-shamanist religion related in many ways to that of Siberia; Inner Asia, Mongolia, Manchuria, East and West Turkestan, and China. Because of the lack of extant documents, few details concerning Bön are known with certainty.

The most important figure in Bön was the priest or shaman.[1] Looked upon as a sorcerer or a spiritual guide, the priest or shaman functioned as healer, psychiatrist, guide, and comforter. Having the power to communicate with deities, he could ask for their help on behalf of an individual or the people as a whole. His unusually powerful status in the community was gained in part through completion of a period of arduous initiation rituals, such as meditation, fasting, purification, the imbibing of specific alcoholic beverages and/or natural drugs, the ingestion of certain mushrooms, and dancing. During the course of his training, the shaman learned to enter into trance states, to communicate with spirits, and to attain superconscious levels and transcendence of terrestrial spheres. Unlike ordinary mortals, who made contact with heavenly beings through prayer, incantation, and offerings, the shaman was endowed with magico-religious powers enabling him to levitate or to "fly," as such a condition is termed, in order to reach the "Plain of High Heaven."

Because it was believed that an elemental force existed in all objects, the shaman, whose knowledge of magic was profound, had been granted a very special power: that of subduing and dominating whatever forces he considered detrimental to him and his people. To prevent disasters, for example, he not only pronounced conjurations and incantations, but by entering into a trance state, he gave credence to the notion that he was possessed by his tutelary deity. Dreams, visitations, apparitions, and hallucinations were therefore frequent experiences for shamans (and for individual meditators as well). Since the prognostications emerging into the shaman's consciousness were considered to be "signs" sent by his deity, life was made difficult for shamans who failed to alleviate the suffering of the people.

Little difference existed between Bön priests and shamans in ancient times. Both, for example, availed themselves of the drum in the performance of their religious rituals. Drums were looked upon as vehicles able to convey shamans through the air, and "flying" in this way allowed them to communicate with the gods (Eliade 1972, 632ff.).

The practice of animal and human sacrifice during the highly solemn Bön's ceremonies was designed to placate ever-present evil powers. If a prince fell ill, it was not infrequent for one of his subjects to offer himself as a sacrifice to assuage the demon that was believed to have caused the illness:

> The soothsayer seized the man by the feet whilst the Bön-Po took his hands. The black Handha then cut open the life orifice and tore out the heart. The two, the soothsayer and the Bon-po, then scattered the blood

and flesh of the victim to the four corners of the heaven. (Hoffmann 1961, 22)

After Buddhism gained ground in Tibet, such violation of life, human or animal, was strictly forbidden. Nevertheless, even today, the practice is carried on, albeit in mitigated form by substituting animals in the form of drawings or carvings as sacrifice to the deity (22).

The terrors and joys preoccupying Tibetans were personified in their gods, *dakinis*, *tulkus*, and demons. As is implicit in other religions, the worshipper intent upon appeasing a god or an evil power evoked the deity or demon in the hope of winning his or her favor.

Three spheres existed in the Bön cosmos, each of which plays a part in *Gesar of Ling*. Heaven was inhabited by the deeply revered King of Heaven, who was surrounded by supernatural spirits and gods, and by the White Goddess of Heaven (gNam-lha dkarmo) who lived near Mount Everest together with the five Sisters of Long Life, each having her own different-colored pool (18ff.).

The other two spheres were air and earth, the latter sometimes referred to as the underworld. Each sphere had its own inhabitants. Residents of the lower domain, in rivers, lakes, and wells, the kLu are reminiscent of Westerners' water sprites. Because they could transform themselves into serpents, they were said to be guardians of secret treasures and were identified with the Indian Nagas. The gNyan, who populated trees, rocks, valleys, and mountains, were believed to be related to mountain gods. Easily disturbed by humans, the gNyan set upon them plagues, disease, and death. The Sabdag, or Masters of the Earth, lived aboveground. The fearful Sri, who resembled vampires, lusted after small children (17ff.).

> The kLu kings are in all streams,
> The gNyan kings are in trees and stones,
> The Masters of the Earth are in the five kinds of earth:
> There, it is said, are the Masters of the Earth,
>   the kLu and the gNyan.

> What kind of company is theirs?
> Scorpions with long stings,
> Ants with notched waists,
> Golden frogs,
> Turquoise-coloured tadpoles,

Mussel-white butterflies,

These are their company.

(Hoffmann 1961, 18)

The Bön Creation Myth

From the void was born a remarkable egg, which after five months burst open, yielding space, heat, fire, oceans, and mountains. There emerged, in the form of a snake or dragon, a man or woman (depending upon the text) who was declared to be the ancestor of the Tibetan race. In other documents, whose authors were apparently influenced by Buddhism, the claim was made that the Tibetans were the offspring of a monkey and a mountain ogress. The monkey, a disciple of Avalokiteshvara (the Compassionate: a principal bodhisattva of the Mahayana Buddhists and Tibet's patron deity), was sent to the Land of Snows to meditate. No sooner had he arrived at his destination than a mountain ogress, in the guise of a gorgeous woman, sought to couple with him. Determined in his spiritual mission, he resisted her temptations until she threatened to copulate with a demon and populate the land with nefarious creatures. Returning to his master for counsel, the monkey was advised to marry the mountain ogress. The six children they bore multiplied so rapidly that they soon faced starvation. Again the monkey returned to Avalokiteshvara for advice. Pitying these "victims of desire," the master picked five kinds of grain growing on Mount Sumeru and had them sown in a field, where they took root and grew. When the apes ate the grain, their tails became smaller, their body hair vanished, and they grew shorter. It was believed they inherited their virtues from their father and their vices from their mother (Shen and Liu 1953, 19).

Other versions of the creation myth exist: one, dating from the fourteenth century, tells of an unnamed Indian prince who, disguised as a woman, had fled his homeland during the great war between the Kauravas and Pandavas (described in the *Mahabharata*). Twelve herdsmen (evidently offspring of the original monkey population), standing in a circle, saw him descend the sacred mountain (Yar-lha-sham-po). Upon asking him whence he came, and misunderstanding his answer, they concluded that he had descended from the top of the sky by means of a sky cord (Shen and Liu 1953, 20).

The sky cord, in keeping with rope symbolism, is an *axis mundi*, a miraculous stairway enabling not only humankind to communicate with heavenly spheres but gods to descend and ascend from celestial to earthly domains.

From mid-sky seven stages high,
Heavenly sphere, azure blue,
Came our king, lord of men,
Son divine, to Tibet.
Land so high, made so pure,
Without equal, without peer,
Land indeed! Best of all!
Religion too surpassing all!
                    (Snellgrove and Richardson 1968, 23)

Having decided that the unnamed Indian prince should be proclaimed king of their land, they named him Nya-Khri bTsan-Po (Neck-Enthroned Mighty One) and carried him down the mountain on their shoulders in a palanquin (Shen and Liu 1953, 19).

He came as lord of all under heaven.
This centre of heaven,
This core of the earth,
This heart of the world,

Fenced round by snow,
The headland of all rivers,
Where the mountains are high and the land is pure.
                    (Snellgrove and Richardson 1968, 24)

Although texts vary, scholars apparently agree that twenty-seven kings reigned after Nya-Khri bTsan-Po. The title bTsan-po (Mighty One) was awarded to most future kings of Tibet, thus endowing their persons with sacrality and lending a mystical cast to their rule. After the kings' earthly sojourn, they ascended to heaven by means of the sky rope, indicating in so doing a "recollection" of, and a need to recapture, a "lost paradise." Following their departure, no trace of their physical being was left on earth. Understandably Bön priests considered the heavenly rope to be the "rope of divination," identifying it with the shaman's "soul-guiding" power (Eliade 1972, 431).

The physical ascent of kings to heaven ceased after the reign of Grigum (Slain by Pollution). Arrogant, argumentative, and vicious, he sought to challenge all those around him to a fight. According to one text, his master of the horse, Longam, after much cajoling, finally agreed to Grigum's demand to fight, if he, in turn, would give up his magical weapons. When the contenders met, Longam indulged in subterfuge and killed the monarch, but not before the latter cut the ladder, thus making a return to heaven impossible (Snellgrove and Richardson 1968, 25).[2] Because he was the first king to leave his body on earth, so the legend goes, people henceforth not only buried their monarchs' mortal remains in royal tombs but began to concern themselves with earthly matters (Hoffmann 1961, 19, 20).

The Advent of Buddhism in Tibet

Because Buddhism, founded by Siddhartha Gautama (566–483 B.C.E.), is so complex a religion, we can, unfortunately, only get a glimpse of its extraordinary spiritual message. Tibetans uphold that in the Buddhist doctrine happiness and salvation result from inwardness, and are not dependent upon transitory exterior phenomena; life on earth is the product of imperfection and sorrow; the annihilation of desire leads to salvation and "perpetual enlightenment" (nirvana).

Although a group of monks allegedly brought some Buddhist texts from India to Tibet in the fifth century, these remained unknown to the mostly illiterate nomadic population. Only under the reign of the powerful conqueror Srong-btsan sgam-po (609–50) did Buddhism become a significant force in Tibet. Of his five wives, two played a significant role in the spread of Buddhism in that country: Wen-ch'eng, a T'ang princess from the Chinese imperial house, and Bhrikuti, the daughter of the king of Nepal. Both fervent Buddhists, they converted the Tibetan king to their faith. By the eleventh century, they were deified, worshipped as two forms or incarnations of Supreme Wisdom (Prajnaparamita), honored by metaphysicians and ascetics under the Tibetan name of Dölma and known more popularly by the Indian name Tara (Savioress or Goddess of Mercy), Tibet's protective divinity. Bhrikuti was identified as the Green Dölma; Princess Wen-ch'eng, as the White Dölma (Davy 1972, 4).

The amalgamation of Buddhism and Tibet's shamanist-animist Bön produced a unique religion: Lamaism, so named for its lamas (superior ones). The lama (equivalent to the Indian guru) enjoyed such importance that certain exceptional spiritual values were attributed to him: as a moral authority, he became the director of monasteries and performed rituals. But he was also endowed with the qualities of the *tulku* (a person who, after undergoing specific tests, was considered to be the reincarnation of a god or a dead master). Some Tibetans believed a lama to be the incarnation of a bodhisattva, a person hoping to attain Buddhahood but refraining from entering nirvana until all humans have been saved. Because the lama was considered the defender of the faith and protector of his people against ever-present evil powers, through the ritual of the "dance of the lamas" and the recitation of the *Bardo Thödol* (The Tibetan book of the dead), he could effect a diminution of noxious forces.

The fundamentals of Tibetan Buddhism were established by the Indian sage Padma Sambhava during the reign of Khri-srong Ide-btsan in the eighth century. The rising power of Buddhism and the alliance of the kings of Tibet with the new faith threatened the privileges of the old Bön aristocracy, understandably provoking their resentment. Indeed, the king was using Buddhism to affirm his political power, as the Bön priests had in former times to strengthen theirs. Although the Buddhist/Bön struggle was intense and did not preclude bloodshed, it nevertheless had its positive sides: Tibetan religion and culture were further enriched by the construction of the first monastery, the bSamyas, completed in 787. It was laid out according to Buddhist cosmography (Hoffmann 1961, 47).

Padma Sambhava—as his name, the Lotus Born, indicates—was not the offspring of earthly parents, but was born miraculously, out of the heart of a lotus in the middle of a lake. An Indian Tantric and cofounder of Lamaism, Padma is also known as Guru Rinpoche (the Precious Teacher). After having been summoned to Tibet in 747, his reputation grew as a wise and deeply committed man, but also as a sorcerer and exorcist. Having been initiated into the secrets of Tantric necromancy by some *dakinis*, his ability to destroy demonic forces was believed to be overwhelming.

Miracles or feats of magic, such as transforming barren into fertile land by diverting rivers and conjuring waterways, dematerializing rocks and other hard matter, and restoring life to the dead, were attributed to Guru Padma. One ceremony, called the *rolang* rite (rite of the rising corpse) is described as follows:

> The celebrant is shut up alone with a corpse in a dark room. To animate the body, he lies on it, mouth to mouth, and while holding it in his arms, he must continually repeat mentally the same magic formula, excluding all other thoughts.
>
> After a certain time the corpse begins to move. It stands up and tries to escape; the sorcerer, firmly clinging to it, prevents it from freeing itself. Now the body struggles more fiercely. It leaps and bounds to extraordinary heights, dragging with it the man who must hold on, keeping his lips

upon the mouth of the monster, and continue mentally repeating the magic words.

At last the tongue of the corpse protrudes from its mouth. The critical moment has arrived. The sorcerer seizes the tongue with his teeth and bites it off. The corpse at once collapses. . . .

The tongue carefully dried becomes a powerful magic weapon which is treasured. (David-Neel 1931, 135)

A student of cosmology, "triple yoga," levitation, philosophy, logic, and secret sciences, Guru Padma was awarded the immortal "Vajra" body. Let us note in this connection that within Buddhism there existed such divisions as Hinayana (the Lesser Vehicle) and Mahayana (the Greater Vehicle). The former and more ancient emphasized individual redemption; the latter preached salvation for all. About the eleventh century, Mahayana Buddhism branched out to emphasize a doctrine answering the Tibetans' fundamental need for magic: Vajrayana (the Vehicle of the Thunderbolt). Although constituted around the guru (master) and his disciple(s), Vajrayana stressed the importance of Tantra ("threads woven on a loom," or scriptures), of mantra (repetition of the mystical syllables or phrases *Om mani padme hum:* "Ah! The jewel is indeed in the lotus!"), and of mudra (symbolic signs, gestures).

The Vehicle of the Thunderbolt, esoteric in essence, amalgamated in its corpus yoga, animism, the symbolic power of light, and the cult of sexuality. It also stressed the importance of the feminine element, namely, the power of the wives, helpers, and/or disciples of the Buddhas and bodhisattvas. For the Vajrayana Buddhist, a knowledge of the *Prajnaparamita* (the sutra of "Perfection of Wisdom") was essential. In time, this concept was personified and transformed into the Goddess Prajnaparamita, and worshiped in the shape of an icon. She is depicted as follows:

Perfect Wisdom spreads her radiance, . . . and is worthy of worship. Spotless, the whole world cannot stain her. . . . In her we may find refuge; her works are most excellent; she brings us to safety under sheltering wings of enlightenment. She brings light to the blind, that all fears and calamities may be dispelled, . . . and she scatters the gloom and darkness of delusion. She leads those who have gone astray to the right path. She is omniscience; without beginning or end is Perfect Wisdom, who has Emptiness as her characteristic mark; she is the mother of the Bodhisattvas. . . . She cannot be struck down, the protector of the unprotected, . . . the Perfect Wisdom of the Buddhas, she turns the Wheel of the Law. (De Bary 1958a, 180)

The Great Mother in Tantrism

Tibetan Tantrism is fourfold: the Tantra of action, the Tantra of practice, Yoga Tantra, and supreme Yoga Tantra. The progression from a lower to a higher mystical state depends on the adept's evolution or knowledge of a previously hidden teaching: the understanding, for example, of the vacuity of all things experienced as illumination. During the training period, when the practitioner's most terrifying and violent sides are unleashed, he must become cognizant of the pulsations or energies inherent in his physical, sexual, and passional nature. Replications of one's darker, or shadowy latent, or hidden character traits, these frequently negative forces not only must be dominated and channeled but must be transformed into positive powers or systems. To attain the Vajrayana state in Tantrism is fraught with obstacles, since it requires the actual transformation of evil characteristics or life courses into good ones (Davy 1972, 30ff.).

Shocking to many a Westerner is the fact that divine feminine beings or forms iconographically or metaphorically in sexual union are frequently conveyed to Tantric meditators. What the Westerner fails to understand is the fact that these feminine beings are personifications of feminine aspects of Buddha's own energy: his maleness is *upaya* (skillfulness), while his femaleness is *prajna*, (wisdom and knowledge in a static and passive state). Each personification, in his (active) or her (passive) way during sexual union, is, in fact, engaged in transmitting the Buddha's teaching (36; Hoffmann 1961, 124).[3] Although demarcations between male and female are implicit in the empirical domain, male and female are considered fused—as one—in transpersonal spheres. Not sexual experience alone, however, can lead to unity: the act must be performed within an esoteric framework. For the Tibetan, the coupling of the Buddha's dual aspects on earth—as Divine Father and Divine Mother—is looked upon as the highest form of mudra: the hand gesture and/or position representing the nondualist concept of Oneness. To consider the posture of sexual union as obscene is to misconstrue the teachings of Tantrism.

Tibetans venerate the Great Mother (Shakti Sa-trig er-sangs), not as "subordinate to the life circle of development," but as participant in the sacred Tetrad (Hoffmann 1961, 102). In the incantation formula of the *gZermyig*, a polemical lamaist text, "the trinity is extended by the addition of the Shakti Sa-trig er-sangs," who is depicted as follows:

Therefore first veneration for our great Mother!
The Mother of space Sa-trig er-sangs
Is like in colour to essence of gold.
Her finery, her clothing, her Heavenly Palace
Is golden and beautiful through golden light.
In her right hand she holds the heroic letters of the "Five
    Seeds,"
In her left hand she holds the Mirror of Shining Gold
She sits on the throne of two strong lions, who shine like
    jewels.
Through blessings she effects the well-being of creatures.
Veneration to the great Sa-trig er-sangs!
                                        (Hoffmann 1961, 102)

Because an individual or a material object "is regarded as the accumulation of its parts and has no self-essence or soul," it is "void of self or ego." Because of its essential emptiness or voidness, it is considered "the primary matrix of existence" and is referred to as the "Mother of Creation." In that primordial space penetrates all matter "and undermines the ego and voidness," it is also considered an aspect of perceived space. "The principle of the Great Mother, is then, the space which gives birth to the phenomenal world. The permeating space and boundary, the fundamental form, is the Great Mother or the source of *dharmas*," of righteousness (Majupuria 1990, 26).

The Great Mother is referred to as the womb, the "cosmic cervix," or the "gate of all births"—that is, the primordial feminine of all creation. Trungpa Rinpoche depicted her as follows:

In the phenomenal experience, whether pleasure or pain, birth or death, sanity or insanity, good or bad, it is necessary to have a basic ground known in Buddhist literature as the mother principle. Prajnaparamita (the perfection of wisdom) is called the mother-consort of all the Buddhas. . . . As a principle of cosmic structure, the all-accommodating basic ground is neither male nor female. One might call it hermaphroditic but due to its quality of fertility or potentiality, it is regarded as feminine. (Majupuria 1990, 25)

Iconographically, she is depicted as a downward-pointing triangle, symbolizing the "outgrowing and reappearing quality of wisdom" (25). Within this divine feminine force exist the potentials for love and compassion, as well as for rage and destruction.

With the advent of Tantrism in Tibet, a whole erotic side of religion became manifest, which interrelated and diminished the distance between earthly and celestial worlds, and permitted access to Illumination. A fusion of the sacred and profane could be achieved through the love/sexual experience—earthly intercourse being a replication of a similar act between divine pairs.

Dölma/Tara

Dölma/Tara, who was born from the tears of the bodhisattva Avalokiteshvara, was protector against natural catastrophes and grantor of fertility. Manifested in twenty-one different forms, Dölma assisted her male counterpart, Avalokiteshvara, in his work. Iconographically, each of Dölma's manifestations may be distinguished in terms of color, posture, and attributes. She expressed anger, for example, by displaying her terrifying, destructive side as Queen of the World (Srid-pa'i rgyal-mo), endowed with three eyes and six arms (Hoffmann 1961, 104).

A root mantra for Dölma's worship—"the twenty-one verses in praise of [Dölma] Tara"—consisted of Lord Buddha's words to Manjushri, the immortal bodhisattva of wisdom:

> O Manjushri, this female form (Dölma) symbolises the source of Buddhas of the three times. Therefore, O Manjushri, as all Buddhas of the past, present and future sing this praise of hers, you also should do so in your mind." (Majupuria 1990, 21)

Excerpts from manuals devoted to Dölma worship read as follows:

> If we worship this sublime and pure-souled goddess when we retire in the dusk and arise in the morning, then all our fears and worldly anxieties will disappear and our sins [be] forgiven. She the conqueror of myriad hosts will strengthen us. She will do more than this! She will convey us directly to the end of our transmigration—to Buddha and Nirvana!
> She will expel the direst poisons, and relieve us from all anxieties as to food and drink, and all our wants will be satisfied; and all devils and plagues and poisons will be annihilated utterly; and the burden of all animals will be lightened! If you chant her hymn two or three or six or seven times, your desire for a son will be realized! Or should you wish wealth, you will obtain it, and all other wishes will be gratified, and every sort of demon will be wholly overcome. (Waddell 1967, 435)

The Bengali teacher Atisha ("The Nobleman," 980/990–1055), consulted Dölma, his tutelary deity, as to the wisdom of embarking on a long and perilous journey to Tibet. Although she warned him that his life span would be diminished, his trip, she added, would benefit humanity. Upon his arrival in the Land of the Snows, he was received with supreme honor by King Od-Ide, after which he began his missionary work. As evidenced from his writings entitled *Lamp for the Way of Enlightenment*, he preached the most spiritual and inspirational form of Mahayana Buddhism (Majupuria 1990, 23; Hoffmann 1961, 121).

Dakini or Khadroma

A *dakini*—a being that takes on consistency in the supreme sphere of reality when invoked by an individual or a group—is called a *khadroma* in Tibetan. *Kha* represents celestial space, the void becoming image; *dro* is associated with walking or displacing oneself; and *ma* with the feminine gender. The concept of the *dakini* originated in the mystic land of Orgyen, the birthplace of Padma Sambhava and of Tantric credos.

In *Gesar of Ling*, the *dakini* represents a personal divinity whose mental and behavioral character traits correspond to those of the adept invoking her. Her manifestation—the visualizations formed by the inner eye of the meditator—can be beautiful or horrific, taking on peaceful or belligerent characteristics. As an aspect of the personality of the individual calling her into existence, she becomes a means of transforming a negative into a positive condition.

As emanations of the Great Mother's energetic powers, *dakinis* not only are endowed with expertise in magic, but are the purveyors of mystic doctrines to earthly worshipers. For practitioners of Tantra, specific disciplines (for example, rituals involving nerves, breath, or essence) are able to conjure the dynamic feminine power sought for at the moment. If an adept understands the symbolism of a certain *dakini* (in terms of color, form, objects carried by her) and identifies with her, the energy inherent in the visualization may not only be channeled along definite paths and used for specific purposes but may also be directed to perceiving that which exists within matter. Thus, hidden treasures such as sacred texts or esoteric Tantric signs and codes may be revealed. It is believed that Padma Sambhava discovered crucial secret writings in unknown languages and succeeded in deciphering these thanks to the mystical inspiration of *dakinis* (Majupuria 1990, 37). Similarly, our hero, Gesar, will make discoveries of concealed treasures.

Tibetan rulers, wise men, and mystics have since time immemorial consulted *dakinis*—these natural apparitional beings—to gain greater understanding of magical arts, rituals, and eroticized positions. Apparitions of such *dakinis* or tutelary deities are psychological realizations, as previously mentioned, of the person evoking them (Evans-Wentz 1960, 122). The visualization of the deity is a means of thinking about or calling into being qualities for which the worshiper yearns. Thus she is not only instrumental in helping to find solutions but may also lead the meditator to eventual enlightenment.

In some meditations, the practitioner has been known to advance to such a profound state of consciousness or awareness that he reaches beyond the world of appearances into the domain of metaforms. Certain mystics, so it has been recorded, have observed their own bodies divested of flesh and contemplated their own skeletons. The *dakini* may ask the meditator to think of his body as a corpse and his mind as a manifestation of her angry side. In one sacred text, her hands hold a knife and a skull: "Think that she severeth the head from the corpse . . . and cutteth the corpse into bits and flingeth them inside the skull as offerings to the deities" (Eliade 1972, 436).

In another text, the yogin sees himself as "a radiant white skeleton of enormous size, whence issueth flames, so great that they fill the voidness, the Universe" (436).

In a third document, the yogin is asked to look upon himself as follows:

> Visualize thyself as . . . that thou . . . spreadest it [the skin] out so that it covereth the Third-Void Universe, and upon it heapest up all thy bones and flesh. Then, when the malignant spirits are in the midst of enjoying the feast, imagine that the Wrathful *Dakini* taketh the hide and rolleth it up . . . and dasheth it down forcibly, reducing it and all its contents to a mass of bony and fleshy pulp, upon which many mentally-produced wild beasts feed. (437)

The sharp side of the blade in the cutting up of the corpse in the first quotation represents the yogin's ability to cut through matter; its crescent contour is associated with the moon and its monthly course; its hooked shape implies the instrument's ability "to pull living beings out of the cycles of transmigration." Thus are attempts made to transform humankind's ego-centered vision into cosmic consciousness, the above paradigms (skeleton, a severed head, and a hooked knife) symbolizing potential and enlightened masculine energy that the yogin projects onto the *dakini* (Majupuria 1990, 34).

The feminine principle in the form of Dölmas, *dakinis*, and *tulkus* intervenes in *Gesar of Ling*. As positive forces, these beings contribute to the success of the Tibetan hero. As negative powers, their function is to destroy those who would impede humankind's evolution. Each time a feminine power appears to Gesar in a dream, an apparition, and/or a visitation, she takes on the role of a guiding force, opening up his intuitive faculties to greater insights.

Archetypal Analysis

Only incomplete fragments of *Gesar of Ling* are extant. Some of these cycles, sung by bards in the Kahm country in eastern Tibet, Gesar's native land, or in Lhasa, Mongolia, Turkestan, or western China, date back to the eighth and ninth centuries. For purposes of our discussion, reference is made exclusively to Alexandra David-Neel's version of *Gesar of Ling*.[4]

Archetypal Mother/Ancestress/Catalyst

Appearing first as a personal mother, the ancestress or catalyst of *Gesar of Ling* later takes on collective or divine dimension in order to play her determining role as archetypal Mother. While the personal mother has only limited import, etiologically speaking, the collective (Divine Mother) is of crucial significance in our epic.[5] Of such magnitude was her role that she would activate her daughter and grandsons to follow an evil course, subsequently transformed into a good one, which would invest her with both authority and numinosity (Jung 1968, par. 83).

As a personal mother, the ancestress spent her waking hours tending her herd of cattle on a mountainside. One day, she suddenly saw "a supernal light shine at the spot where the Bodhisattva [had once] lived at the foot of a tree." Immediately she sensed the presence of this saintly man who had practiced austerities continuously during his earthly trajectory. So deeply did she regret not having learned from him the Doctrine—the "Wheel of the Law"[6]—that she decided there and then, despite her advanced age, to go to India to listen to the preachings of him who was reborn as a Buddha (*Gesar*, 49).

The "light" that elicited a powerful mystical experience in the mother, interpreted psychologically as a projection, may at first appear antinomic in character. As a projection, however, the saintly man emerged from her own, long-dark subliminal spheres, and finally sought manifestation. The vision of

light may be understood as an unconscious attempt on her part to differentiate what may be termed an archaic and/or unredeemed mass within her—
that is, she needed to experience the Bodhisattva's saintly qualities cognitively.
This kind of transference suggests that the dark or unknown areas in the
psyche seeking expulsion were instrumental in paving the way for her illumination. Aren't metaphysical assertions dependent upon an individual's and
a collective's levels of consciousness? (Jung 1963, par. 833).

The personal mother in *Gesar of Ling* had been living in darkness until
she suddenly saw *the* light shining at the foot of a tree. Why did she instinctively heed the message she had intuited? Trees not only were considered
ascensional symbols, taking shamans skyward on a celestial journey, but they
also possessed holy aspects in and of themselves. Their roots reaching deep
into the earth and their branches high above it served to link terrestrial to
heavenly spheres. Such communion between high and low gave Tibetans
fluid access to heretofore inaccessible polarities. The tree came to symbolize
a living and regenerating cosmos—death and rebirth.

By gaining enlightenment, the woman would die in her role of personal
mother. The supernal light had become visible to her in response to her
deep-seated need for sacrality. The birth of the archetypal Mother not only
necessitated the shedding of her previous state; it would be the prelude to
her cosmic experience.

Upon returning home with her flock, the personal mother apprised her
daughter of her visitation and also informed her of her plans for both mother
and daughter to travel to India. So completely had she been swept up in the
dazzling light of her vision that all cognition had been blocked out. That her
daughter might be unwilling to give up her comforts and material possessions—her herd, headdresses, amber beads, and necklaces—and refuse to
endure the cold and starvation such a journey entailed never crossed the
mother's mind. Much to her chagrin, the daughter did reject the idea of
visiting sacred places and performing ascetic rituals in order to earn a possible
future beatitude. Only here and now counted.

After intoning her mantra—*Om mani padme hum!* and "May I be reborn
in Nub Dewachen!" (the Western Paradise of Great Bliss)—the aged mother
left home alone to face her rite of passage. Suffering incredible difficulties,
including intense cold, near drownings, and grave loneliness, she arrived in
India years later. Her physical and spiritual travail, instrumental in the successful
completion of her journey, had taken her from a condition of darkness or
ignorance to one of illumination. The archetypal Mother was in the process
of being born: she had "advanced to the entrance of the Path" (*Gesar*, 51).

As she listened to the preachings of the Buddha and heeded his principles of deep meditation and strict mind control, there appeared before her "the first ray of sunlight," as a trail of brilliant white light. Her spirit, unveiling "the red Amitab[h]a [Infinite Light] seated on his throne in the Western Paradise, surrounded by a thousand and twenty-two Buddhas," had begun its ascent. This was the moment when the mother's spirit escaped from its body and attained beatitude (52).

Even while the archetypal Mother successfully completed her rite of passage, her daughter was faced with adversity: her three sons died, disease killed her herd, and her material possessions were stolen. The daughter, ascribing these calamities to Buddha's desire for retribution because she refused to go to India, vowed to fight the master and his Doctrine (53).

Guru Padma Sambhava, having heard the daughter's oath from on high, had intervened unsuccessfully on her behalf. The spirits of the woman after her demise, and those of her dead sons were ordered to wander in *bardo* (limbo, between death and rebirth), after which they were to be reborn as demoniacal beings bent upon destroying the "true Religion" (55).

In his wisdom, Guru Padma knew that only *one* hero was capable of annihilating the evildoers. Calling a meeting of the gods, extraterrestrial beings, and magician-sages, he asked them to single out by divinatory means *(mo)* the one capable of destroying the demons. Thubpa Gawa, the son of two lama deities, was designated, but he resisted the challenge of earthly incarnation, preferring to remain in his blissful abode (56). Even after Guru Padma finally persuaded him of the importance of upholding "the true Doctrine," Thubpa Gawa, displaying a mind of his own, posed eighteen demands, including:

1. That the father of Thubpa Gawa's earthly incarnation be a God, and his mother a Nagi (in Tibetan, a *lu* or *klu*: a demi-goddess inhabiting the ocean, lakes, streams).
2. That he must be given a winged horse (Tulku) able to under stand the language of humans and animals; a saddle studded with gems, a helmet, cuirass, sword, and bow and arrow, none of which must have been made by human hands.
3. That two companions (heroes) be made available to aid him.
4. That he must be awarded the most beautiful wife. She must know how to inflame men's passions, and thus "incite" them to fight for her.

5. He also asked that some Gods and Dakinis, now residing in paradise, be incarnated so that he could count on their help if necessary. (*Gesar*, 57)

Thubpa Gawa's conditions were met, and we will continue his story after observing that the personal mother's visitation and her quest for deeper knowledge of Buddha served as an irritant, or catalyst, precipitating events to come. The daughter's disdain of her mother's religious credo had, metaphorically speaking, given birth to demons who would contaminate the land. The demons may also be understood as latent characteristics within the daughter, which took form because of resentment of her mother's abandonment of her for "higher" matters. She may have transferred her anger to her sons, arousing negative characteristics in their psyches. The incarnation of a hero, then, became a dire necessity: change had to occur to rout the rapidly spreading scourge of evil and to restore goodness.

A Virgin Birth

Thubpa Gawa was born miraculously to the virgin Dzeden (a Nagi) after she drank a "chalice of consecrated water."

Dzeden was a woman who lived in harmony with her Nagi nature— that is, in a fluid relationship with all dimensions of her personality. Tibetans consider the Nagis (serpents) mystical water deities who make their habitat at the bottom of an ocean or lake. Like the serpent who sheds its skin yearly, a Nagi represents renewal and eternality. Within their richly furbished aquatic palaces, Nagis guard sacred Buddhist texts placed in their care until humanity is mature enough to receive them.

The Nagis, like all things in nature, are endowed with both healing powers and destructive powers, which involve them in the world of humans. The potency or importance attributed to the Nagis in *Gesar of Ling* stems from the Tibetan concept of redemption (Jung 1963, par. 768).

Better to understand the importance of redemptive power, let us note the disparity between the Easterner's and the Westerner's views of this concept. In the West, "man is incommensurably small and the grace of God is everything; but in the East, man is God and he redeems himself" (par. 768). Despite the fact that the gods "of Tibetan Buddhism belong to the sphere of illusory separateness and mind-created projections," *they exist*. For the Westerner, "an illusion remains an illusion." C. G. Jung writes:

> With us a thought has no proper reality; we treat it as if it were a nothing-
> ness. Even though the thought be true in itself, we hold that it exists only
> by virtue of certain facts which it is said to formulate. We can produce a
> most devastating fact like the atom bomb with the help of this ever-chang-
> ing phantasmagoria of virtually non-existent thoughts, but it seems wholly
> absurd to us that one could ever establish the reality of thought itself. (par.
> 768)

The East considers psychic reality, or the psyche, "as the main and unique
condition of existence" (par. 770).

Guru Padma, using the great store of mind power at his disposal, succeeded in convincing Dzedeb's Nagi family that his motives for extracting
Dzeden from her watery bed and bringing her to earth were impersonal,
transcendent, and "incomprehensible to the vulgar," but not to those initiated into the domain of higher understanding (*Gesar,* 64). The pain she
experienced upon leaving her family and her watery world for the vagaries
and sufferings of life, however, was to be excoriating. Nevertheless, she understood that she had no choice but to comply with her destiny.

Arriving at the "peaceful and happy" country of Ling, most naturally
Dzeden went in search of water, and so happened upon Gyasa, a married
woman, who had brought her flock of animals to the same watering hole.
Not overly surprised by the meeting inasmuch as her husband had had a
premonitory dream about the passage of a young girl in the vicinity, Gyasa
invited her to stay a few days with them in their yurt (67–69). Dzeden'd
charm and amiability enabled her to get along well with the family until
Gyasa's husband, Singlen, grew increasingly fond of Dzeden, and she of
him. Despite the Tibetan practices of polygamy and polyandry, Gyasa re-
sented the presence of a rival. The climate of harmony in the household
yielded to one of discord. Unwilling to hurt his wife, Singlen controlled his
sexual desires by undertaking a pilgrimage. During his absence, Gyasa planned
to rid herself of her rival by sending her to distant grazing lands that she
knew to be replete with demons.

Although aware of the dangers facing her, Dzeden complied and left.
On her way, she took stock of the magnitude of the demonic forces she
would encounter and wept bitterly. Meanwhile, the deity called Kenzo,
having been chosen to become Gesar's father, believed it was time to involve himself in earthly matters. Descending on his gray courser together
with six hundred gods "along a golden rainbow," he moved "in dazzling
light" (71). The supernal vision terrified Dzeden. Dismounting, Kenzo

brought her a gold vase filled with peacock feathers steeped in holy water. At this very moment, Thubpa Gawa from on high "looked at himself in the consecrated water" and imprinted "his image on it" (71). Kenzo poured the contents of the vase into a jade cup and Dzeden drank from it. The miracle occurred: she became the vessel by means of which Thubwa Gawa would be incarnated in the person of Gesar, as confirmed by Kenzo before he departed: "By this act a kingdom will be founded, the demons will be overcome, you will obtain the fruit of the sublime Doctrine, and all your wishes will be realized" (72). The god then departed.

The blending of consecrated water and peacock feathers in the above image may be identified, on the one hand, with Dzeden's Nagi essence, and on the other, with the sun, fire, and "dazzling light" created by Kenzo during his descent. As a mediating force between Heaven and Earth, Kenzo was in effect linking infinite and finite worlds, the impossible and the possible. That shamans have associated peacock feathers with ascension, clairvoyance, and divination further underscores the numinosity of the event. The peacock, an animal of supernal beauty, served, according to the *Bardo Thödol,* as Amitabha Buddha's throne, and it participated in transformatory processes. Important as well is the notion that peacock feathers, associated with the highest of values, such as sun and flame, have been endowed with the power to absorb humanity's venomous impulses and deeds. Thus Dzeden's vision, fusing celestial light/fire with earthly water, also triggered an alchemical mutation concluding with the future birth of the savior Gesar.

Following the miracle—the deposition of Thubwa Gawa's image as he looked down onto the consecrated water that Dzeden had imbibed, or the symbolical insertion of the treasure (semen) into the secret cavern (Dzeden's uterus)—she returned to her mistress much to the latter's dismay. As the mystery of virgin birth pursued its course, Dzeden became a prey to violent head pains and lay ill for three days. Fearing that neighbors might think her heartless, Gyasa sent for a lama and a doctor. Their curative agents, however, were to no avail. Nature took its course until Dzeden was again visited by celestial powers in an annunciation. She

> saw the end of a white rainbow touch her head. At the same time, from her body rose a light that joined the rainbow, and a male child as white as a conch emerged from the summit of her head. He encircled round her three times, keeping her on his right, and said:
> "Mother, one will come who will recompense you for the goodness you have shown in giving me birth." He then flew away in the sky. . . .

The next day, a red gleam coming from the sky rested on the young girl's right shoulder. Out of this shoulder sprang a boy, flame red, who circled round her, said the same words that his brother had uttered, and, in a red light, ascended to the Marmized paradise.

The day after, it was a blue light that touched her left shoulder. Out of it leaped a male child blue as a turquoise. He circled round her and repeated what the other two children had said, then, on a path of blue light, mounted to the paradise of "Perfect Joy."

At the dawn on the fourth day after the beginning of this strange series of marvels, a ray of sunlight touched the Nagi's heart and, almost at once, a little girl of extreme beauty came from it. She wore a headdress displaying the images of the five Dhyani Buddhas and was adorned with necklaces and various other ornaments made from the bones of human beings. She prostrated herself three times before her mother, said the same words as her brothers, and, ascending along the ray of sunlight, went to Dölma paradise.

The fifth day, a faint light showed on the navel of the nagi [Dzeden] and out of it came a sack. (73)

Because illusions, which obliterate demarcations between the perceptible and the imperceptible, play such a significant role in the Tibetan credo, Dzeden should have become accustomed to the ghostly happenings forever occurring around her. But rather than extend her psyche outward toward cosmic experience, she based her reality on her personal and limited understanding of things. So terrified was she at the sight of the sack emerging from her navel that she called Gyasa, who was equally stunned.

Like the uterus, the sack may be understood as a protective covering in which the fetus develops unharmed until it is ready to be born or expelled from its normal hiddenness. By analogy, the work of the mystic—the initiated—is carried on in secret, protected against the hostility and ignorance of the collective, which is unprepared to receive its message.

Unheeding of the virgin's protests, Gyasa took the sack to her uncle, Todong, also a *tulku,* who was destined to speed up Gesar's coming and test his mettle. Todong recalled having read a manuscript informing him "that a young girl would arrive bringing five animals with her, that she would become the mother of several gods, then of a man who, as King of Ling, would conquer many countries" (*Gesar,* 74).

Fearing that his power might be usurped by the unidentifiable, troublesome "thing" that had the form of a sack, Todong scolded Dzeden:

Never was such a thing born of woman. . . . You are a bad girl, that is why this dreadful thing has come out of you. If this sack remains here any longer it will bring misfortune upon Ling. It must at once be thrown into the river. (*Gesar*, 75)

He then ordered three lamas, three heads of families, and three married women to take the sack and throw it into a river. His act not only cut off the object's simple identification with the personal mother's uterus, but when the sack was plunged into a collective body of water, it became associated with the atemporal and limitless universe of the Nagi. Consequently, this terrestrial "thing" and its contents were ennobled in preparation for the advent of the god.

On the very evening the "thing" had been cast into the river, King Kurkar of Hor, Gesar's future enemy, dreamed he "saw a jewel that sparkled in the river." Acting on the message emanating from his unconscious, he ordered that the bag be caught in a dragnet and brought to him. The learned man who was called to court to examine the sack pronounced it "a human matrix" and cut it open. Three children emerged: the first was as "red as flame," the second as "blue as turquoise," and the third black. The three were awarded, respectively, to the three brothers of the king, who were *tulku*s and, we now learn, progeny of the daughter who had blasphemed against the Buddha. Unbeknownst to them, however, was the fact that the infants were also *tulku*s, emanations of the gods whose function was to help Thubpa Gawa, incarnated as Gesar (75, 76).

*Tulku*s, or reincarnations of dead masters, were considered by Tibetans to be supernal transmitters of the "true religion," and instrumental in handing down living doctrines from one generation to another. Masters perceiving great spiritual potential in a child might recognize him as a *tulku*. In such cases, he was trained intensively by his master, or guru, and spent his life absorbing secret, traditions that he then transmitted to the next generation—to future *tulku*s.

Like *dakini*s, *tulku*s are psychological manifestations, or projections, of subliminal contents within the individual to whom they appear. Their presences, as apparitions or visitations, enable them to speak out their messages and shed light on heretofore unrecognized qualities in the adept's psyche. The energy charge inhering within the mental image perceived by the worshiper, passing into his or her body/psyche complex, infuses it with increased self-confidence. Thus may the adept become equipped to intercede in an event and change the course of life by rectifying dangerous and/or disrupting situations.

The mystery of form, as concretion in a vision or image in dreams, or simply in fantasy images, may be looked upon in a larger frame of reference as a meeting or an embrace of Heaven and Earth, or of air and matter. Appearing first in the form of diffused particles, the visualization later takes on the opacity of a dense and recognizable concretion. Thus, projection takes on sacrality, becoming vision and/or visitation.

Dzeden—now to be viewed as the symbolic vessel connecting temporality to eternity and/or the unmanifest to the manifest—had not yet completed her travail. Terror again seized her when she heard a voice emanating from "the upper part of her heart" say to her: "Mother . . . is it now time for me to be born? Shall I come out from the summit of your head?" (76).

Anxiously she told the voice that if he were a demon, he should emerge from her head, but if he were a God, "I pray you to be born in the natural way" (76). Reassuringly, the voice told her that it would be best for him to come out of her head. He then asked her to go outdoors to see whether the animals under her guard had had any young, whether white rice had fallen from the sky, whether golden flowers had blossomed, and whether the ground had been covered with yellow, red, blue, and black snow. She obeyed.

> Near to each of the beasts that her father Menken the naga had given her lay a little one just born. A powdering of different coloured snow: yellow, red, blue, and black, out of which rose golden flowers, covered the ground with a fairy carpet; and from the sky fell a rain of white rice, the grains of which sparkled as silver spangles. (77)

Returning to her dwelling place, Dzeden was surprised when "out of a white vein, which opened on the top of her head, came a white egg marked with three spots that resembled three eyes" (77). She wrapped the egg in a rag and put it in her dress, after which the egg broke, and there emerged a male child with three eyes. Believing that a three-eyed child would be a source of torment, with her thumb she put out the eye in the center of the child's forehead.

The head represents ardent mental activity, and authority as well as spirituality, and because of its spherical shape may be considered both a microcosm and a macrocosm. Like a celestial body, it contains the most primitive undifferentiated elements as well as the potential for differentiation in the most complex of spheres. The egg that emerged from Dzeden's head suggests the coming into being of a germ/seed, an entity that would have to develop in keeping with its genetic structure.

Eyes as organs of perception play a significant role in Buddhist and Hindu religious texts. Lord Shiva of the Hindus, for example, had three eyes, two of which looked outward, that is, into the world, while his third, frontal eye accorded him inner vision; the three together endowed him with cosmic perception. In that the eye for Buddhists represents fire, it has been identified with Amitabha's powerful contemplative nature. Let us recall in this regard that the peacock's feathers with their multiplicity of eyes served as his throne. That Dzeden drank of the sacred water in which peacock feathers had been steeped suggests the birth of a supernal being. Dzeden perhaps put out one of her son's three eyes in her desire to diminish his earthly suffering, aware that if an individual differs from the majority, he or she is singled out for ridicule by others.

During a conversation Dzeden had with her son, she asked him why he had been born to her. His response:

> For a great number of years I was an Indian hermit practicing unheard-of austerities in dense forests. In virtue of these practices I was reborn in the world of gods. . . . and my name is Thubpa Gawa [Gesar]. (77)

Identifying himself as a reincarnation of the hermit who had instilled religious fervor into the mother of the apostate daughter, the son informed Dzeden that the animals who had just been born were all helpful *tulkus*; he also revealed that the goal of his present mission was to wage war against demons and malevolent beings through her instrumentality.

Although the enemies of the "true religion" sought to kill the child by burying him alive and believed they had succeeded in doing so, Gesar's voice rang out from underground, announcing his return in three days. Meanwhile, the *dakinis*, demigoddesses protective of the newborn, ran to the child's grave, removed the earth, carried him up to the gods and then back to earth to his mother, who wrapped him in a white silk scarf and put him in her dress (82). Although she feared for her son's life as well as for her own, the child calmed her anguish by telling her that despite attempts on his life by enemy magicians, he (and she) would escape all harm. So it came to pass that for the next three years mother and son lived together in poverty and fed on rats.

Although one looks askance in the West at the eating of rats, carriers of disease and death, in Siberia, China, Japan, and Tibet these rodents have positive connotations. In that they feed on foods growing within the earth, they are harbingers of fertility, abundance, and prosperity. Not only may they be assimilated to positive mother figures because they are nourishers, but they are healers as well. The absence of rats in Eastern society is cause for deep disquietude.

Guru Padma, after calling a meeting of the Gods, declared it was time to *awaken* the *tulku* incarnated as Thubpa Gawa. Thereupon, he folded a rainbow into the shape of a tent, "entered it and descended to the place where the young boy dwelt." The "precious son of a God" was then informed that his father was Kenzo, a deity, and his mother Dzen, a Nagi; and that he, who had once lived in celestial spheres, had now been incarnated for the purpose of ridding the world of evil (90).

> Henceforth thy name is Gesar, King of Ling. Become conscious of thy strength and of the destiny to which thou art called. Go and take possession of thy throne. The people of Ling must all become thy subjects and the brave among them thy warriors. In order to attain this end use all the resources that wisdom and ability offer thee. (90)

Guru Padma then enumerated the gifts that would be given the child; they included a thunderbolt scepter *(dorje)*, a heavenly sword made by Dölma, ninety-eight arrows, and a bow of horn (91). The wife bestowed upon him was the *tulku* of the White Goddess Chomden Dölma, Dölma the Conqueress. At the propitious moment he would have to accomplish a difficult task: take possession of her father's incalculable treasures.[7] These included a bronze statue representing Chenrezigs, "the Great Compassionate One of Penetrating Vision," a statue of Dölma, "the Mysterious Mother of Beings," and twelve volumes of religious texts (91).

Now aware of the "intelligence and divine insight" bestowed upon him, the child Gesar conquered his bride, Sechang Dugmo, queen of Ling, and had a palace built for her, his mother, and himself, while he lived for a brief time in happy contentment (98). But periods of tranquility were, for Gesar, all too ephemeral. He would, like most mythical heroes, be called into action.

Manene (Anima): A Visitation

Unlike other heroes, such as Aeneas and Roland, Gesar was not catalyzed by a male figure, but by a feminine power or anima figure. In psychological terms the anima image, defined as "an autonomous psychic content in the male personality," is alluded to frequently as "an inner woman," a "psychic representation of the contrasexual elements in man" (Edinger 1968, 5). Having appeared in dreams, legends, myths, and literary works throughout the centuries, anima figures are usually the repository for feelings or notions that are not discernible in man's outer attitude. Because anima figures transcend categories, they have been iconicized in symbolic imagery as women ranging from harlots to saints.

Gesar's anima figure, the goddess Manene, appears to him amid rays of light. Her energy (she is a part of nature) flows directly into the man whose projection brought her into being. As long as Gesar is in contact with Manene, she remains a living power within him, helping him to evolve and to forge ahead. Playing the role of psychopomp, she points out to the hero the right path: the one leading to the highest levels of consciousness. As anima, she is the carrier of the life experience. Triggering his activity, not only does she guide and encourage him to face opposition actively and openly, but she also activates his thinking principle. She encourages him to discriminate, to use his reason each time he encounters new situations. When, due to feelings of well-being or security, Gesar's projection recedes, the enormous energy implicit in this archetypal image diminishes in power and what she symbolizes lapses into the unconscious (Jung 1968, par. 174).

Manene, appearing to Gesar at night as he sleeps, has been sent to convey "the decisions of the Gods." Such a vision suggests not only the hero's attachment to divinities and to his anima figure in particular, but also the onset of the *numinosum*. That gods, psychologically speaking, are identified with the Self (the total psyche) indicates Gesar's readiness on both conscious and subliminal planes. Both planes work as a cohesive whole and in mutual trust, endowing him with unity of purpose and harmony of spirit.

The following description of Manene is highly revealing: "She rode a white lion, and led a buffalo in leash behind her; in one hand she held a bow, in the other a mirror" (*Gesar*, 99). That Manene is astride a white lion identifies her with the attributes associated with this animal: divine power, wisdom, nobility, and indomitability. As such, she also represents a form of what the Tantrics call *shakti*: energy implicit in each of the six chakra (subtle energy centers or points of encounter and interpenetration between a human's physical and psychical systems). As subtle energies pass through the body in stages in keeping with the individual's psychic or spiritual progress, they are redistributed and transformed. That the lion is white, as is Manene's clothing, signifies both the absence and the sum total of colors: the beginning and end of life's journey, or Gesar's mission and Manene's visitation. As a supernal power, she carries a bow, symbolizing combat and prefiguring Gesar's earthly activities of exorcising and expelling evil powers. The mirror, like the consecrated water on which Gesar, as Thubpa Gawa, has imprinted his image, not only reflects celestial knowledge but in the Tibetan epic is an instrument of supreme wisdom. Form, then, as a reflection of supernal spheres, is merely an aspect or fragment of the infinite Void. If the mirror were covered with a "thick deposit of dust" it would represent the mind enveloped by nescience (Evans-Wentz 1960, 211).

Because Manene was Gesar's counselor and guide, her visitations and dictates, unlike those dispensed to the archetypal Mother and Dzeden, were assertive in tone and specific in directives. She told Gesar that the time had come for him to acquire the storehouse of treasures that were to be his, and to distribute a portion of them liberally to his warriors. Admonishing him to begin his mission, she vanished.

Events unfolded in keeping with Manene's command. Gesar first informed his wife, Sechang Dugmo, herself a *tulku,* of the visitation, after which he prepared for his mission. She, in turn, arranged for the complicated rituals preceding her husband's departure. Luxurious carpets, gold and silver vases, and priceless objects of all types were set out to welcome the different tribes of Ling. Upon the great lama's arrival on the scene, he celebrated the greatness of the gods and their subjugation of demons (*Gesar,* 100).

The following day Gesar left under the guise of an "air spirit." Rising to the top of a mountain, he came face to face with a "pure crystal" rock surrounded by dark ones from which flames issued. Shaped like a huge ritual vase, the pure crystal contained consecrated water, the very element onto which he, as Thubpa Gawa, had bestowed his image. Grasping his ritual dagger, an instrument designed to cut and thereby modify passive matter, he drew the "mudra of anger." The mystic sign he so carefully traced with his hand served symbolically to connect and sustain that which had been severed or interrupted. In the redness and heat of his angry passion, he spoke in a thunderous voice:

> Here are the treasures hidden by Padma Sambhava. They are guarded by the twelve goddesses of the earth. I, Gesar, son of gods, am the legitimate owner of them. According to the bidding of Manene, I come to claim them. (*Gesar,* 100)

The hero then took the gold *dorje* given him by Guru Padma and used it to strike open the crystal rock.

Empowered by the fulgurating energy implicit in Manene's directive to acquire the treasures, Gesar's will, flexed to the extreme, enabled him to step through a doorlike passageway into a magnificent hall. A mandala (in the form of a magic pentacle) lay on a large gold throne, in the center of which "shone the vessel containing the water of immortality, which bubbled up and overflowed." Most important of the many precious objects contained in this inner sanctum was the supernatural armor destined for the hero (101).

Before continuing with Gesar's story, let us make two observations. The first concerns the mandala. This complex circular image, within which a square is usually imprinted, is used for meditative purposes by Tibetan Buddhists. While focusing their gaze on one or on various centers within the image, they are concentrating their psychic energy (libido) within a given area or areas and are also activating their psyches. Thus they are laying the groundwork for their own self-renewal and self-restoration. Because their libido during the process is contained and not dispersed or fragmented, the mandala, like the magic circle, has implications of protection and shelter. Therefore it has come to be identified with the Mother archetype, and by extension with places and vessels of birth, such as the lotus flowers from which Buddha and Padma Sambhava came to life. Understandably, then, exposure to a mandala is considered a psychologically unitive experience that revitalizes an individual's rhythms, sounds, and feelings in a synchronous whole.

Secondly, let us observe that the hidden treasure that Gesar discovers—symbolically construed as his heretofore unmanifested divine essence—represents esoteric knowledge. Because treasures, as they appear in myths, have been equated with immortality, spiritual teachings, and mnemonic deposits—a whole inner world or life—it is natural that they be placed in remote areas and guarded by dangerous beings or animals. Accordingly, the discovery and acquisition of treasures requires extreme effort on the part of a hero. Indeed, it is in the very effort expended by Gesar that his psychological and metaphysical progress or evolution will take place.

Manene/anima appeared to Gesar once again during the week he spent removing the treasures. As *logos*, a thinking and rational factor, she warned him to be aware of the many evil spirits haunting the area. Reason must be forever on the alert in ferreting out good and evil. Gesar could not allow himself to be blinded by the dazzling light emanating from the treasure; vigilance and discrimination were essential.

Manene's warnings were of extreme psychological urgency. Dazzlement by glitter, or submersion under affects, suggests a hero's natural propensity for hubris or inflation. So many heroes, consumed by arrogance, have been undone after winning a battle or discovering a treasure. The conviction that their victory has been achieved solely by their ego (center of consciousness), without the participation of the Self (total psyche, or the Divine within) diminishes their power of discernment and thus leads to their undoing.

Gesar learned yet another lesson from Manene's visitations. After she vanished, the area she had occupied was again cast into darkness. This compelled him to act with greater care to avoid stumbling in the physical sphere, and enabled him to perceive a deeper reality in an inner world. Demon-infested realms thus became learning instruments.

Gesar's *tulku* horse, Kyang Gö Karkar, helped his master throughout the epic. Recognizing enemy spirits in the form of a musk deer, a monkey, and a boar, he killed them instantly with a swift kick (101). As an instrument of raw, unbridled, instinctual energy, Gö Karkar may be regarded as an appendage of the warrior, symbolizing the confidence he placed in his own physical ability. Not simply called into action in a moment of need or fear, the horse in this instance may be looked upon as an iconization of the hero's character traits and psychological attributes. Not only does he stand for his strength but for the kind of wisdom needed to slay demons—that is, enemies in the guise of cowardly minds that populate the world (Trungpa Rinpoche 1981, 10–12).

Every battle or struggle that Gesar waged against a negative influence revealed how seriously he took Manene's advice. Never did he allow himself to bask in the luxury of complacency or solipsistic joy. Indeed, to avoid falling into the abyss of narcissistic apathy, the lot of so many heroes, he turned to the enriching experience of meditation, whose purpose is to achieve increasing awareness of the *way* or *path* leading to expanded consciousness. The Tibetan, unlike many a Westerner, does not consider indwelling a goal, but rather a healing device that paves the way for expanded consciousness—and "Voidness, . . . the state transcendent over all assertion and all predication" (Jung 1963, par. 838). The *way*, then, is the goal; the experience, the process.

> Having realized the "Void" [in lamaist terminology, the "Inexpressible reality"] they become emancipated from the illusion of the world and, as a consequence, liberated from rebirths which are but the fruit of that creative delusion. (David-Neel 1971, 261)

Meditation frees and calms the spirit/mind complex, enabling it to reach the state of transparency of the smooth surface of a crystalline river of imperceptible depth. The multiple becomes one through meditation; the individual becomes collective, and the earthly, transpersonal.

Indwelling, psychologically speaking, may lead to an assimilation and ordering of an immense horde of acquired riches, permitting the individual ego to integrate the newly acquired elements into the personality as a whole. It permits the individual to distance or to objectify him- or herself from what could subvert clarity of mind/feeling—that is, from affective charges that might pulsate within subliminal spheres. Thus it is rare that identification between ego and Self leads to inflation, which fosters psychological imbalance in the individual. Avoided too are domination of oneself by an all-empowering will, activation of a sense of authority, or morbid need for domination of others, all of which could compromise an urgent mission.

Wisely, then, did the young Gesar listen to Manene/anima—his all-wise Mother—and withdraw from society into deep meditation. During his period of introversion he saw only his wife, who brought him his meals, and a few ministers who sought his directives for the country's administration.

During his seclusion Gesar experienced another optic phenomenon, this time not in slumber, but at dawn, at a moment of deep mental fixity. Appearing to him in a luminous glow, Manene spoke to Gesar as follows:

> Thy rest has lasted long enough. Much work awaits thee; it is time that thou didst begin it. Thou drawest near to thy fifteenth year, the one during which thou hast to pierce with an arrow the forehead of Lutzen, the black demon of the north, and to subdue his numerous subjects. (*Gesar*, 103)

The cutting off of oneself from the phenomenological world for an extended period of time threatens the life experience as much as the complete lack of any inward journey. One-sided attributes may lead to psychological decomposition—that is, to an inability to function in the pragmatic domain.

Manene—and Gesar by extension, if we consider her presence as a projection in the outer world of aspects of his inner, as yet unrecognized needs—declared him ready to undertake his mission. Should he not act immediately, his kingdom and the neighboring states would be ravaged by physical and spiritual darkness. Fear of disease—certainly based on the actuality of dreadful plagues at the time—was uppermost in Manene's mind: "pestilential mists" and "deadly vapors" were controlled by "the black demon of the north," as King Lutzen was called. So formidable were his power and expertise in magic that he could spread sickness (physical as well as spiritual) to other lands. To combat his death-dealing weapons—or, in modern day parlance, germ warfare—Gesar would have to avail himself of special medicines that were guarded by the Mutegspas (Brahmins or Jains), who forbade their exportation. Equally ominous was the fact that the chief of the Mutegspas and his Kashmiri and Nepalese disciples not only preached false doctrines and resorted to blood sacrifices, but had also secreted the authentic sacred writings of the "true religion" (104).

Knowing that the well-being of the kingdom of Ling depended on the obliteration of both physical and spiritual disease, Manene indicated to Gesar how to obtain the crucially needed medicines, which were kept hidden in a sandalwood box in a monastery. The turquoise key to unlock this treasure store had been entrusted to Padma Chös Tso, the daughter of Lungjags Nagpo, one of the invincible Mutegspas chiefs. Because Padma Chös Tso was a *tulku* (of the celestial fairy Yeshes Kahdoma), Manene advised Gesar to comport himself so that she could be won over to his side (104):

> Beware, O Hero! The Mutegspas' magic skill is about to manifest itself effectively. Assume, without delay, the form of the god of their maternal ancestors *(mo lha);* that is, of a young seer astride a *khyung*; thy horse will take on the appearance of this bird. Thus shalt though go to Lungjags Nagpo and endeavour to mislead him by thy predictions. If thou dost not succeed in deceiving him with false prophecies, thou wilt never be able to defeat him. Pay great attention to my counsels and be happy. (107–8)

Heeding Manene's advice, Gesar "produced a phantom," a *tulku,* or emanation from himself. Assuming a divine form, he sat majestically on his winged mount, his horse having now been transformed into a gigantic bird, and left to perform his heroic deeds (106).

Padma Chös Tso: Tulku of a Dakini

Dakinis—inspirational forces—are frequently referred to as "mothers," "magicians," and diamond-hearted hermits, and they are sought after in their quality of holders of secret doctrines (23). Not created for man's sexual pleasure, they came into being to help him deepen his aesthetic and spiritual understanding of life. As representatives of divine wisdom, *dakinis* are, understandably, frequently rendered iconographically as fearsome, wrathful, vengeful, and violent powers, whose task is to break through the hardened thought and rigid ways of their worshipers and set them on new paths in worldly and spiritual matters. It is with the *dakini* that the devout seek to unite for the purpose of expanding their consciousness.

Padma Chös Tso, a *dakini's tulku* or "phantom body," was placed on earth or in Gesar's mind's eye to help our hero fulfill his mission. Described as the "lotus ocean of religion," Padma Chös Tso had a personality that conformed to the highest qualities of her prototype. She was wise, well versed in magic, and in this case guardian of the treasure (medicines). Custodian of the sacred turquoise key to the treasure, she may be identified with snakes, dragons, and other guardians of precious objects. Symbolically, keys may unlock or lock the doors of secret earthly or celestial areas, or by extension, of the mind. They are fundamental in blocking or linking a whole network of inner and outer realms, or abstract and concrete spheres. Padma Chös Tso was to be the harbinger of mystic doctrines and the provider of divine offerings (David-Neel 1931, 120).

Gesar, under the guise of an "engaging feminine personality," addressed Padma Chös Tso in a carefully worded speech designed to inspire confidence: "Our mothers are sisters, therefore we are sisters" (*Gesar*, 115). To impress her with his wisdom and power, he told her that "the Precious Master, has deputed me to give you, on his behalf, this crystal *dorje*."

Overjoyed at the thought of possessing the crystal *dorje*, she misunderstood "the meaning of Gesar's last statement," and believed "she was soon to die in this world to be born again in the paradise where she had lived in her previous life" (115). Gesar, as "the sham goddess," continued:

> I know that the Mutegspas possess medicines of immortality that are concealed in a sandalwood box, the turquoise key of which is in your keeping. The Precious Master has told me that whosoever looks upon them and pays them homage is freed from the cause of death (becomes immortal). I beg that you will let me see them before I go back to Zandog Palri. (115)

Padma Chös Tso acquiesced to his wish to see the medicines/treasure. Gesar, by sleight of hand, seized the substances designed to heal the ills of humanity, leaving imitations in their place.

Upon returning to his maleness, Gesar pursued his cause by creating five *tulkus*: mental phantoms symbolizing Mind, Word, Body, Knowledge, and Actions (116). The first four were placed in front of the four gates of the Mutegspas citadel, while the *tulku* of actions was sent to warn Padma Chös Tso to prepare for her escape. Meanwhile, the *tulkus* "representing Gesar concentrated their minds on the *phowa*, the mystic process by which the malevolent force that animated the Mutegspas would be transmuted into benevolent energy and their reincarnated spirits transported on to the path that leads to spiritual illumination" (*Gesar*, 120).

To transform these emanations of Gesar's mind from inactive into active energetic forces, he had to concentrate his thoughts most powerfully on each of the *tulkus'* specialties. In so doing, he was following the Tantric meditative disciplines of *phowa* and of *tumo* (inner heat), introduced into Tibet in the eleventh century by Naropa and contained in "The Six Doctrines of Naropa." While Tibetans maintain that the discipline of *phowa,* which is designed to transmit thought from one person to another or from one area to another, demonstrates "the power of the mind," A. David-Neel refers to it as "auto-suggestion." The practitioner of *tumo* must first assume the proper posture of "squatting with the legs crossed, the hands passing under the thighs and then clasped together" (David-Neel 1931, 225ff.). Emphasis is then placed on breathing techniques, such as exercises for the retention of the breath, since breathing determines the amounts and rate of energy currents dispensed throughout the physical system, affecting both bodily and psychological functions. The acolyte must also concentrate his meditative powers on various regions of the body (chakras, centers through which subtle energies pass), from the umbilicus to the head. During the process the acolyte must make mental images of the letters RAM ("seed of fire," as in Tibetan mantras). Such mystic syllables are not to be construed as "mere written characters, or symbolic representations of things, but as living beings standing erect and endowed with motive power" (220). The combination of the visual and respiratory disciplines results in the heightening of body heat—to the point that the entire body feels as if it were aflame.[8]

When Gesar practiced *tumo* to overcome the Mutegspas, so focused and intense did his meditation become that the currents of energies within him reached incandescence. The heat and light radiating from his brain waves, directed against his enemies, set aflame the monastery fortress in which the Mutegspas had sealed themselves. Frantically they tried to escape, but not one succeeded.

Now, having been saved from harm, Padma Chö Tso recognized Gesar as an avatar of Thubpa Gawa. Now she understood the reason for her own creation: to help Gesar fulfill his mission. After such expenditure of mental energy by Gesar (and by Padma Chö Tso, by extension), the two spent a week together in a "luminous sun-lit cave" in deep meditation. This period of introversion allowed libido to withdraw from the light of consciousness and secrete itself anew into collective subliminal spheres. Just as the archetypal womb protects and feeds the fetus, so the oxymoronic "luminous sun-lit cave" provided nourishment for Gesar and Padma Chös Tso (*Gesar,* 121). After the two left their retreat, Gesar gave Padma Chös Tso in marriage to King Dharma Mani, entrusting to the couple's care half of the sacred writings he had found in the storehouse of treasures (121). He also commanded the people to build many *chötens* (religious monuments) on the sight of the burned monastery. Gesar then took the precious medicines to the people of Ling, for which they blessed him.

Transpersonal Imagings of Wife and Mother

Following these and other valiant accomplishments, Gesar again withdrew for meditation, in preparation for another awakening or illumination. While he meditated in darkness, the "ray of light" entering his room seemed once again to transport him into a realm midway between corporeal and incorporeal states. This time Guru Padma came into his mind's eye and said that now that he was fifteen years old he was ready to fulfill the next step of his mission: the destruction of the "giant" Lutzen, the leader of a powerful demon state. To eliminate this formidable power—whose "tongue was a living flame," whose head "reached the sky," and whose feet touched the earth—would be no simple task (123).

Gesar kept his plans secret, except from his wife, Sechang Dugmo. Apprising her of his departure, he requested that she harness Kyang Gö Karkar with his gold saddle and his bridle studded with turquoise ornaments. Although Sechang Dugmo was distressed at the thought of Gesar's absence and terrified by the dangers of his mission, she obeyed the higher and collective authority that had commanded him to destroy evil. Following Tibetan custom, Sechang Dugmo placed her hands on the courser's saddle, invoked her husband's tutelary gods, prayed for his success, and opened the courtyard door through which he went forth (124).

Upon learning of Gesar's departure, Dzeden, along with many courtiers, set out with the intention of persuading him to return. Their supplications were to no avail; the fearless hero stood steadfast in his determination to fulfill his mission.

Note must here be taken of Dzeden's evolution. Her immediate impulse as personal mother was to follow her son and beg him to return. But the archetypal Mother prevailed. Reaching into her collective unconscious, she understood that interests broader than the feelings of a personal mother were at stake: that of the well-being of a people. The expansion of her consciousness put her in touch with her Nagi essence, bringing her to the realization that just as she had been snatched from her family in order to live out her destiny, so Gesar must carve out his own way in life.

O Gesar, golden god, what you say is the exact truth. The precious Guru came himself to the country of the Nagas, and made me leave it in order to become your mother.

One night . . . a god descended from the heavens and gave me a magic potion to drink. I miraculously became the mother of several gods, who vanished as soon as they were born. Then you came into the world one morning, when golden flowers blossomed through the multi-coloured snow that covered the tableland. Many times people have tried to kill you, but, always, even when you were buried in a deep pit, you have reappeared alive.

We have both been destined for a work that we must accomplish. Go and be victorious. (125)

Like Sechang Dugmo, Dzeden placed her hand on her son's saddle and wished him success in silence.

Betrayal or Bewitchment?

Arriving in Lutzen's kingdom, Gesar realized almost immediately that he would have to resort to magic to succeed in his formidable task. To escape the jaws of the cannibalistic Lutzen required that he and his courser become invisible. Accordingly, they transformed themselves into cairns (stones). Because stones were not considered inanimate but rather living elements fallen to earth from celestial spheres, they were believed to be divinely sent. As such, they contained godlike elements, and they served also to link high and low, spirit and matter, passive and active elements. Understandably, shamans considered stones instruments of clairvoyance and signs of collective souls. The Dalai Lama received a stone from the King of the World, thereby uniting himself with his spirit.

Concomitant with their assumption of the form and texture of cairns, Gesar and his horse took on their qualities: strength, stability, sacrality, immobility, and, paradoxically, dynamism. The unsuspecting King Lutzen left the stones untouched and returned to his fortress-castle without finding "a being to devour for his meal" (125). No sooner was he out of sight than Gesar and his horse assumed their normal shapes and pursued their course.

Discerning, Lutzen's wife, Queen Dumo Mesang Bumche, on her balcony, Gesar called to her. His aggressive manner took her somewhat aback, but her curiosity prompted her to ask outright how he had avoided being devoured by the king. If the "mystery" were to be revealed, Gesar replied astutely, it would have to be whispered into her ear. The inquisitive queen descended from her balcony and greeted the stranger, who immediately revealed his mission by asking her point-blank the best way to slay her husband.

Although a *tulku* and aware of Lutzen's evil nature, Dumo Mesang was human enough to plead with Gesar that he spare her husband.

> He is my husband and my support; who will provide for me when he is dead? Go, that will be best. The King, he too, has powerful protectors. And the meaning of oracles is always doubtful. If you remain here, you will certainly be devoured by him when he returns home. (126)

Well versed in the art of manipulating humans, Gesar realized that only by impressing the queen with his power and arousing her emotionally would he be able to captivate her. Drawing closer to her, he told her in an "insinuating voice" not only that he possessed great wealth but, more importantly, that he was a god. Were she to help him in his mission, he would take her to his country to live in luxury and happiness. He also assured her that after their demise they would both know the beatitude of the Western Paradise (126). Again speaking as an astute psychologist, he warned her of man's fickle heart: the day Lutzen ceased to love her, he would devour her. Gesar added a well-placed compliment:

> Dost thou not know that thou art beautiful, and that one cannot see thee without loving thee? . . . I have seen thee and I love thee. I am rich, powerful, and a hundred times handsomer than thy husband. Thou shalt be my wife in this life and, later, my companion for centuries without number in the lotus gardens of the blessed Paradise. (127)

Unable to refuse such promises, Dumo Mesang took Gesar into the king's chamber, where she served him dried meat and roasted barley flour *(tsampa)* with tea. Prior to Lutzen's expected entry, she hid him in a hole she had dug in the corner of the kitchen and placed a copper cauldron over his head (127).

Not having eaten "even the smallest living being," Lutzen was understandably ill-humored on entering his fortress-castle. Intent upon learning the particulars of a prophecy foretelling his death at the hands of Gesar, he asked Dumo Mesang to bring him the box containing his magic dice and his books of destiny. Discerning that "an enemy [was] hidden in the house," he told his wife to dig up every hole and search in every cranny in the fortress. Although terrified, the queen wisely repressed her emotions and replied: "It is not under the earth that one finds enemies. Yours is at Ling" (128).

Convinced of the veracity of her statement, Lutzen again resorted to his accessories. Where could Gesar be found? Was he dead or alive? Over and over did the answers point to

> a dark place where the wind does not blow. On his head is a copper caul-
> dron and a mass of maggots swarm about his feet. I cannot discern if he be
> dead or alive. . . . Perhaps he is being tortured by the King of the infernal
> regions. (129)

The mention of "wind" in this context refers to the practitioner's "per-fect command over the mind," his ability "to produce at will the powerful 'one-pointedness of thought' on which the phenomenon depends." Unless highly advanced, practitioners of this magical or "scientific" art of divination fail to obtain the sought-for results. Because "wind" is considered the carrier of mental messages, and Lutzen aimed his "thought" at a land where none blew, he was evidently not "tuned into" the sought-for wave length. The results of his "volitional telepathy" or "transmission of thought" were insuf-ficient in seeking to ferret out the intruder (David-Neel 1931, 230ff.).

Cleverly, however, Dumo Mesang bolstered her husband's self-confi-dence by feigning admiration for his aptitude and concluding that the dead Gesar now occupied "one of the tenebrous hells" (*Gesar*, 129). To celebrate Lutzen's newly won peace of mind, husband and wife enjoyed tea together and went to bed in peace. Once assured that Lutzen was sleeping deeply, Dumo Mesang rose to apprise Gesar of the situation. Immediately the hero donned his helmet and magic armor, and placed a magic arrow in his bow. "Shoot your arrow" at the vulnerable spot on his forehead, she told him, "and he will die instantly" (129).[9]

Only after Gesar had killed Lutzen did Dumo Mesang, now unafraid of reprisals from her husband, speak laudably of him.

> Lutzen . . . was always good to me. When he ate human flesh, he gave me
> mutton for my meals. When he drank blood, he gave me milk. He pro-
> vided for all my needs. I received from him dresses made of fine cloth,
> beautiful Chinese brocade, and cloth of gold, also ornaments for the hair
> and necklaces of precious stones. You declared he was an enemy of the
> Religion, that is why I have helped you kill him; but my intention was to
> permit you only to destroy his body. I crave pardon for his "spirit" and beg
> you to send him to the Western Paradise. (*Gesar*, 129)[10]

Dumo Mesang had not acted irrationally. On the contrary, as a *tulku,* she deemed what might be considered duplicitous or even treacherous as justifiable. Claiming to be partisan of a higher cause, her religion, she believed herself to be free from blame and even heroic. What convinced her to side with Gesar—and in support of humanity—was determined subjectively and was motivated by what best suited her needs.

Gesar's destructive act is transformed into a positive one, thus ennobling his murder of Lutzen. "The spirits of the demons whom I conquer must be enlightened and purified; good must take the place of evil." The transformation process is described as follows: Lutzen's spirit first enters the *bardo* (the state between death and rebirth), after which, avoiding the wrong directions ("openings") on its way to transcendence, it unites with the "terrible Machig" (130).[11]

Machig is depicted as follows in *Gesar of Ling:*

> Below, is the terrible Machig. Blue of complexion, she sits cross-legged, arrayed in a silk robe of many colours and adorned with "cemetery bone ornaments." In her right hand she holds a hand drum, in her left a sweet sound bell. Lutzen, may thy spirit unite with her and, with her, rise to the second node.
>
> There, dwells the victorious white Dölma [principal goddess in the Lamaist pantheon; Tara of the Hindus]. Whiter than the whitest conch, covered with sparkling jewels, she is seated in the lotus position; with her right hand she points to the earth, placing the world in subjection, and in her left she holds a blue lotus and a crystal rosary. May thy spirit unite with her and, with her, rise to the third node.
>
> There, sits the Universal Mother. Her complexion is red. Her red hair, divided in four parts, hangs down her back, over her two shoulders, and over her face. At the top of her head burns a red flame. In her right hand she holds a blood-stained human skin, and with her left she puts to her lips a *kangling* [a trumpet made from a human femur], from which she produces terrifying sounds. Her skirt is a tiger skin and her tunic is of red silk. Upright on an elephant, she dances frantically. May thy spirit unite with her. From her dwelling-place starts the path that leads to the Western paradise where reigns the red Amitaba. Proceed that way. (131)

Not only had Gesar's supernatural power transformed evil into good; it had also allowed Dumo Mesang to feel that, as a *tulku,* she had acted for the good of humanity and not egocentrically. Inner joy was also hers upon observing Lutzen's arrival at "the Paradise of the Great Beatitude" (132).

Once her mission had been fulfilled, however, Dumo Mesang reverted to her human side. No longer gratified by cosmic experiences, she became possessive of Gesar, reminding him of his promise to marry her and to take her into the beatific Western Paradise. His cold retort was that her "hour ha[d] not yet come," and he humiliated her by adding, "I am not of those who can be conquered" (132). Indeed, Gesar gave the impression of having simply used Mesang Dumo, and his sole concern, seemingly, was "to evade the promise he had given to make her his wife" (133). But then, are not most heroes—and heroines—essentially pragmatic? Do they not willingly resort to subterfuge to achieve their goals, frequently excusing their crassness by pointing to higher motivations?

The Compassionate Chenrezigs

Dumo Mesang would not remain passive. Just as she had betrayed her husband, she would lead Gesar astray. Refusing to accept his imminent departure, she compelled the divine hero to remain by imprisoning him both physically and psychologically, with the complicity of Lutzen's warriors.

Appealing to his human side, she made Gesar as comfortable as possible by "slipping under his pillow some cushions on which they [other people] had sat and rested their feet. (To place one's head on a cushion, carpet, or on any other article upon which another person has sat or rested his feet appears abominable to the Tibetans.)" (133).

She gave him tea with such powerful "defiling effect" that it clouded his mind, immobilizing and debilitating the once dynamic and courageous hero. "He forgot Ling, his mission, his own personality. Each night, he created a magic emanation, which resembled him exactly and which shared the Queen's couch; while she lived in happiness, believing that she possessed the Hero's love (133).

Only in a condition of mental stupor or of psychological stasis could Gesar have remained captive to Dumo Mesang for six years. Stasis implies physical, mental, and emotional inactivity—immobility to the point of paralysis. Although a seemingly negative condition, it may have a positive aftermath if the rest and relaxation permit active people to recoup their energies. Extensive physical and mental immobility, however, atrophies muscle and mind—body and psyche. Rigidification of any system may lead to its disintegration and rot.

Thanks to Chenrezigs (the Compassionate; or She Who Looks with Clear Eyes), a Tibetan avatar of Avalokiteshvara, Gesar was spared such a fate. Chenrezigs dissipated the clouding of his mind, awakening the hero from his stupor or what may be identified as a long and paralyzing dream state.

No sooner had his awareness returned than Gesar journeyed home to

Ling, despite Dumo Mesang's sobs. On his way he learned that Ling had been invaded by Kurkar, the king of Hor, and that this monstrous individual had slaughtered many of his people, transported Gesar's wife, Sechang Dugmo, to Hor, and reduced his mother, Dzeden, to slavery. Kurkar had left his henchman, Todong, to reign in Ling as his delegate and vassal.

Gesar's principal concern was to learn his mother's fate. Dressed as a lama, he happened upon a beggar woman whose straits were so dire that she was reduced to eating roots to survive. Gesar recognized her as his mother. Rather than complain of her poverty, she begged the "stranger" to resort to magic so that she might learn her son's whereabouts. In a mock ritual, he told her that her wish would be granted if she threw her sack of roots into the air. After complying, she questioned, then guessed, the lama's identity. "I pray you tell me if you be Gesar. Many years I have wept for my child, not knowing if I should ever see him again. Why leave me in suspense?" (140).

So affected was the hero by his mother's pain that he revealed himself "in his shining armour and . . . celestial weapons." Overcome with joy, she apprised him of the sad events she had lived through and he in turn re-counted the reasons for his long absence (140, 141).

Not long thereafter, Gesar was again awakened during his sleep "by a great light." Manene appeared to him "wearing a headdress bearing the images of the five mystical Buddhas and adorned with flashing jewels." She admonished Gesar to leave immediately for the demon-ridden land of Hor to annihilate King Kurkar and his two brothers, who had taken an oath to destroy the true and good Doctrine (147, 149).

Sechang Dugmo

Despite Sechang Dugmo's valiant attempts to resist King Kurkar's advances during Gesar's long absence, her efforts were to no avail. Her only hope rested on Gesar's prompt return. It was not to be.

Loneliness, threats, deceit, and violence had forced Sechang Dugmo to act overtly, and at times deceitfully, to safeguard her interests and her person. The day she left for Kurkar's kingdom as his captive, unbeknownst to her retinue she stopped on a mountain where she hid some magic vases contain-ing holy water. Upon Gesar's return, she reasoned, his superhuman insight, enabling him to see through matter, would lead him to the buried treasure and, by extension, to her whereabouts. Her hopes vanished with the passage of years. Feelings of abandonment, even rejection, took possession of her, accounting in part for her change of heart toward her abductor. Indeed, she not only fell deeply in love with the king of Hor, but bore him a son as well.

When news came of Gesar's possible return to Ling, Sechang Dugmo was aware of her dangerous situation. How would Gesar react to what could appear as a betrayal? Justly fearful of his anger, she nonetheless failed to apply caution. Instead of indwelling and internalizing her libido (psychic energy), she comported herself extrovertedly and somewhat irrationally, stifling whatever new insights might have protected her from psychological blindness.

What Kurkar sought most to discover was whether Gesar was in the vicinity. To assuage his anxiety as well as her own, Sechang Dugmo herself offered to reconnoiter. She alone, she apprised the King, would recognize his distinguishing mark, "a white hair that stands erect between his eyebrows" (160). Although confident that his wife would succeed in her mission, Kurkar was also convinced that even if she should fail to discover Gesar's whereabouts, he and his brothers could easily kill the hero.

During her search for Gesar, Sechang Dugmo met a caravan. After being ushered into their yurt, she demanded tribute for the grass and water they used to feed themselves and their animals. "Elder Sister," one of the men replied, "I am only a servant"; he asked her to follow him into his master's yurt. Having observed the men in the tent, she assured herself that Gesar was not one of them. The man seated in the place of honor asked her about Kurkar's health, then continued:

> So you are the beautiful Sechang Dugmo. I have heard people speak of you. Drink some tea and eat something. You will present a scarf on my behalf to Kurkar and tell him that I think of remaining here about six days. (161)

As an offering to King Kurkar, the attendant brought in boxes containing a gold saddle, a gold bridle, two iron chains with an enormous iron nail, and a pair of gold earrings for Sechang Dugmo (162). At home again, she assured her husband that he had nothing to fear.

So thick was the deceptive veil that Gesar used to curtain Sechang Dugmo off from the truth of things that she and her husband settled into complacency. Kurkar, adhering to his rational function, had obliterated intuition. As for his wife, she had embarked on a course of deception that had imprisoned her in a visual maze. Only the king's brother understood the real meaning of the strange gifts given to Sechang Dugmo for Kurkar, and he said to the king:

I am very inclined to think that they come from Gesar. He will put the saddle on your back, and will drive you with the bridle; it is a symbol of your subjection. The chains will be attached to your walls to help in the escalade. The nails will be driven into the hearts of your ministers. As to the ear-rings, with which Dungmo has adorned herself in such haste, they signify that Gesar will recapture her. (163)

The king refused to listen, and accused his brother of rambling.

Your gloomy predictions lack common sense. Leave to the lamas the task of unveiling the future, it is not your business. Tomorrow, as I have commanded, the women shall go and take beer to those chiefs. (163)

Only after carrying out Kurkar's commands to recompense the caravan people for their kindness by bringing them beer did Sechang Dugmo understand the immensity of the deception perpetrated on them all. No trace of the caravan existed: "Clouds, like fringed scarves, slowly crept up the mountains, and then, to the women's astonished gaze, the great grass valley appeared in front of them, empty and desolate." Humiliated by her lack of discernment, Sechang Dugmo spoke with bitterness: "I allowed myself to be taken in . . . by Gesar's magic power (164). Her failure to be forthright and decisive and her choice of an invalid middle course in the hope of placing both husbands made her position even more hazardous.

Having reached a crucial juncture in her life, and unsure of how she should handle her problem, Sechang Dugmo, somewhat like the wife of the cannibalistic King Lutzen, failed to consult her own groundbed. She lost sight of her identity and the solidity that one draws from such an inner authority. Her untruths led Kurkar into an imbroglio of faulty reasonings and fed Kurkar's own arrogance.

Gesar and his glittering army battled on until one evening he stood before the evil Kurkar who had invaded Ling, abducted his wife, and slain innumerable people of his kingdom. The hero took his sword and in a single stroke cut off the king's head. He directed Kurkar's "spirit," like Lutzen's, into the Western Paradise (196). Later Gesar also slew the "demon" child born to Sechang Dugmo and her abductor. Finally, he reestablished the "true religion" in the country of Hor and elsewhere, and Sechang Dugmo returned with Gesar to Ling (201).

The epic continues with Gesar's many victories in his continuous endeavor to better the lot of humanity. Never deviating from Manene's sage advice, he completed his earthly mission. The evils he had destroyed were transmuted into "beneficent energy"; his victims were sent to the Western Paradise, where they would again become manifest in a new form of being.

In time Gesar, Sechang Dugmo, twenty other women, twenty-five chiefs, and eighteen relations established themselves on the slope of a mountain facing east. The many grottoes and caves on this ascending part of earth served them as hermitages. Gesar lived alone in his cave, while Sechang Dugmo dwelled among the twenty women. Living for over three years in a state of profound meditation, each in her and his own way, they became masters of, among other disciplines, the Tantric practice of *Tsa lung gom* (play of air in the arteries). Such a discipline enables the yogin to reach a state of consciousness and bring about his or her own death in "a state of ecstasy" (263).

On the fifth month of the fourth year of their retreat, Gesar called his wife and four others to him. He reminded them that they, like him, were *tulkus* and that since their earthly work had been completed, they should "dissolve their fictitious personalities and return to the paradise whence they had come" (264).[12]

For three days they remained without food or drink and in perfect concentration; then they uttered a wish for the happiness of all beings—from the highest to the most fragile of insects. Because it was impossible to enter paradise with bodies, Gesar said: "Tomorrow we will detach the 'spirit' from them by the rite of *pho lang*." (The "rite that effects the liberation of the 'spirit' by separating it from the body and its 'double'" [265].)

Motionless and in profound concentration of thought, the following morning,

> before dawn, the many deities, playing different instruments and throwing a rain of flowers, appeared on a white rainbow.
>
> The first sunbeam shot an arrow of light above the distant mountains. Without a movement, without lifting their lowered eyelids, Gesar and his companions uttered the piercing *hik*, then the grave *phat*; and, on the rocky terrace of the white mountain, there remained only five empty robes, aureoled in light. (265)[13]

The many feminine voices in *Gesar of Ling* each in their own way play a significant role in Gesar's life. They reveal themselves to be not merely messengers but independent spirits as well, displaying profound insight and intelligence, particularly at crucial periods during Gesar's incarnation in terrestrial existence. Fascinating as well is the fact that Sechang Dugmo, who not only had fallen in love with the enemy during Gesar's absence but had even borne him a child, was accepted back by her husband and lovingly resumed her place as the hero's wife.

Although Tibetans, like Buddhists in general, frequently consider the woman's moral character inferior to that of the man, it is said that "a women contemplative, if she is any good at all, is more often than not the superior of a man" (Beyer 1973, 47).

2 Kalidasa's Sanskrit Drama, *Sakuntala:* From Passivity to Adamantine Essence

Kalidasa's *Sakuntala*, a Sanskrit dramatic ritual, draws its viewers into a love sequence played first on an earthly plane and then reaching a supernal realm of bliss. Sakuntala, a passive, unconscious, and withdrawn archetypal Maiden during her earthly trajectory, evolves to become a conscious, decisive, strong spiritual Mother—with an adamantine essence. Functioning within the parameters of the patriarchal Hindu society of the time, she catalyzes her own psychological and spiritual evolution as well as that of the king, her husband. In this regard, she is comparable to Lord Siva's wife, Sakti, an energetic cosmic force whose activity and vigor generate change. Neither Sakuntala nor the king, however, are to be viewed as humans in their own right. Both are personifications of dual powers, identified with deities or cosmic principles that make for spiritual and psychological growth in the existential domain. Sakuntala and her husband play their terrestrial roles: each fulfills a function.

Sakuntala is not only a play; it is an exercise in ascesis. Each dramatic sequence indicates a step forward in the individual's growth—a progressive extraction from the *prima materia* and hence from bondage to the phenomenological world. A close interplay between material and cosmic domains, personal and impersonal worlds, is therefore implicit in *Sakuntala*. Whether animate or inanimate, visible or invisible, the performers interact onstage as individuals in their material form and as collective divinities. Because gods and mortals act in consort with the mineral and vegetable worlds, lower and higher forms of life cohere in a giant symphony of varying dimensions and multiple tonalities. The entire spectacle—a microcosm of the macrocosm—may be understood as a manifestation of Absolute Reality or Universal Oneness. Humankind needs such manifestations because we apprehend the unknowable and the ineluctable only through tangible signs and feelings, during an end-less "sea of change" (*samsara*) or "vicious circle of existence" (Younger n.d., 140).

Scholars know virtually nothing about the author of *Sakuntala*, the Indian poet and dramatist considered the most distinguished figure in Sanskrit literature. It is surmised that he lived sometime between 100 B.C.E. and 414 C.E., and some exegetes believe his birthplace to have been Ujjain, the capital of Chandragupta II's kingdom in central India (Coulson 1981, 29). Others see the court of Matrigupta, king of Kashmir, as the most likely background for his poetic genius (Lal 1959, 10). Kalidasa's play *Rakshasa's Ring* is drawn from the dramatist's imagination, while *Sakuntala* is based on a mythological event narrated in the first part of the *Mahabharata,* the Sanskrit religious epic begun about 200 B.C.E. that reached its nearly final form by 350 C.E.

Sakuntala combines liturgical drama with the elegance and sensitivity of Sanskrit theater. Kalidasa, skilled in the use of metaphor, eidetic verbal descriptions, and delicate poetic harmonies, brings into being the protagonists' inner landscape—a mysterious and tremulous realm that is reflected in the natural surroundings onstage (Berriedale 1964, 161).

Ectypal Analysis

Since the period of time to which Kalidasa belongs hypothetically spans four centuries, it may be useful to briefly to mention the names of some of the most distinguished rulers who notably contributed to India's history during the time. Asoka (273–232 B.C.E.), one of the country's most important kings, not only set the ethical standards during the Mauryan dynasty but was also instrumental in uniting most of India and in making Buddhism its state religion. The eight stupas built during his reign were said to have enclosed what remained of the Buddha and his possessions.

Perhaps the two most important Mauryan sculptures for our purposes, although there were many remarkable ones, represent a *yakshi* (female earth-spirit) and a *yaksha* (male earth-spirit). The former was discovered in the environs of Patna, and the latter at Patna itself. Both sculptures are realistic and emphasize the sensual aspect of the body, suggesting the importance accorded to animistic and fertility cultures in the India of the pre-Harrapan period (3000 B.C.E.) (Craven 1976, 45).

After Asoka's death and the collapse of the Mauryan empire in 185

B.C.E., disorder prevailed and invasions from neighboring lands continued for nearly two hundred years, even as Hinduism grew in strength and Buddhism declined.

The inception of the new and vital Gupta dynasty in Bihar in 320 C.E. ushered in prosperity and the flowering of what is considered India's "classical" period: the sciences and the visual, performing, and literary arts reached their apogee during the reign of Chandragupta II (375–415 C.E.). The mature and tasteful balance between earthly and otherworldly domains that is manifested in the arts of this period is evident in the dramas of Kalidasa, and especially in *Sakuntala.* Indeed, this Sanskrit playwright, who was purported to have adorned the court of Chandragupta II, instilled in the work serenity and transpersonal understanding (Craven 1976, 111).

Women in Society

The situation of women in India during the Vedic period (c. 1200–600 B.C.E.) was better than that of later times. During the early centuries of this era men were so involved in conquest that they relied extensively on women to tend both to agriculture and the manufacture of bows, arrows, and other armaments. Not only did women run the home and raise the children; they also engaged in such activities as weaving, basketry, embroidery, and the dyeing of materials. With the rise of class consciousness, however, many of these tasks were relegated to the lower strata of the population.

Despite the importance of the above-mentioned functions, women were regarded for the most part as chattels. If it was politically and/or economically expedient, for example, they were given away in marriage. In the *Mahabharata,* Dhritarashtra suggested that he give a hundred female slaves to Lord Krishna as proof of his admiration of him. Because husbands had proprietary rights over their wives, as recorded in the *Rig Veda* (c. 1200–900 B.C.E.), a husband could pay a gambling debt by handing his wife over to the winner (Altekar 1983, 213).

Nevertheless, it is fair to say that in Vedic times women were treated with respect, and they comported themselves in keeping with the mores of the times. Usually, upon entering her new household, a bride was expected to run it, thereby sparing her husband's elderly parents the effort of doing so (90).

Women, not being obliged to marry until the age of sixteen, could be educated and function positively in family life. In some families daughters were taught to direct and organize large households (9). Some women chose to remain unmarried and to follow a profession, thus acquiring economic independence.

In post-Vedic times—from 500 B.C.E. to 300 C.E.—the situation changed drastically. Girls married at the age of six or seven, and thus were denied any but the most basic education. Because they were unable to read, write, or even recite their prayers, their legal and social status in the homes of their husbands declined calamitously. Moreover, since the bride was too young for her marriage to be consummated, she was forbidden to remain alone with her husband, adding to her extreme loneliness, sense of isolation, and feelings of rejection. When finally she did come of age, she lived in total submission to her husband. So unsure were these children of their comportment and so ignorant of household planning and organization that mothers-in-law frequently abused them, beating them with a pestle—sometimes with fatal results. To avoid mistreatment, some Hindu daughters-in-law chose to become Buddhist nuns. One of these wrote of her days as a wife:

> My salutations morn and eve I brought,
> To both the parents of my husband, low
> Bowing my head and kneeling at their feet,
> According to the training given to me.
>
> (Altekar 1983, 921)

Higher-class women, however, were at times allowed to become teachers, the most gifted among them choosing theology, philosophy, poetry, and literature as their subject matter. Others specialized in grammar. Some of the women admitted to Buddhist and Jain nunneries became well-known preachers. Lady doctors specialized to a great extent in midwifery; some practiced Ayurvedic medicine. Women in industrial and business circles also pursued their families' trade. Although music, dancing, singing, painting, and instrumentation were cultivated in the home by high-class women, there is no information suggesting that these arts were taught or practiced outside of the family compound. Courtesans who were fine artists were often held in high esteem, and women attached to shrines and temples as entertainers, considered sacred prostitutes, were generally treated well.[1]

In some ruling families daughters were given military and administrative training. Such instruction was greatly valued in the case of dowager queens, such as Nayanika of the Satavhana dynasty (second century B.C.E.), who administered kingdoms during the minority of their sons (23). Only infrequently, however, did women become heads of state. Queen Didda did rule as sovereign and not as regent of the state of Kashmir for twenty-two years, but in the *Ramayana* (c. 500 B.C.E.), although the crown was offered to his wife, Sita, during Rama's fourteen-year exile in the forest, she chose instead to accompany her husband.

These examples of successful women were rare, and the birth of a girl since earliest times had been generally experienced as an unenviable event. The increasing complexity of the caste and subcaste system resulted in fewer opportunities to select sons-in-law. Unmarried daughters frequently added to their parents' financial burdens, and since widows were forbidden to re-marry, daughters unable to earn money represented a severe drain on family income. On occasion, a widow would take up the spinning and weaving of cotton and woolen yarn and piece goods to support her family. Parents grieved empathetically over their daughters' loneliness and feared even more the hor-rendous possibility that a widowed daughter might follow the custom of suttee by throwing her self on her husband's funeral pyre (Altekar 1983, 5, 23).

Although suttee came into existence only in the early centuries of the common era, references were made to this ritual even in the *Ramayana*, the *Mahabharata*, and some Puranas. It was not, however, encouraged, nor was it considered a religious duty. The custom took on amplitude among warriors and ascetics, self-sacrifice being the most sublime way of living an *imitatio Dei*. However, poets such as Bana (625 C.E.) and Tantric writers opposed the custom vehemently, maintaining that since woman was a manifestation of the Supreme Goddess, her cremation on her husband's pyre warranted con-demnation and eternal punishment. Although the British prohibited suttee in 1829, it still exists in some remote areas in India (Altekar 1983, 122ff.).

The marriage that takes place in *Sakuntala* dates to the Vedic age and is referred to as a Gandharva marriage, a name inspired by celestial musicians, the Gandharvas, known for their beauty and their amorous relationships. The marriage, considered a love match, was consummated prior to religious rituals (42). With the growing impact of religion, however, Gandharva mar-riages came to be frowned upon and demands were made for the ceremonial ritual to be performed before sexual acts.

The Brahma form of marriage was considered a sacred union: the father selected a husband for his daughter and offered him presents, and the future son-in-law swore that he would be a good husband, caring for and never ill-treating his wife. The father then made ritual offerings of "sacred gifts in the presence of the Divine Fire," the entire ceremony being looked upon as a binding commitment undertaken in the presence of the Creator of the Universe (39–47).

As conveyed in the *Laws of Manu* (about the second or first century B.C.E.), the wife was forever tied to her husband in marriage, but a husband's abandonment of his wife could be interpreted as a divorce, in which case she could remarry. Although men were permitted several wives, if a wife loved or married another man, grave sin devolved on her. If a woman was barren, a husband could not only take a second wife but could expect encouragement in this respect by his first wife. According to the *Laws of Manu*, a husband always ruled supreme over his wife (Altekar 1983,108).

There are some passages in Vedic literature that mention cases of polyandry. In the *Mahabharata*, for example, Draupadi was married to the five victorious Pandava brothers. One explanation for her polyandrous marriage—a historic event—was that she had uttered five times in a prayer, in a previous incarnation, the following words: "Give me a husband" (*Mahabharata* 1:213). In later centuries polyandry still existed, and seemingly it even is practiced today in certain tribes of Kashmir and Tibet.

Although a few segments of society advocated the veil for royal ladies in ancient times, the custom of purdah (seclusion and the wearing of the veil) was virtually unknown in India prior to Muslim rule. Nevertheless, it was written in the *Ramayana* that when Sita went into exile with her husband, she regrettably did not wear a veil, and thus "became the object of public gaze." The adoption of purdah by the Hindu ruling class and aristocratic families became customary after the advent of Muslim rule and increased in popularity thereafter. The notion of seclusion in the king's palace was nowhere mentioned in the *Mahabharata*, as attested to by the story that tells of the student Uttanka's visit to the queen in her harem (Altekar 1983, 169).

Ambiguity and contradiction is seemingly inherent in the male's relationship to women in India—and in other lands as well. Although, according to the *Laws of Manu*, the killing of a woman was punishable by death, to defend a woman and die in the process insured the male repose in a beatific sphere. On the one hand, women were to be protected, perhaps like an endangered species; on the other hand, they were denied their freedom and most basic human rights. In the words of the *Laws of Manu:*

> Her father protects her in childhood, her husband protects her in youth,
> her sons protect her in old age—a woman does not deserve independence.
> (De Bary 1958a, 228)

Sanskrit Theatrical Conventions

Sanskrit theatrical conventions are all-encompassing—a complex blend of philosophy/religion, music, dance, and the visual image. Hindu scriptures declare that Brahma—who was called "the Breath" or "Master of the Word"—revealed the mysteries and delights of theater to Bharata, the earliest theoretician of Sanskrit drama (first century B.C.E.). His revelations, handed down orally from generation to generation, were inscribed in the *Natyasastra* (Canons of the dance and drama) between the second century B.C.E. and the second century C.E. Siva, "the Master of the Dance," it was disclosed, had taught Bharata that all theater was part of a cosmic process. All matter, visible and invisible, moved about in a dance pattern in eternally transforming particles. Everything that is created, even that which does not enter the manifest world, is subject to destruction; nothing is permanent except the All, called Absolute Reality or the original Brahman, which is the "source, sustenance, and end of the universe" and "partakes of every phase of existence" (Prabhavananda and Manchester 1957, 60). Siva also made it known that his consort Sakti, experienced as an energetic force in the universe, was a projection of his own feminine nature into the manifest world. It is she who, like Agni, the god of fire, consumes (as do passions), titillates, and illuminates. Together with Sakti, Siva is eternal motion, solar activity, the process of fusion and dissolution. The *Rig Veda* describes the Master of the Cosmic Dance as consisting of white, red, and black flames. Symbolizing the union of time and space, color and the absence of it, matter and nonmatter, Siva incarnates the universe's creative principle—that force which enables humankind to transform itself into God and God into humankind.

For the Hindu, the theater is a spiritual venture/adventure, a rite of passage taking its participants on a journey from one state of being to another. The spectacle, therefore, is not to be considered merely as a work of art, entertainment, or a representation of fine craftsmanship and expert character delineation, although it may be understood in these terms, but rather as an experience to be absorbed and assimilated. It gives its participants spiritual nourishment. Through the multiplicity of theatrical conventions—that is, created forms—the participants in the theatrical spectacle become integrated as individuals into a collective sphere of complex forces implicit in the cosmic plan.

There is a double movement during this conjunction of forces in a theatrical performance: the voluntary destruction of the primal state of unity existing prior to the enactment of the spectacle, and the birth of multiple forces onstage (decor, actors, lights, sound, and so forth), each struggling for its own expression within the framework of the performance. The experience dramatized during the course of the play, with its vicissitudes and complex series of identifications, concludes with the annihilation of the personal ego—or personal consciousness—and its assimilation into cosmic being (Brahman), Absolute Reality, Universal Oneness. The movement onstage, then, ranges from monism to plurality back to monism—that is, from construction through dissolution and reconstruction (Daumal 1970, 8–30).

The fluidity in the stage happenings indicates the process of the continuous alteration of matter in form and consistency. According to Hindu philosophy, atoms, as single units, live on eternally; as aggregates or compounds, however, they change perpetually in form, potency, and consistency. When grouped together as elements onstage, they become part of the phenomenological world and are subject to birth and decay. Each dramatic production is viewed by the Hindu as a combining and recombining of elements or atoms, a reworking of these tangible and intangible forces in single or aggregate forms (66). In a numinous experience, the condensation, distillation, and crystallization of feelings are not isolated expressions of humankind's inner world of passions. They are, rather, manifestations of nature's eternal flux—its disappearance from view and reappearance in the universe—as experienced by humankind's limited understanding. Buddha understood the duality inherent in the so-called instability of the phenomenological world and the "nonchangefulness" (nirvana) of the eternal condition. That notion is expressed as Brahman in the *Upanishads*. Brahman is transcendence, or Absolute Reality:

> He wakes with the waking man, dreams with the dreamer, and sleeps the deep sleep of the dreamless sleeper; but he transcends these three states to become himself. His true nature is pure consciousness. . . .
>
> The Self being unknown, all three states of the soul are but dreaming—waking, dreaming, and dreamless sleep. In each of these dwells the Self: the eye is his dwelling place while we wake, the mind is his dwelling place while we dream, the lotus of the heart is his dwelling place while we sleep the dreamless sleep. . . .
>
> O thou self-luminous Brahman, remove the veil of ignorance before me, that I may behold thy light. (Prabhavananda and Manchester 1957, 60)

As in Brahman, words, gestures, sounds, and lighting in the theatrical world are both changeable and immutable, evolving and dissolving. They build situations, conjure up moods, and impregnate the listless particles with kinetic impulses and cognitive abstractions. The dynamism triggered by this multidimensional language, consisting of visualizations and sonorities, quickens the affective systems of both protagonists and viewers, enabling them to absorb and assimilate the mixtures and blendings occurring onstage.

Philosophical/Religious Notions Embedded in Sakuntala

Kalidasa's characterizations, which are in keeping with Sanskrit dramatic theory, naturally differ greatly from those of Occidental theater. Paradigmatically, he did not consider pain and distress suffered by his protagonists to be rooted in some moral or psychological defect inherent in their personalities, nor did he deem the anguish they felt to be tragic. Unlike writers of Western drama based on Aristotle's *Poetics,* who maintain that the hero's undoing is caused by a fatal flaw in his character or some error in judgment or the like, Kalidasa believed that life's experiences were manifestations of the individual's karma or "cosmic justice." Aristotle's theory of catharsis, purification through purgation, has no place in *Sakuntala;* nor does the concept of tragedy, with its accompanying notions of pity and terror.

Theater for the Sanskrit dramatist in general and for Kalidasa in particular is a dispassionate enactment of pleasurable or painful experiences, during which audiences view impersonal sentiments on stage interwoven in a harmonious spectacle. For Kalidasa, moods are more important than actual events. Inasmuch as feelings, sensations, and optical experiences stir the Indian playgoer, images, symbols, and signs in *Sakuntala* progressively illuminate the protagonists and the audience and contribute to the spiritual growth of both.

A religiously oriented play, *Sakuntala* may be considered a theatrical rendering of the Hindu's search to realize four aims in life, each of which has a spiritual and psychological equivalent. The first period of search, *artha,* represents the phase of material well-being, in which the acquisition of worldly possessions and a reputation seem to be life's goal. Extroversion is usually the rule: a seeking "out" for fulfillment and spiritual development. During this period of search, the flowing forward into life becomes a virtual necessity for the individual: fluidity marks her or his understanding and emotional malleability furthers the evolutionary process. The opening scene of *Sakuntala,* for example, is a forest, the *prima materia* of the Hindu's *prakriti*—the undifferentiated world of phenomena or matter—where the protagonist steps out of an enclosed world into life's swiftly coursing currents.

The second period of search, *kama,* is the period dominated by the pleasure principle. Kama, the Hindu equivalent of the Roman God Cupid, strikes the unsuspecting protagonist with feelings of joy, love, sensuality, and attachment. A virtual art of loving is lived out in this sequence, but it is always delineated with the utmost delicacy and tenderness. It is during this stage of psychological evolution that a fixing or coagulation of emotions occurs with the focusing of energies and desires on one person. In the ashram, or religious retreat, where Sakuntala dwells, the dramatic action follows a course of progressive interiorization, paving the way for her initiation into the life process with all its dualities and tensions.

The third stage, *dharma*, is the period during which religious and moral obligations must be fused. Order and structure take shape on both the terrestrial and the cosmic planes. The tension between society's religious dictates and the individual's instincts and passions burns the protagonist, destroying all peripheral sensations and emotions that might lead her away from the strict code of ethics imposed upon her by society. The palace, or worldly order, with all of its constrictions and injunctions, is the scene of the protagonist's submersion in pain and suffering.

The fourth and last phase, *moksa*, is the phase of eventual salvation, redemption, or liberation from the phenomenological condition that besets Sakuntala during her earthly trajectory. A higher sphere is brought into play, ushering in the experience of cosmic connectedness or superior understanding. The protagonist is no longer viewed in terms of her fleshly body but as a purified, adamantine, incorruptible being. The celestial sphere, a fitting background for the sublimation stage, is depicted in this sequence.

Reality for the Hindu—including stage reality—is comparable to the Westerner's unconscious. Thus, the Hindu considers thought, nightmares, fantasies, and colors to be empirical truths; they enable her or him to become integrated into the All. Tibetan, Buddhist, and Hindu gods are archetypal forms/thoughts, projections of humankind's mind that nevertheless exist also in the empirical world. In direct contrast is the Occidental view of thought and the thought processes, which takes them to be abstractions possessing no concrete reality; they are and remain illusions (Jung 1963, par. 480).

The goal of Indian disciplines, dramatic or religious, is to teach individuals more about themselves so that they may perfect their spiritual and physical essences, deepen their understanding of the sensory world, and comprehend more fully why they are required to experience samsara. Such instruction encourages them to objectify, to refrain from identifying with objects and people in the phenomenological world where the nonilluminated live out their existences. It also emboldens them to search out ways of transcending the sphere of illusion and eventually to reach *samadhi* (absorption in Self). The dramatic ritual, as well as certain religious disciplines such as yoga, instructs human beings how to enlarge their scope of being—providing them with the ability to experience themselves in the uniqueness of their individuality as well as in their collective nature (paras. 480–82).

Archetypal Analysis

Sakuntala is an initiation ritual by means of which the protagonists, although given human form, are also part of a transcosmic sphere. They are, then, incarnations of superhuman or subhuman forms that touch, irritate, and terrify those with whom they come into contact.

Artha: *Mother Nature and the Forest Experience*

Sakuntala opens as King Dushyanta, ruler of India, is hunting in a forest. Preparing to wound a stag, he hears shouting voices offstage, after which he is stopped by a hermit who tells him that the animal is sacred. The king is offered hospitality in the neighboring ashram. Its beautiful flowering plants, trees, and tame animals set the tone for Sakuntala's entrance.

Nature, and specifically Mother Nature as featured in the opening scene of *Sakuntala*, is not present simply for background purposes or to fill empty stage space. It is implicit in the play's very organism—an important means of expressing the intensity, pitch, and timbre of the emotions inherent in Sanskrit drama. The Hindu scriptures teach that plants are dormant or exist in a state of latent consciousness; they are, therefore, capable of both pleasure and pain (Brahenda 1958, 175). Similarly, animals have feelings that, if not as well developed as those of humans, are nonetheless powerful and worthy of reverence. Animals are frequently seen in Kalidasa's play as holy and sacred beings.

We learn that the king is Siva's earthly counterpart. Symbolized by the *linga* (phallus, or procreative force), he is a generating principle—creator and destroyer. Like the divinity identified with the *lingam*, the king, hunting in the forest, is in search of his procreative power in nature, or his Sakti, or *yoni*, the female element with its rounded and containing features (Eliade 1973, 355).

Unlike Siva, who with his wife, Sakti, is a total being, the king is incomplete. The "quintessence of Siva," according to scriptures, contains the female principle, or ovum. The two together, then, generate the "glorified body"—the existence of the godly being (Eliade 1971, 128). Devoid of the energetic principle in life—that is, the female force—the king has developed only one side of his personality: the patriarchal, rigid, masculine conscious-ness that manifests itself in aggressive acts. Isolated, despite his numerous wives, he has not as yet experienced a profound relationship with a woman. He understands the female principle only in the most limited way: a woman represents sex and a beautiful decoration in his harem. Although he is the head of the social and spiritual world of his realm and the possessor of great riches, the king experiences a void because he has never known love. He does not yet possess what Jung calls the "treasure hard to attain"—that is, the feeling or relating principle that will allow for fluidity and malleability within the psyche.

A balance between patriarchal and matriarchal domains was necessary if the king—the archetypal man or the ruling consciousness of political and social order—is to evolve spiritually and psychologically. His hunt in the forest implies that he is actively searching for prey in Mother Nature—the matriarchate. Metaphysically, it indicates that the one (king) will have to become two (male and female) in order to create a dynamic state of tension that will precipitate the next step of the evolutionary process.

At the outset of *Sakuntala*, the charioteer informs the king: "You are like Siva on a deer hunt: / Bow and arrow in search of the antelope" (Lal 1959, 3). Hunting, which indicates a quest on both the physical and meta-physical levels, may also represent the beginning of the growth process. The forest, with its uncontrolled and uncultivated flora, fauna, and various min-erals—the domain of the Great Mother, of which Sakuntala is but an as-pect—is the focus of the king's attention. Animals, aquatic plants, and trees mirror nature's fertile aspects; they also create a liquid atmosphere. The king's experience in this elemental realm, where instincts roam free, will enable him, through the feminine principle, to develop that "diamond body," that Golden Essence which will expand his worldly experience and lead him to his spiritual salvation.

Approached symbolically, the woman will make it possible for the king to gain entry into his own subliminal depths, where he will arouse his still-untapped forces. By pushing further on in the life experience, his whole physical and spiritual mechanism will become attuned to cosmic rhythms and tensions. As the "Lord of Beasts and Prince of Yogis," Siva, by means of his Sakti, will lead the king to the source of nourishing forces, drawing an ego-centered individual into the pleromatic sphere of cosmic consciousness (Eliade 1973, 355).

The antelope that the King is hunting outruns his arrows. He orders the charioteer to overtake his prey, but animals excel even the gods.

> This speed is a miracle, it plays tricks with my eyes—Small objects put on size, the crooked becomes straight. I seem to be nowhere and everywhere. (*S*, 13)[2]

The element of speed brings into play these opposites that lead to the drama's action and "savor" (Zimmer 1974b, 450). *Rasa* (savor, taste) is that dynamic principle which gives immediate perception of the essence, or inside, of the dramatic ritual and the "innate architecture" of the artistic creation (Daumal 1970, 15–27). In keeping with this vitalism, the text mentions animals, grasses, flowers, and a speeding chariot, evoking the continuous circuit of organic and inorganic life, which plunges the protagonists and viewers directly into mythical time, where past, present, and future cohabit with an eternal present. The transient exists only as measured by the continuous; to the perishable is juxtaposed the immortal. in infinite cycles.

The antelope or deer may be associated with Buddha's so-called Deer Park Sermon, the first one preached at Benares (now Varanasi), treating the subjects of causation and illusions (Campbell 1974, 169). He informed his followers that all entities, both manifest and unmanifest, may be likened to a mirage—to the moon reflected in water or to an echo. They are neither real nor unreal. Buddha spoke of the terrestrial, personal, and subjective condition of the ego-centered or unenlightened being preoccupied mainly with momentary worldly desires rather than with the eternal and pure spirit *(purusa)* and the transcosmic (in Buddhist parlance, the nonbreath or nirvana stage). That the antelope is running at high speed underscores the king's preoccupation with the moment rather than with the "eternal," the individual instead of the collective, ego-centeredness rather than Self-centeredness. The notion of celerity arises in the world of duality (the empirical domain), where polarities as such pave the way for tension. The king's localization in the world of the particular and his concentration on his prey nevertheless serve a cosmic purpose. A dynamic principle is awakened within him, and serves to counteract inertia. It is his destiny to act as he does: to hunt for that which will complete him. He is the product of his past incarnations, and, as such, part of the process whereby potentials are lived out and finally consummated in keeping with karmic law. Only after one's earthly experiences have been lived out can one be "awakened"; only with such illumination can the king, paradoxically, be annihilated and nirvana realized (Eliade 1973, 34).

Just as the yogin meditates to experience deeper levels of consciousness, so the king's senses now see the outward configurations of objects, animals, or plants as dilating, expanding, and altering to become dynamic inhaling and exhaling principles in an active universe. As the yogin enters the world of nonduration through physical and spiritual disciplines, so the king, dazzled by the speed of his chariot and disoriented by the novelty of his new experience, "burns" temporal time and annihilates history. He divests himself of the "blackness" and "ignorance" of his inherited lives—and glimpses nontime (*S*, 83, 185).

Kalidasa's visual images as well as his use of metaphors underscore the world of duality on stage and the tensions to which it gives rise. The deer leaps into the air like a woman, breathing freely and gracefully. Plants and seeds alter in their form, consistency, and temperament. The notion of freedom—of an unconstructed and unobstructed existence—now emerges. The subtle elements of air, breath, and wind also come into play. Indian mystics frequently allude to Vayu, the god of wind, as "vital breath": that force which dominates bodily functions. Hatha yogic treatises, such as *Rasarvana*, emphasize the importance of breath because practitioners of this discipline believe that the body may remain alive for an indefinite period of time through the proper control of the vital force (*S*, 283).

The king begins his initiation into another modality of karma, or universal causality. He must now experience the world of illusion—that is, life with all of its pains and joys. Conflict, which mystics, psychologists, and alchemists translate as a process of trituration, may lead to knowledge. Now that he has successfully completed the disciplines associated with his material well-being, the king may pass beyond his artha condition and be awakened to the *kama* stage of development.

Kama: *Sakuntala's Secret Flame*

When the king hears voices cry out "The sacred stag!" (*S*, 13), he immediately stops hunting. The stag must not be harmed. For Buddhists, the stag—looked upon as the Golden Stag—is the prototype of all stags; it is a bodhisattva, a helping savior type, a hierophany, instrumental in enabling humankind to become liberated from worldly passion. Aware that he is approaching a sanctuary, the dominion of divinity, the king will sever himself from the temporal sphere to contact transcendency and thereby find his own spiritual center, represented by the sanctuary, or ashram (Hopkins 1971, 12). Putting away his bow and arrow, for he has left the external world of matter with its sports and the ardor associated with them, the king enters the internal domain of the ascetic where the inner fire is kindled.

Fire, for the Hindu and the Buddhist, is an element of that secret force that lies asleep in the umbilical region. The kindling of this inner flame so that all parts of the body may experience its ardor and warmth permits humans to transcend their limitations. In Kundalini and Tantric yoga, the initiate believes that a divine power (Sakti) inhabits his being and remains dormant within him in the form of a coiled serpent (Kundalini). Through specific meditative practices and physical techniques, he is able to arouse and lure upward this energetic force as "heat" capable of stirring the "fire" of feeling within whatever area of the body he chooses to activate. Kundalini may be regarded, then, as a manifestation of Agni (the fire god), Surya (the sun god), and Indra (the atmospheric deity); these are manifested on earth as fire, sun, and thunder. For the Indian practitioner of Kundalini and for Tibetan Tantrists, inner fire, created either through the body itself or by artificial means (in an athanor, or oven), reduces subtle matter to ashes and the impure to its pure state.

Although considered the incarnation of Siva, the king also embodies Kama, the Indian counterpart of Cupid. This god carries the "flower bow" and shoots the "flower arrows" in Hindu cosmology. By activating heart, feeling, and desire, he is considered creator of the arts, love, and passion. It has been said that early in his life Kama was ordered by Indra, the king of the gods, to aim his arrow at Siva. Instantly, the meditations of Siva—"master yogi and archetypal ascetic-solitary" within the Hindu pantheon—were interrupted. He was filled with love for the divine daughter of the Himalayan king, the female principle, an externalization and concretization of his own energy as projected onto nature. In his new condition, Siva had to contend with this force in the outer world; he had to recognize its existence and learn to deal with it. Thus diverted from the "timeless contemplation of his innermost supernal luminosity," Siva gave vent to his anger by shooting flames from his third eye and reducing Kama to ashes. In desperation, Kama's wife, Rati, begged Siva to return her husband to her. Not able to produce him physically, Siva did incarnate him as a force thenceforth known as Ananga (Zimmer 1974b, 141). It is the unseen Kama—in his invisible and nonmaterial presence—who propels the twists and turns, the pirouettes and the sensual gyrations, throughout Kalidasa's drama.

At the point of the drama where the king approaches the ashram, an atmosphere of serenity, relaxation, and inactivity reigns. The "fruit lies rotting," the grain remains untouched, "the deer gaze nonchalantly," and the "paths and pond are wet" (*S*, 15). The Great Mother is at rest; she awaits the king; the Great Wheel will be put into motion (Zimmer 1974b, 158–60).

Now the king is beset by a "strange omen": his arm involuntarily trembles. He wonders why, in this sacred area where discipline and tranquility reign among the ascetics, he should fall subject to such tension, but quickly realizes that "fate has doors everywhere" and that Brahma's omnipresence may be experienced in infinite ways (*S*, 15).

Two elements are at work in the ashram: the spiritual fire of the ascetics and the water (moisture) of the enclosure. The lush vegetation produces its own heat, which mixes with the dampness of the enclosed area, causing vapor to form. Concomitantly the stage happenings take on an intangible quality: solids seem to vanish through the vaporization. The atmosphere is conducive to love—the shooting of Kama's darts.

In this "Forest of Penance," the king's arm still trembles. His allusion to the "doors of fate" connotes the mysteries surrounding him (*S*, 5). In Tibetan meditative practices, doors symbolize the hierophant's passage from one sphere of consciousness to another, and elsewhere doors have been identified with the female principle. In the context of *Sakuntala*, the ashram is a type of door—or female image—the opening of which the king must experience, not only in the visible realm but within his own psyche. Ashrams have also been compared to mandalas—those circles and squares that represent, psychologically, humankind's impulses toward wholeness. Metaphysically, they are meditative devices used by initiates to concentrate their energies on a central point. The initiate sets his gaze on the outer circles or squares of the mandala images, which represent the polarities in life: life and death, attraction and repulsion, and so forth. Sometimes the four cardinal points of mandalas depict terrifying demons or "guardians of the doors," whose task it is to protect the meditator from the intrusion of disruptive forces. These monsters aid the initiate to overcome inner pollution, restraining the destructive thoughts and sensations that emerge from his subliminal world to diffuse his powers of concentration. In the king's search for his spiritual center, the ashram/mandala may open the door to experiences and dimensions heretofore unknown to him.

The king is apprised that the head of the ashram, the sage Kanva, is away "on a pilgrimage to ward off the evil eye from his daughter"—in reality his foster daughter, Sakuntala (*S*, 14). Eyes, associated with luminaries such as the sun and moon as well as with Siva's third eye, may destroy, reducing everything in sight to ashes, or they may illuminate. Since demons have invaded the ashram since Kanva's departure, it follows that the creative center—the point of equilibrium in a mandala image and by extension within the religious retreat—has been displaced. Imbalance prevails. That the ashram, the seat of humankind's spiritual world, is being invaded by demons indicates that some spiritual sickness has overcome the area.

Sakuntala enters with two friends. Having been requested by her foster father to water the ashram's plants during his absence, she is associated with water from the very outset of the play. She is a diminutive of the Great Mother, a source of nourishment, a symbol of fecundity and of life *in potentia*. In the *Chandogya Upanishad* we read, "Only this water in solidified form are this earth, the atmosphere, the heavens, the mountains, plants and trees, wild animals, even to worms, flies and ants—they are all only this water in solidified state" (Stillman 1960, 108).

The king is immediately captivated by Sakuntala. He observes her every motion as he stands protected behind a clump of trees, implying that he is immersing himself in the divine, and therefore the collective, sphere. For the Hindu and Buddhist, trees are sacred. It is said that Buddha gained illumination under the Bodhi-tree, and he is frequently represented as a tree. A tree may be used as an altar and it may represent as well the world axis, encompassing all cosmic spheres: its roots are Brahma, its trunk is Siva, and its branches are Vishnu.

Through the forest—or Mother Nature—with which Sakuntala is identified, the king will be able to fulfill his karma and experience heightened consciousness. Similarly, she will advance from the stage of passive/personal and earthly understanding to cosmic consciousness because of his presence. But since Kalidasa's upbringing is patriarchal, his emphasis at the outset of the play is understandably placed on the male's feelings, and only later on the female's.

Mesmerized by Sakuntala's countenance, the king compares her to earthly and celestial spheres, to matter and spirit, to the lotus and the moon: "The lotus is lovely though filth-covered / The moon prettier for her dark spot" (*S*, 16). The lotus, representative of the female principle because of its rounded form and its watery environment, is used for meditative purposes (Zimmer 1974b, 96). Concentration on its shape may lead the initiate to experience "the heart of the lotus," or his own inner radiance—his supernal point. The eight-petaled lotus symbolizes cosmic harmony and is frequently featured in Hindu iconography with Vishnu asleep on the surface of the flower, or "causal ocean," the aquatic element in nature. In the *Bhagavad Gita,* the lotus is a manifestation of Brahman (Parrinder 1975, 31). For the Buddhist, the lotus represents Buddha-nature; the center of the flower remains unbothered by the muddied environment, implying that samsara in no way detracts from its eventual absorption in nirvana. As the smooth and oily surface of the lotus leaves lets the mud slip from its petals, so should a person allow life's vicissitudes to detach themselves from his being.

Sakuntala will become that lotus image upon which the meditator focuses his attention in order to experience superior centers of being where time becomes timeless and the microcosm unites with the macrocosm. In her lotus association, Sakuntala will develop her levels of experience, and in so doing, evolve from the lotus with two petals to the lotus with four, six, eight, sixteen petals . . . until she becomes that thousand-petaled lotus which has passed through all the other phases of existence. Like Sakti, who, having fulfilled her potential, transcended her previous incarnations and joined with Siva, Sakuntala will be drawn to the king (Zimmer 1974b, 584).

That the king compares Sakuntala to the lotus also indicates that her presence has given birth to another dimension within his universe. The cosmic waters in which the mystical lotus grows have allowed the previously dormant "radiant sun," or Golden State, to emerge. For the mystic/alchemist, gold and the lotus both represent immortality. As gold is associated with divinity and spirit, so the lotus coincides with that force within human beings which seeks to liberate them from material existence, from perpetual transmigrations. Before *moksa* can come into being, however, gold must be absorbed; it must be mixed and incinerated, reduced to ashes.

A spiritual atmosphere has been prepared for the meeting of the king and Sakuntala. As previously mentioned, the two are the earthly counterparts of Siva and Sakti. Sakuntala, the future thousand-petaled lotus, will become "the door," the "womb," the "mouth" through which universal waters flow. She will participate in the creation of that incorruptible gold, the highest form of Mother Earth, "Goddess of Moisture," the procreative and maternal manifestation of the Absolute (Zimmer 1974a, 91–96). In her water/lotus aspects, Sakuntala will be the bestower of beauty, purity, and happiness. The vaporous condition created at the outset of the scene couples with the ardent fire of spiritual growth and is transformed into the burning sensations of passion.

The king again compares this radiant virginal figure to natural forces:

Her lips glisten like new leaves,
Her arms are shoots
And her youth sprouts a glory of glittering flowers.

(*S,* 16)

He will experience her as he does a flower, absorbing her essence, inhaling her feelings, and taking in her beauty. According to Tantric belief, man must not only accept nature as it is, but also use it well and not divest himself of it. The *Kulamava Tantra* depicts her as metaphor: "As one falls into the ground, so one must lift oneself by the aid of the ground." Passion is very much part of the earth experience. "Every function is part of the Divine Action (sakti) in Nature." When a man "eats, drinks or has sexual intercourse, he does so not with the thought of himself as a separate individual satisfying his own peculiar limited wants, an animal filching as it were from nature the enjoyment he has, but thinking of himself in such enjoyment as Siva" (Zimmer 1974b, 576). Mortals, therefore, experience themselves as gods, and in so doing, accomplish their destiny. Thus matter is thoroughly absorbed and experienced in order to be surpassed, so that the metauniverse may become a reality. Intellect *(buddhi),* an aspect of the empirical world, aids in the process of gaining autonomy over oneself—in becoming that smooth lotus leaf from which all cares slip.

The frequent repetition in *Sakuntala* of water images to describe vegetation of various kinds coincides with the Indian mystics' and alchemists' extensive use of drugs and medicines. These they extracted from nature's own storehouse in order to remedy a condition of imbalance or sickness in the body. Lotus juice, they believed, had magical powers. Called "soma" after the divinity of the same name, it was capable of restoring health and improving longevity. A gift of the gods brought to man by an eagle, soma enabled mortals to communicate with Divinity: it brought on the state called "divine drunkenness" (Eliade 1973, 278). To imbibe soma, as the king was doing visually and emotionally, was to pave the way for the coagulation or firming up of his relationship with Sakuntala.

Soma, then, "awakened" the king from his strictly patriarchal activities and laid the groundwork for the Golden Essence to be. The *Avatamsaka Sutra* (150–350 c.e.) teaches that the drug called *hataka* may also prepare for the purest of conditions: "One *liang* of it [*hataka*] will turn a thousand *liangs* of bronze into pure gold." In the *Mahaprajnaparamitopadesa*, Nargarjuna, the great second- or third-century c.e. Buddhist teacher, alchemist, and magician, wrote: "By drugs and incantations one can change bronze into gold.

By the skillful use of drugs silver can be changed into gold, and gold into silver" (Eliade 1973, 279).

By visually imbibing the juice from the lotus, or soma, plant in the form of Sakuntala, the king triggered a whole new interplay of emotions and relationships. A fresh chemistry within his being set his libido ablaze, as the flames in the alchemist's athanor were set ablaze when fed wood and coal. The inner heat he now experienced brought about a redistribution of particles within the king's physical and emotional system, altering substances and powers and transforming inertia into kineticism. Sakuntala, as the all-embracing unsullied nature principle, became the focal point of the king's meditation; as such she gained magical power over him, transmuting him into malleable metal, into a loving and gentle soul. The same operations used in alchemy to alter the consistency and powers of metals are used in Tantrism and yoga, where they are called the "force of *samadhi*" (280).

The king feels "pulled" toward Sakuntala. *Kama*, the world of desire, form, and impulse, was being activated (*S*, 17). Buddhist alchemists consider the drawing of one individual toward another to be the effect of magnetism, and it is likened to a burning fire that must be experienced so that it may be extinguished. Only when the Buddhist has felt the heat of passion may an awakening be experienced and detachment be known (Zimmer 1974b, 472).

Sakuntala shoos away a bee. The bee in this context may be considered a person inebriated with the pollen of life, flitting from one source of nourishment to another, extracting the sacred juices of life from every beautiful flower. Unable to remain still or silent, the king emerges from his hiding place behind the tree. He reproaches Sakuntala and her friends for disturbing the peace of the ashram with their chatter and childish games. They have not violated any rituals or rites, they retort. Then they welcome the stranger. The king, however, hides his identity and introduces himself as one of his own officers.

Kama's power has made itself known to Sakuntala as well. Her ultrasensitive nature seems suddenly troubled; she cannot understand her new feelings. A desire that neither plant nor animal can satisfy has entered her world for the first time. She is disturbed and disoriented because her sexual longings have been awakened. Kama, the begetting power, is pursuing his course. Sakuntala will become the instrument through which matter, abundance, and multiplicity will make themselves known, as distinguished from the nonmanifest cosmic realm of Brahman (*S*, 143).

Alchemical forces are at work. The king, as mercury, is associated with

Siva's semen; Sakuntala, as sulfur (Sakti), coincides with the earth/body and earth/fire (Agni) principle, the combustive element in nature. In the *Kamasutra,* the "book of rules" for lovers and courtesans written in the third or fourth century C.E., love and sexuality are not considered sinful nor are they relegated to hushed and hidden areas. On the contrary, in Tantric mystical disciplines sexuality is vitally important. It is when uniting sexually that man and woman transcend their mortal condition and become archetypal forces: man is Siva (*lingam,* phallus), while the woman is Sakti (*yoni,* vagina). As sulfur and mercury, they will unite to make gold, thereby transforming the polarities of the empirical world into the oneness of the nonmanifest domain. The fusion of male and female as universal principles is understood in Hindu scriptures as the welding of thought and breath, spirit and matter.

When the king first entered the Forest of Penance, the hermits were preparing for his sacrificial fire ritual—a prelude to the initiation into his *kama* phase. In keeping with alchemical recipes, the king will have to endure burning sensations, trituration, and a kind of dismemberment so that the vulgar or earthly male-female condition may be transmuted into its aristocratic and golden equivalent. Just as the practitioners of Tantric and hatha yoga attempt to absorb the earthly counterpart of the solar force —their Golden Essence—into their systems through breathing techniques, fasting, and muscular discipline, so the king will attempt to purify his emotions and absorb the spiritual metal into his system.

The yogin's work is designed to direct and channel bodily impulses into higher visions. When the king first saw Sakuntala, a fire glowed within him. The more he observed her, the more that fire blazed: "This is not fire, but a gem: / I must make her mine" (*S,* 20). Like the mineralogist or the alchemist, the king will take this gem Sakuntala in her elemental state, dark from the blackness of the surrounding earth, cut her to size, polish her, concentrate the fire of his energies upon her, and transform her into a sparkling diamond of adamantine essence.

The coagulation operation has begun. No longer hunting at random or filling his days with frivolous pastimes, the king concentrates his vision and life force on Sakuntala, his luminous center. He gives her a ring with the royal seal, ostensibly to free her from her obligations to friends. (It seems she owes them a plant.) Representing infinity, the Eternal Wheel of Buddhism, and Brahman's void, the ring is a bond linking sulfur and mercury, sun and moon, woman and man. As an earthly counterpart of an infinite process, it is subject to creation and dissolution, to the vicissitudes of life. The king's gift marks the beginning of his circular trajectory, his initiatory procedure, and his cosmic dance reminiscent of Siva's *tandava* that united space and time and engendered the creative act.

Voices are heard offstage. The king's "horses are kicking up brown dust that settles like a film of locusts on the ashram trees"; an "elephant is scattering the deer" and "is lunging at the trees"; and because "he is blinded by torn creepers, he is charging into the holy huts" (*S*, 21). The atmosphere of play and frolic has now given way to turmoil. In the *Rig Veda* the horse is associated with Agni; it is a fiery, impetuous, and valorous steed, one "nobly born." Indra, the atmospheric god, became associated with stallions, accounting for traumatic situations, eruptions of instinct, and searing and fiery forces in the world. The elephant, a sacred animal identified with Buddha because of its stability and immutability, or with the forces of chaos and disruption when driven mad, is also identified with Ganesha, the son of Siva. It often wears a gem on its forehead, a parallel to Siva's third eye, which sparkles with wisdom and enlightenment, but which, under certain conditions, can also incite and destroy. That the animals are now wreaking havoc in the ashram, uprooting trees and shrubs in their fury, implies that the energy that has been released, were it to remain unchanneled, could bring chaos and not cosmos to the couple.

Dharma: Sakuntala's Calcination

Dharma, the god of justice, ushers in the reign of individual and collective order on both terrestrial and cosmic levels. According to the *Dharmasutra* (The book of laws) allegedly written by Manu, who was a legendary figure as well as being the prototype of man, certain regulations and rituals must be followed if evolution into higher spheres of being is to come about. The king, in the dharma phase of his life, will bow to the strictures imposed upon him, and in so doing, will experience what alchemists refer to as the *calcinatio*. The events to follow will inevitably bring pain first to Sakuntala and later to the king—pain being considered necessary for the spiritual ascesis leading to *moksa*.

The king now speaks to the jester, who complains of his physical discomfort because they are camping out in the forest rather than enjoying the comfort of the palace. A subtle psychologist, the jester listens carefully to the king as he speaks of his love for Sakuntala. The king maintains that she looked at him "out of the corner of her eyes." He muses on the lightness of her step and the grace of her stance and is surprised at her "quick anger." He confesses, as he attempts to articulate his feelings:

Words are poor things.
God made her as beautiful as a painting.
She is flawless, created out of whatever is lovely, precious, and
    simple. . . .
She is a virgin flower, a serene leaf,
An uncut diamond, untasted honey.

(S, 26)

Again the image of the diamond is used: "flawless," Sakuntala represents perfection in an unpolished state. As an "uncut diamond," she is still part of the earth principle, the *prima materia.* In this state she is still "ungraspable," an impersonal force rooted to the *nigredo,* or black earth; living ferment sprouts from her natural habitat, awakening a force within the king. Though buried in darkness, she is light; thought opaque, she is bright; though identified with matter, she is radiant and sparkling. The diamond—the mystic's "luminous center"—is that area within each individual where spiritual riches are stored. Only through protracted attention and discipline can this creative point be experienced. To reach it, the initiate must shape, pare, and smooth the blackened carbon and transmute it into a luminescent, even dazzling, gem. According to Indian alchemists, such transmutation on a physical as well as a spiritual plane has parallels in the poetic or artistic process, when the amorphous idea is transmuted through its realization on paper or canvas. The diamond, identified with the philosopher's stone, represents immortality, that inalterable, invincible, immutable spiritual substance known as Buddha-nature. Buddha's throne under the Bodhi-tree was said to have been made of a single diamond. The adamantine world buried within matter, as yet unmanifested, lives *in potentia* in Sakuntala, the female, sulfuric force within nature. In conjunction with mercury, the unfulfilled Sakuntala, living in the sacred protective atmosphere of the ashram, will evolve into her next phase of development.

The king questions the jester about the best method to enter the ashram unnoticed so that he may captivate and capture Sakuntala. The jester answers:

Easiest thing in the world! Next time come as the king, to collect your taxes—order the hermits to bring one sixth of their grain, as others do. (*S,* 27)

The king replies:

That's foolish. Their payment is more precious than gold. The taxes we collect come and go, but their tax is their prayer and penance—things that are imperishable. (*S*, 27)

Their hermits' disciplines of prayer and penance, the king suggests, indicate their self-mastery and detachment from the mundane world's ephemeral desires. They have broken the bonds that enslave spirit to the material world and therefore are invested with the purest of essences—gold—and not merely funds to keep the government wealthy.

Two young hermits enter the scene. They inform the king that demons have been harassing their ashram since their guru, Kanva, departed to do penance in the forest. Demons or monsters are frequently found in myths and legends that feature ascetics attempting to renounce the world in order to conquer themselves. The demon or monster, representing an instinctual force that lies buried in the unconscious or in the universal void, may symbolize a fear, an impulse, or some unresolved latent content with which the conscious mind has not yet coped. During an initiation period, whether in Oriental or Occidental disciplines, the initiate must experience death followed by rebirth—chaos leading to cosmos. As supreme monarch, the archetypal governing principle, the king is called upon to expel the demons and purify the ashram.

The king has come to a turning point in his life. The world of multiplicity is upon him. The hermits insist that he remain with them to lead them in the absence of Kanva. They are not strong enough to pursue their holy work without the protection of a temporal figure. But the king receives an urgent message from the Queen Mother demanding that he return to the palace to celebrate "the Fast of the Son's Homage," which is to take place in four days. He is torn between his head (the mother and the society and government offices she represents, the obligations to his other wives, and so forth) and his heart (his love for Sakuntala, the Earth Mother as manifested in her pristine form).

The jester advises the king to "stand in the middle" (*S*, 29). Hindu and Buddhist ascetics use this term to mean abstention from extremes. To cling to any mode of action for selfish or personal aims indicates an enslavement to the philosophy it represents. The Middle Way was the path of Siddhartha Gautama (the Buddha), who warned of extremes and their nefarious results. The summons from the king's mother forces the king to act, to take a stand, and to become conscious of the depth of his feelings. Kama, the spokesman for the bride, has plunged his arrow deep into the king's heart. The stab will not only solidify the liquidity of the first encounter but will cause tension and friction to reach incandescence.

Remaining in the forest, the king sends the jester, whom the Queen Mother has always treated as a son, to the palace in his stead, giving proof that he considers his governmental obligations lighter—almost clownish—in comparison with his feelings. As the generative principle, the mercurial life force, he focuses and fixes his emotions on Sakuntala. The heat of his passion burns all peripheral matter—the pure flame alone remaining. Worthy of attention is the fact that upon the king's decision to remain in the ashram, the demons no longer disturb the serenity of the sacred domain.

Sakuntala has withdrawn for the night. Alone, the king sighs for his beloved in an apostrophe to the moon.

> O Moon, how many of the lovesick you deceive!
> Your arrows are not flowers, nor is moonlight cold.
> It burns, and the arrows are as sharp as rock.
>
> (S, 30)

The king has called upon the goddess of the moon, symbol of nature's immortal and regenerative forces, universal rhythms and time cycles, to help him measure his own course. In Tantric rituals, a parallel is made between lunar and feminine forms. Complex analogies are also drawn in hatha yoga between luminous bodies and various body parts, including arteries, genital organs, heart, stomach, and liver. The goal of these correspondences is to find the harmony between a person's bodily centers—that is, the seat of bodily rhythms and transcosmic forces—and her or his energetic impulses. If such a fusion does take place, an absorption in primal unity may occur at least temporarily (Eliade 1974, 179).

The moon is also identified with water, dew, and tears—those fluids circulating about the universe in the form of sap, milk, and blood to nourish creatures, as does the god-given soma. In the same way, the divine waters of the Ganges rehabilitate and purify those who bathe in them. Tender and understanding at certain periods, the moon lightens humanity's through the dismal spheres of primeval life; it fosters dreams; it refreshes from the intense heat of summer and the harshness of daylight. In the *Brihadaranyaka Upanishad* we read:

> The moon is honey for all beings, and all beings are honey for this moon.
> The intelligent, immortal being, the soul of this moon, and the intelligent,

immortal being, the soul in the individual being—each is honey to the other. Brahman is the soul in each; he indeed is the Self in all. He is all. (Prabhavananda and Manchester 1957, 90)

Illuminated by the forces symbolized by the moon, the king walks to the cane bower and there, in the enclosed, protected, and womblike area, discerns Sakuntala surrounded by flowers and resting on a bed of stone. At peace with nature, she becomes the living incarnation of its nutritive forces: the honey, water, and milk of life. The king overhears her speaking to her friends of her love for him; with her nails she scratches a love poem onto a lotus leaf described as "soft as a parrot's breast." The lotus is referred to in the *Upanishads* as "the lotus of the heart"; it is not surprising that she should have chosen it to articulate her feelings. Overjoyed by the knowledge that his love is reciprocated, the king will no longer remain passive. His mercurial nature will emerge. "The god of love gave me sorrow, but he can heal it too / Like black clouds that burst in rain" (*S,* 32). Declaring his love to Sakuntala, although he "cannot break tradition" and repudiate his other wives, he will marry her according to Gandharva rites and declare her his favorite. Gandharvas, the heavenly musicians, believed that marriage could be contracted by an exchange of garlands between the couple and that no other ritual, either religious or civil, was necessary.

Following the marriage, the king leaves for his palace, planning to have Sakuntala join him later. But the bride's joy is so great that she neglects to pay proper homage to Durvasas, an ascetic who comes to visit at the ashram. He curses her and declares angrily that her husband will forget her until she returns the ring he gave her. Meanwhile, Sakuntala's foster father, Kanva, the ashram's guru, returns. He has been told of Sakuntala's marriage and of her pregnancy. He realizes that she can no longer remain at the ashram and must join her husband. A painful parting is enacted between father and daughter, and between Sakuntala and her friends, the animals she has raised in the forest, and the plants she has always tended. The protective, paradisiac world of the young girl recedes to give way to the harsh collective sphere of wife and mother. Before her departure, the hermits bring Sakuntala gifts of grain, flowers, and tree branches. "You deserve diamonds and golden bracelets," they say to her. A holy sage asks her to circle the sacrificial fire they have just lit in her home, thereby purifying her: "May your sins dissolve in the fragrance of these sacred offerings" (*S,* 42).

Terrified and pained at the prospect of her voyage into the world, Sakuntala experiences for the first time the vertigo that arises from the unknown. Nature mirrors Sakuntala's disorientation and distress: Sakuntala's pet fawn follows her sadly down the path, the deer no longer munch the grass, the peacocks have given up their dance, and the dew falls on the branches like crystalline tears. When the shriek of the chakravaka sounds in the forest—strident and terrified because she cannot find her mate—an ominous atmosphere descends upon the scene.

In the palace, the king sits in court busying himself with the affairs of state. He is told that hermits and a young girl wish to see him. He receives the visitors. Sakuntala stands before him veiled. Strangely enough, though he neither recognizes nor remembers her, he is drawn to her. The curse has taken effect. The hermits are aghast at this turn of events, while Sakuntala, deeply pained, laments her lot. "I am lost. He can't even remember what happened" (*S,* 51). Disgrace is heaped upon her. The hermits insist that Sakuntala remain in the palace despite the king's denial of her as his wife—or even as an acquaintance. As a last resort, Sakuntala remembers the ring. She will show it to him and he will certainly recognize it and remember he gave it to her. She makes the gesture of taking the ring from her finger when she suddenly realizes that it has been lost, perhaps when she was bathing in the Ganges prior to her visit to the palace.

That Sakuntala has lost her golden ring implies that her quest for mystical union, in the alchemical sense, has been thwarted; the single focus, or central meditative point, that the ring represented has vanished, dispersed in the world of multiplicity. Fragmented spiritually and psychologically, Sakuntala lacks the power to pursue her quest. Gold, the mystical body representing sacrosanct words and feelings, absolute truth, and the purest of principles, has been lost amid the sacred waters of the Ganges— that is, her own unconscious. In the depth of her sorrow Sakuntala accepts the fact that "Fate has intervened" (*S,* 51). The fire of pain sears her. In vain she repeats certain conversations she had with the king when they were walking together in the forest; in vain she attempts to help him recall a past that no longer exists for him. A sage now intervenes to predict that the king's "first son will be blessed with a circle in his palm." If Sakuntala's child "has this sign, take her as your queen. If not, send her back to the ashram" (*S,* 53). The king agrees. Sakuntala will remain in the palace until the birth of her child.

Memory, for the Hindu and Buddhist, is of prime importance. Whenever the gods lose their memory temporarily, it indicates a fall from the divine condition. An inability to recall personal events is equated with an inability to remember previous existences; thus it is a loss of perspective toward eternity, the gods, and oneself. Only with a perfect memory can one reach "the beginning of time" and thereby transcend it. For Buddha, memory was knowledge; it represented illumination, a person's most precious faculty. To make use of memory and to develop its power through concentration was advocated by the Buddha. To allow this vital instrument to weaken is to yield to dispersion, distraction, and ignorance. Memory enabled the Indian to recall, recognize, and develop that sacred zone within him, the central point where Nonbeing and Absolute Reality may be discovered. The *Isha Upanishad* reads: "Let my life now emerge in the all-pervading life. Ashes are my body's end. OM . . . O mind, remember Brahman. Remember thy past deeds" (Prabhavananda and Manchester 1957, 28).

The king's loss of memory is symptomatic of his lack of equilibrium. Without perspective, unable to differentiate one situation from another, he is devoid of any scale of values. Sakuntala's pain heightens. She longs for "the earth" to "swallow" her up, to moisten her heated countenance, to extinguish the fire of life. She leaves the king of her own free will. Shouts are heard offstage. A priest enters. He recounts the strange happening he has just witnessed. "Suddenly a white light in a woman's form swept out of nowhere and picked [Sakuntala] up and took her into the sky" (*S*, 54).

A policemen enters. He is castigating a fisherman, accusing him of having stolen a royal ring. The fisherman claims to have caught a fish, cut it open, and found the ring in its belly. The ring is brought to the king, who recognizes it immediately. The curse's poison is annulled and he remembers Sakuntala, his marriage, and his passion for her. It is too late, however. Sakuntala has been taken to heaven, to her mother's abode; her mother, the audience learns, was a nymph who had stayed on earth only long enough to give birth to her. Grieving over Sakuntala's disappearance, the king is visited by the fire of grief and the blackness of remorse. "She was a dream, an incantation, a breath of lovely air. / Such things don't come back" (*S*, 61).

Moksa: *Sublimation*

During the *moksa* phase of spiritual evolution, the hierophant attempts to find release from worldly entanglements and to experience an "emancipation of the soul." Having fulfilled his potential on earth, he reaches the condition that alchemists term *sublimatio*. The metaphysical meaning of this spiritual release has been summed up by the sixteenth-century philosopher Vijnana-bhiksu: "Just as the statue, already existing in the block of stone, is only revealed by the sculptor, so the causal activity only engenders action by which an effect manifests itself, giving the illusion that it exists only in the present moment" (Eliade 1973, 23). The king, now in a state of depression, is catalyzed by Indra, the atmospheric god, who asks his help in fighting his enemies. The battle takes place and the god is victorious. The king is seen onstage in Indra's chariot—a singular honor for a mortal—earning him the admiration of his people, who have now erected monuments and written songs in his honor.

Indra's charioteer takes the king to higher regions, where he will gain insight into cosmic matters. Indian alchemy speaks of a fifth element—*akasa*, which has been identified with Aristotle's ether—in addition to the four recognized by Occidental alchemists. *Akasa,* or the "soniferous ether," can only be heard and not experienced by the other senses. It is composed of unchanging and infinite atoms. Some mystics consider it to be the *prima materia* out of which all other elements were born. The *Upanishads* say:

> From the Atman [the universal soul or Brahman] arose akasa, from the akasa the wind [from wind, fire, from fire, water, from water, earth]. When this earth shall pass away, the reverse order of changes will take place, earth to water, water to fire, fire to air, air to akasa, akasa to Brahma. (Quoted in Stillman 1960, 119)

The moment the king accepts Indra's invitation to participate in divine wars and mounts the god's chariot, he breaks with the mundane world; like the yogin who claimed to be able to levitate and thereby experience transpersonal spheres, the king reaches akasa and *sublimatio.* The charioteer stops at a celestial ashram. The king notices that

> The bathing water is golden with the pollen of lotuses.
> Meditation is practiced on heaps of gems,
> Here there is self-discipline near bewitching girls,
> Other sages practice austerity for gain:
> Here they scorn it.
>
> (S, 69)

Suddenly the king's arm involuntarily throbs, as it had before he first met Sakuntala. He sees a little boy teasing a lion cub. Little girls, wearing the dresses of the hermitage, look at the boy with annoyance. They see the king and ask him to intervene. As the king looks at the boy, he experiences a sensation of emptiness: he has no son. He looks more closely and notices the sign of royal birth on the boy's hand. Certainly the boy is his son, he thinks. He questions the girls, who tell him that the boy was born in this celestial palace and that his mother is related to a heavenly nymph. The king picks up an amulet that has fallen from the boy's wrist and returns it to him. The girls look at the king in horror. Anyone except the boy's parents who touches his amulet, which was given to him at birth, will die. It contains a rare herb called *aparajita*, which turns into a poisonous snake. Nothing happens to the king, however, indicating that he is the boy's father. The boy and his father embrace.

Seeing a stranger embracing her son, a young lady wearing a saffron-colored robe, with her hair tied in a hermit's knot, approaches. The boy runs to her and tells her that this stranger calls himself his father. The king recognizes her as Sakuntala and his joy knows no bounds.

> Forget the sad past of separation, my beautiful wife.
> Delusion filled my mind.
> To a blind man a garland is a snake.
>
> (S, 73)

He asks her for forgiveness in the gentlest terms as she murmurs her happiness.

> Be still my heart.
> My fate pities me, having done its worst.
> This is my husband.
>
> (S, 72)

She begins weeping as she whispers to her son: "My son, a star is dancing." The king falls to his knees before her. He now knows the feeling of freedom that comes with fulfillment. The *sublimatio* or vaporous atmosphere in these celestial regions has allowed him to experience a transcosmic sphere of life without impediment. Not oblivious to the rigors of existential conditions, he has earned *moksa* through the disciplines imposed upon him: in the feeling domain by Sakuntala, in the governmental sphere by his duties as monarch, and in the military area by his battles. All facets of his earthly stay have now been integrated. Only one more desire remains to be fulfilled. Of the sage offering Indra's blessing, the king asks

May the lord of the earth seek the good of my subjects.
May the wise be honored.
And may I be released from further lives.

(*S,* 74)

The king has lived out his karma. The seeds of his destiny, present in his former incarnations as well as in the acts dramatized in Kalidasa's play, have now germinated. *Artha, kama, dharma,* and *moksa* have transformed the king's unconscious contents into the deeds of his life.

In hatha and Tantric yoga, as well as in Buddhist and Tibetan disciplines in general, an occult correspondence exists between matter and humankind's "physio-psychic body" (Eliade 1973, 282–83). Each element in its own way attempts to find the elixir leading to spiritual and physical immortality. The practitioners of religious rituals seek to create a "body of diamond"—that is, a body "incorruptible" and strong enough to be able to experience its last transmutation into immortality. They quest for the Transcendent Principle, the Self that is eternal, immutable, and surpasses the world of causality and linear time to become the "adamantine Self" (Zimmer 1974a, 140–48).

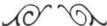

Throughout *Sakuntala* it is the woman who is irreparably faulted; it is she who stands guilty of having offended society and kingship. Yet it is she as well who has been the catalyst for the king's—and her own—spiritual and psychological growth. She has been brought up in an ashram by Kanva, the sage head of the community of ascetics, and her life has been used to prove an abstract concept. Like the body of the Hindu ascetic, it is her body that has been used as a laboratory. The special disciplines (breathing, fasting, and so forth) that she practiced in the ashram have taught her to free herself from her physical dependency on others and have encouraged within her a condition of immutable wisdom and multidimensional consciousness. It is she who left the palace of her own volition after having been granted the right to stay until the birth of her child. The return of the ring—that Golden Essence—activated feeling and sentiment in the king, thus earning for her and for him release from the entanglements of life. To convey such spiritual evolution alchemically, it may be said that mercury, contained within Siva's semen (and incarnated in the king), united with sulfur, or Sakti's ovum (as represented by Sakuntala). A son was born from this *complexio oppositorum,*

thus insuring humankind's future existence. No longer bound by temporal rhythms or earthly matters, the king and Sakuntala existed in a "deconditioned" state leading to Nonbeing or Absolute Reality.

Although the king and Sakuntala disappear from earthly view, the savor of those precious moments spent in the empirical domain lingers. In the *Brihadaranyaka Upanishad* one may read:

> As a lump of salt when thrown into water melts away and the lump cannot be taken out, but wherever we taste the water it is salty . . . so . . . the individual self, dissolved, is the Eternal—pure consciousness, infinite and transcendent. Individuality arises by identification of the Self, through ignorance, with the elements; and with the disappearance of consciousness of the many, in divine illumination, it disappears. Where there is consciousness of the Self, individuality is no more.

> This it is, O my beloved, that I wanted to tell you. (Prabhavananda and Manchester 1957, 88)

3 The *Nibelungenlied:*
Kriemhild and Brunhild—
The Obsessive/Compulsive
Stress Syndrome

The *Nibelungenlied* (Song of the Nibelungs), an anonymous Middle High German epic poem written in about 1200, is a blend of heroic poetry and courtly romance. Beyond the artistry of the depiction of Siegfried's courageous and perhaps not so courageous acts are the intriguing, complex personalities of the two heroines: Kriemhild and Brunhild. The former is Siegfried's beautiful wife; the latter, her brother Gunther's spouse. To explore the psyches of these two archetypal women is to enter the realms of both sun and shadow, the lightened regions of consciousness and the deep interiors of primal darkness.

Like women of stature throughout the ages, Kriemhild and Brunhild as archetypal figures show certain behavioral patterns that reveal the universality and eternality of reactions stemming from devastating psychological hurt and an obsessive/compulsive stress syndrome. Kriemhild's and Brunhild's character traits—like DNA—may lie latent in contemporary women, and, depending upon the intensity of their incandescence, may provoke incredible extremes of violence.

Myths that touch on the Nibelungs appear in the eighth-century Anglo-Saxon epic *Beowulf;* in the songs of the Icelandic *Elder Edda,* composed between the ninth and twelfth centuries; and in the *History of the Danish People* by the Danish historian Saxo Grammaticus, the *Younger Edda* compiled by Snorri Sturluson, the *Volsunga Saga,* and the Norwegian *Thidreks Saga of Bern,* all of the thirteenth century. Although the plots are varied and frequently contradictory, it may be said that the myth of the Nibelungs was relatively well known in the medieval period.

The legend dramatized by Richard Wagner in his opera cycle *Der Ring des Nibelungen* (The ring of the Nibelung) is different from the one formulated in the *Nibelungenlied*. Whereas Wagner's version of the myth stresses the divine and the supernatural, the *Nibelungenlied*, although far from devoid of otherworldly happenings, deals mainly with formidable existential events as well as with the mysteries of the human heart. Brunhild of the *Nibelungenlied*, for example, is neither the Wagnerian daughter of the god Odin nor a Valkyrie maiden, but the queen of Iceland. Nor is Siegfried, as in the opera, the fruit of an incestuous marriage between deities but the lord of the Netherlands, Norway, and "Nibelungland." His capital, Xanten, is on the Rhine. Although the action in the *Nibelungenlied* takes place mainly in the western and eastern areas surrounding Danubian Austria, part 1 is lived out in the city of Worms, the capital of the Burgundians, and part 2 in the city of Gran, in Etzel's Hunland (Hungary). Stressed in the *Nibelungenlied* is the ethos of the age of chivalry: the performance of deeds of valor and great love motifs, with a panoply of accompanying characteriological tendencies, such as possessiveness, passivity, hatred, jealousy, greed, and thirst for revenge.

Ectypal Analysis

The events depicted in the *Nibelungenlied* take place in the fifth century, a highly unstable age of mass migration. Among the ethnic groups flooding Europe were German tribes, which overran the Roman Empire, and Slavic tribes, which occupied that part of Germany east of the Elbe. Attila, king of the Huns, while sweeping across the Balkans, Germany, France, Milan, and Pavia, plundered and devastated the land with even greater vigor than had the other migratory groups. A century later the Avars, nomadic Mongols, traversed southern Russia, the Balkans, and Bohemia and settled in Hungary. The progress of the migratory movements saw the establishment of the Saxons in Britain and of the Franks in today's France, west and south Germany, and Thuringia.

The atmosphere of mobility injected into the *Nibelungenlied* mirrors the tenor of the times and is of historical import. Highlighted is Attila's defeat of the Burgundians, a Germanic people from the Baltic shores, in the second quarter of the fifth century. The political rivalries between the three important regions and dynasties of the area—Swabia (Hohenstaufen), Saxony, and Bavaria (Guelphs, or Welfs)—also come to the fore in the epic poem (Andersson 1987, 94, 96, 98).

Let us examine briefly the period of history in Germany that furnished the background material for the *Nibelungenlied*. Not until 962, when Otto the Great was crowned Holy Roman Emperor in Rome, was it possible to speak of a kingdom of Germany and of him as its founder. Otto's intention was to become Charlemagne's true heir. The latter, having been crowned emperor in Rome in 800, had extended his immense Frankish empire to include most of Europe: Lorraine, Burgundy, Lombardy, Bavaria, Saxony, Austria, and the northern fringe of Spain. After the Treaty of Verdun (843), when Louis the German, Charlemagne's grandson, was awarded the territories of the Saxons, Swabians, Bavarians, and Franks lying east of the Rhine, boundaries grew increasingly unstable, and Germany could not be looked upon as a political unit.

Thanks to Otto the Great's astute maneuverings, he succeeded in extending his power to include the duchies of Saxony, Franconia, Lorraine, Swabia, Bavaria, Burgundy, and most of Italy. His control of the Church and his assumption of the title "imperator," to mention but two of his subtle moves, proved politically effective. Otto and subsequent rulers were, however, hampered by the German constitution, which was designed to foil attempts on the part of kings to stem the growing strength of the nobility. Feelings of independence and rivalry between the dukes of Franconia, Swabia, Bavaria, Saxony, and Upper and Lower Lorraine were such that disruption became rampant throughout the kingdom. Nor did the virtually continuous state of contention between the popes and kings create a spirit of harmony. Civil wars broke out as political and economic dissension pervaded Europe, and Germany and Italy became increasingly unstable.

The most important ruler of the period, Frederick I, or Frederick Barbarossa (1123–90), duke of Swabia following his election to the German kingship in Frankfurt, was named Holy Roman Emperor in 1155. The goal of this dynamic and frequently farsighted ruler was to bring order to his country and to consolidate the royal holdings. Himself a Hohenstaufen, he not only challenged the power plays of the pope, but tried to end the fighting between the Guelphs (descendants of the Bavarian count Welf I) and the Ghibellines (the Italian name for the Hohenstaufen counts of Waiblingen). In that he was half Guelph and had Ghibelline relatives too, Barbarossa had high hopes of reconciling the rival factions. Although he contracted politically correct marriage alliances, and awarded Tuscany, Spoleto, and other Italian territories to Welf VI (1191), his nearly forty-year struggle against papal imperial interests had been misconceived (Andersson 1987, 100). So, too, was his attempt to subdue the Italian Lombard communes, which concluded with his defeat by the Lombard League at the battle of Legnano in 1176. Instrumental in this military loss was the disloyalty he had suffered at the hands of his Guelph cousin, Henry the Lion, duke of Saxony, nominal ruler of northern Germany. As a result, Frederick I caused his cousin's lands to be partitioned, thus dismembering the formerly great independent German duchy. By 1186, thanks to the marriage of his son, Henry, to Constance, heiress to the Sicilian kingdom, Frederick I succeeded in establishing a power base in Italy. In 1189, two years after Saladin had taken Jerusalem, Frederick joined the Third Crusade and drowned in the Saleph River in Asia Minor.

Barbarossa's son, Henry VI (the Severe), crowned emperor in 1191, earned his fame for taking Richard Lion-Heart of England hostage and for his crushing campaign against the Sicilian rebels. Upon his death in 1197, Philip of Swabia, a Hohenstaufen, acceded to the throne, waging war for the next ten years against a Guelph, Otto of Brunswick.

Thereafter, the power struggles between the pope, the Germans, the Italians, the French, and the English ran their course. Regional principalities as well, vying for control over each other during the twelfth and thirteenth centuries, attempted to crush the frequent thrusts for independence of the local lords (Duby 1977, 179).

Feudalism

Feudalism (from Latin *feudum*, fief) is said to have originated in northern France around the ninth and tenth centuries, with the decline of the Carolingian empire. The fief—land owned by a lord but assigned by investiture to a vassal—in time became hereditary. Requirements were made of the vassal, including military service and counsel. The solemn oath of fealty between lord and vassal, and the latter's obligation to give his ruler counsel, implying consent as well, has led modern historians to believe that the great councils between kings and their tenants-in-chief were the precursors of modern parliaments. Following the feudalization of the monarchy, the ruler enjoyed even greater power as suzerain than previously as head of state. Because the suzerain had obligations to his vassals, as well as rights, absolutism seemingly could not take root.

Knighthood

Among the duties of a knight were that of horseman (*chevalier*, master of his mount) and servant to his feudal superior. The training period to attain knighthood was long and arduous, frequently requiring apprenticeship as a page and squire, knowledge of the use of armaments, and familiarity with elaborate rituals, including the wearing of special clothing. Included in the knight's code of behavior was reverence for religion and for noble ladies, to whom knights frequently vowed their service—perhaps accounting in part for the fusion between the ethos of courtly love and that of the valorous warrior.

Heraldry, the science of blazoning and armorial insignia, included the tracing and recording of genealogies. Hereditary rights and succession to properties were defined through the study of family pedigrees. A knight errant, for example, moving about the land, could be identified by distinguishing marks or designs on his shield or helmet, which not only associated him with his retainer but indicated his descent from a fine family. Later on, the symbols and vocabulary used in blazoning followed complicated and frequently esoteric rules, suggesting such notions as honor, etiquette, and nobility of character. The wearing and use of emblems and blazons during jousts, tournaments, and all types of pageantry, including the bestowal of knighthood, added both color and an aristocratic element to these spectacular events.

By the twelfth century, knighthood not only was identified with upper classes but its concept was enhanced by moral and cultural considerations. Courtly etiquette took on romantic and quasi-mystical notions, as attested to by the emergence of the *chansons de geste* and the *romans d'aventure*.

Literature

Various literary genres flourished in the medieval period— myth, folklore, narrative romance, and so on—to whose specific conventions and general themes authors frequently added a personal twist of their own. Didactic and imaginative poetry was generally favored over prose.

Warrior epics flourished in concomitance with courtly romances: the *Song of Roland*, Chrétien de Troyes's *Lancelot* and *Conte du Graal*, and Lorris and Meung's *Roman de la Rose* in French; *Beowulf* and Arthurian legends in English; the Norse *Eddas*; the *Hildebrandslied*, *Nibelungenlied*, and Wolfram von Eschenbach's *Parzival*, in German; the Celtic *Tristan and Isolde*; the *Cantar de Mío Cid* and Juan Ruiz's *Libro de Buen Amor* in Spanish; and so on.

The cult of love, launched by one of the earliest troubadours, William IX of Aquitaine (1071–1127), gave rise to the vogue of itinerant musicians who sang of both spiritual and bawdy relationships. In the courts of southern France, these poet-musicians celebrated in their romances the notion of *fin'-amors*: "true love," a blend of platonic and carnal love that glorified the woman. Although concepts varied, if such a love were based on *virtue*, it was considered ennobling. Couples were required to observe certain behavioral patterns and adhere to codes of constancy, sincerity, and harmony of character, frequently enigmatic in their imagery and philosophy. The fulfillment of the requirements engendered a love grounded in the worship of the female.

The ritualized code of love also came into its own in Germany, in the art of the *Minnesänger* (*Minne,* love; *Sang,* song). Walther von der Vogelweide and other poet-musicians attested in their works to the ethics and atmosphere of the feudal court, the lover submitting to his lady as the knight submitted to his lord, thereby enhancing his own sense of worth and courage and the nobility of his love. Despite his request to his lady for mercy or pity as well as for a "reasonable" reward for his services, the lady—tied to conventions, as was the lord to his faithful vassals—remained frequently unattainable.

The Status of Women in Society

A dichotomy existed between the idealization of women and their assignment to inferior rank by the Church and in state law. On the one hand, courtly romances and a growing devotion to the Virgin Mary elevated womanhood; on the other hand, the actual lifestyle of wives, mothers, sisters, and daughters indicated a low social status.

The cult of the Virgin Mary, which took root in the eleventh century, rendered an already complex situation even more ambiguous. Mary, looked upon as both divine and mortal, was empowered to play the role of redeemer. By the thirteenth century, however, the joy and abandon she inspired in her worshipers triggered a countermovement. Writings grounded in the misogynist tradition emanating from Saint Paul were also gaining ground. Women came to be looked upon as obstacles to salvation. A more basic and frightening question was posed at the Council of Mâcon in 585: Did women have souls or not? (Jacoby 1985, 110).

That women were assigned inferior rank had already been made patent in Paul's First Letter to Timothy: "Let a woman learn in silence with all submissiveness. I permit no woman to teach or to have authority over men; she is to keep silent. For Adam was formed first, then Eve" (1 Tim. 2:11–13). In his Epistle to the Ephesians Paul wrote:

> Wives, submit yourselves unto your own husbands, as unto the Lord. For the husband is the head of the wife, even as Christ is the head of the church: and he is the saviour of the body. (Eph. 5:22–23)

Such inferiority of social position was confirmed in his *Summa Theologiae* by the thirteenth-century religious philosopher Thomas Aquinas:

> In a secondary sense the image of God is found in man, and not in woman: for man is the beginning and end of woman; as God is the beginning and end of every creature. (Quoted in Warner 1976, 179)

Because women in the lower echelons of society were expected to work hard in the home and in the fields, understandably they died at younger ages than men. Wives of merchants or tradespeople frequently worked selling foods, cloth, and crafts, and in other business ventures with their husbands. If a wife did survive her spouse, she usually carried on his work. There are examples of wealthy widows of burgesses, knights, and nobles who displayed notable organizational talents in running their complicated households.

Marriage contracts, governing the transmission of fiefs to future generations, were accordingly of extreme importance in aristocratic circles. Usually drawn up by the family, the contracts showed virtually no consideration for the proclivities of the future bride or groom. A maiden having reached marriageable age was valued in terms of her dowry and inheritance, and thus was looked upon as an economic asset or drawback. Once married, wives were subjected to floggings by their husbands, "a practice condoned by canon law" (McConnell 1984, 6).

Although late Roman law placed an unmarried women in tutelage, by the tenth century such interdicts were weakening in Spain and southern France. Women could inherit land on the same terms as men, while in Germany females could inherit property and enjoy the privilege of benefiting from, if not the right of transacting, territorial exchanges.

Some exceptions were made to the law of primogeniture. The Merovingian queens Brunhild and Bathild, in the late sixth and seventh centuries, respectively, were rulers of worth who saw to the health and strength of the dynasty and the prosperity of their kingdoms; Urraca became queen of Castile (1109); Empress Matilda inherited the throne of Henry I of England and Normandy (1100); Blanche of Castile (1188–1252), the mother of Louis IX (known as Saint Louis), was twice regent and governed France with wisdom and firmness—or repressively, depending upon the historian's bias. Eleanor of Aquitaine (1122–1204) not only repudiated her pious husband, Louis VII, king of France, but married the English king Henry II, thereby bringing to England the lands she had inherited—the duchy of Aquitaine, including

Poitou and Gascony. Thus she destabilized the balance of power between the two countries (Warner 1976, 141).

The *Nibelungenlied* incorporates in its text certain societal factors and behavioral modes implicit in feudalism and knighthood and contains as well all the psychological underpinnings of heroic epics, romances of adventure, and courtly romances. It remains to be seen how the comportment of the two heroines, Kriemhild and Brunhild, reflects and transcends the weltanschauung of their times.

Archetypal Analysis

Moods swing widely as the *Nibelungenlied* moves forward. In Kriemhild's case, her ego (center of consciousness) seems cohesive and relatively well integrated at first, but, in time, hurt affects her so deeply that her rational sphere is submerged. Like the shattering of a stained-glass Gothic window, Kriemhild's entire personality seems to break apart. Synergy yields to chaos: from tender gentleness she veers to the extremes of cruelty. To use the author's words, Kriemhild is transformed into a "she-devil"; or, in psychological parlance, she lives out her shadow-potential.[1] Clues as to how Kriemhild will react to pain and injustice prior to her actual experience of them are strewn here and there, particularly in the first part of the epic.

In Brunhild's case, we are at first exposed to a "warrior-maiden," to a woman who has found her groundbed, who lives out her joyous and fulfilling existence productively, according to her needs and wants. The archetypal images of Brunhild in the text indicate that hers is a connected and cohesive personality. But the imposition of society's marital regulations and its insistence on conformity injure her sense of identity and spirit of independence. Thus deprived of her self-image and self-esteem, she is reduced to the status of a nonperson.

Kriemhild's Dream

At the outset of the *Nibelungenlied*, Princess Kriemhild, living in the city of Worms on the Rhine in Burgundy, enjoys a seemingly harmonious relationship with her family. Her father, Dancrat, is described as "a man of abounding valour" who had won great fame in his youth. Her endearing mother, Uote, is endowed with an empathetic and loving personality. Gunther, her brother, is senior king of Burgundy; his two younger brothers,

Gernot and Gilselher, are co-kings of the land. Living in the royal surroundings are vassals and warriors of renown—among them, Hagen of Troneck, advisor to Gunther, and his brother, Dancwart. Together, they maintain the "court's high honor" (*N*, 18).[2]

Kriemhild is introduced to the readers as

> a maiden of high lineage, so fair that none in any land could be fairer. . . . She came to be a beautiful woman, causing many knights to lose their lives. This charming girl was as if made for love's caresses: she was desired by brave fighting men and none was her enemy, for her noble person was beyond all measure lovely. Such graces did the young lady possess that she was the adornment of her sex. (17)

Beyond her extraordinary physical attributes, Kriemhild's charm, gentleness, and nobility of character point to an aristocratic upbringing. She lives a sheltered existence under the care of her parents and, as the reader is given to believe, of her three courageous and honorable brothers.

Kriemhild enjoys a particularly close bond with her mother, the loving Uote, a woman fulfilled as wife and mother. Understood psychologically, her mother is the carrier of her daughter's first and basic experience of secure love, and as such, is a nurturing, positive force in Kriemhild's life. Uote's inner contentment has, thus far, kept the components of her daughter's psyche on an even keel. As a feeling person, Uote acts in accordance with her subjective understanding of the family values of the time. The relationship of mutual love, trust, and harmony between mother and daughter may be said to have prolonged an ideal condition of perfect likemindedness throughout Kriemhild's childhood and adolescent years.

Not surprisingly, when Kriemhild has a disturbing archetypal dream at the outset of the epic she confides its contents to her mother: "Kriemhild dreamt she reared a falcon, strong, handsome and wild, but that two eagles rent it while she perforce looked on, the most grievous thing that could ever befall her" (18).

The dream's message clearly conveys a future change in direction in Kriemhild's life. Having reached marriageable age, she is at the threshold between her paradisiac or nonconscious, uncommitted, childlike existence and the age when choices are to be made.

Uote, interpreting the premonitory dream in accordance with her own limited frame of reference, pronounces: "The falcon you are rearing is a noble man who, unless God preserve him, will soon be taken from you" (18).

Vexed, Kriemhild replies petulantly and incisively: "I intend to stay free of a warrior's love all my life. I mean to keep my beauty till I die, and never be made wretched by the love of any man" (18). She fears suffering and understandably so, since the *Minnesänger* sing so frequently of the pain and madness brought on by unrequited or lost love. Rejecting the thought of living out love crises and disillusionments, Kriemhild opts for imprisonment in the childish world of nonengagement. Her desire to prolong a condition of stasis is, symbolically, antithetical to the life experience that is based on change. By avoiding commitment, she sets herself on the path of a regressive psychological condition.

The dichotomy in values between mother and daughter becomes apparent in their differing views concerning love. Warning Kriemhild not to be intransigent, Uote projects her understanding of married life: joy in domesticity and close family ties. Her subjective judgments and limited life experience lead her to believe that real "happiness comes only from a man's love" (18).

Let us now examine the meaning of the imagery in Kriemhild's dream. The falcon, a diurnal bird of prey, was highly prized by kings and knights in the Middle Ages. Trained by falconers to hunt and kill small game, the bird could make power dives at speeds up to 175 miles per hour. Falcons were reputed to kill cleanly, usually by breaking their victims' backs. That Kriemhild had "reared a falcon"—training it to live out its "strong, handsome and wild" instinctual nature—may be, as suggested by Uote, an identification with a future lover who would bring her grief. It may also be understood as a projection of unlived aspects in Kriemhild's own subliminal world. In that the falcon undergoes specific training, an analogy may be drawn between its development and the successive psychological stages a human undergoes in the maturation process. The following may also symbolize an as yet unlived potential, a "strong, handsome and wild" streak in Kriemhild herself, buried beneath layers of repressed instinct.

"Two eagles rent [the falcon]" in Kriemhild's archetypal dream. As king of birds, the eagle is known to be rapacious and cruel, yet on standards and flags it symbolizes military might and power, functioning as a protector of citizens. If representative of high-energy charges guided by instinct alone and not combined with judgment, the eagle symbolizes a perversion that may become a powerful and life-threatening force. Accordingly, the as yet untried contents in Kriemhild's subliminal world may indicate her powerlessness to stem the onslaught of her potential for violence. The eagles incised on some Viking stones on the island of Gotyland represent birds of the battlefield who feast on the slain. Nordic warriors were known to wear helmets adorned with eagle crests, sometimes featuring images of a woman entering Valhalla to greet them. Eagles, then, symbolized not only conflagration, militarism, and war, but death as well—which Kriemhild also projects onto these realities..

Until now, the Burgundian princess has lived within the confines of family and society, but her emergence from these suggests that she has an agenda of her own. Determined to solve her problems preventively, Kriemhild will distance herself from suitors and avoid any experience of extreme sorrow or happiness. Tantamount to prolongation of a sheltered life, her decision signifies a lack of commitment and the continuation of emotional stuntedness.

But fate, particularly in myths, has a way of upsetting well-laid plans. From the city of Xanten in the Netherlands there has come a gallant, handsome, and courageous royal prince—Siegfried, son of Siegmund and Sieglind. For his parents, Siegfried will always nurture the deepest respect as long as they are alive: thus he refuses to accept the crown of the Netherlands that is offered to him (22). Desirous of fulfillment as a valiant knight, he set as his goal the repulsion of enemy incursions into his country. Siegfried has slain two mighty Nibelung princes, Schilbung and Nibelung, subdued seven hundred men of Nibelungenland, and taken their immense treasure for himself (27). He has also slain a fearsome dragon and bathed in its blood, making his skin invulnerable to harm; and from Alberich the dwarf, whom he also subdued, he has won the *tarnkappe*, a magic cloak that will make him invisible when he wears it (28, 64).

The Bridal Quest

Upon hearing of the beautiful Kriemhild and her seemingly "spirited disposition," the ebullient and fearless Siegfried ventures to Worms. Although Kriemhild has rejected many suitors, Siegfried aims to win her hand, and as though preparing for battle he sets out with bravura, zest, and determination to make his conquest (23).[3] In fact, Siegfried aims not only to marry Kriemhild but to obtain for himself the kingdom of Burgundy.

Siegfried's intuitive parents, fearing for their son's life and having "no illusions" about the Burgundian king, Gunther, and his vassals, have already warned him against Gunther's adviser, Hagen. The fearless and self-confident—perhaps in his own way self-indulgent—Siegfried turned a deaf ear to his parents' advice, although he did feel his mother's sorrow and asked her not to weep for him. He brashly verbalized his belligerency: "Whatever I fail to get from them [the Burgundians] by friendly requests, I shall take by my own valour. I fancy I shall wrest their lands and people from them" (24). Realizing the impossibility of changing the youth's decision, the parents yielded, providing him with clothes, companions, armor, chargers, and everything needed for his perilous journey (25).

In Worms, King Gunther, duly apprised of Siegfried's prowess, receives the hero courteously. But the fearless (and thus undiscerning) Siegfried allows his aggressivity to explode. "I will wrest from you by force all that you possess!" he threatens. "Your lands and your castles shall all be subject to me!" (29) To his lack of diplomacy—or better, to his aggressivity—the unctuous Gunther, seemingly a master politician, acts out his own behavioral patterns and replies: "Everything we have is at your disposal, provided you accept it honourably. Our lives and our wealth shall be shared with you in common" (31). Ambiguous in both his actions and demeanor, Gunther, unlike Siegfried, has a character that is hard to fathom. Are his words an attempt to appease Siegfried rather than confront him and run the risk of conflict? Or is his answer simply duplicitous because that is the man's nature?

From the very outset, then, we are dealing with two antithetical personalities: an exuberant, aggressive, fearless, willful, and to a certain extent, thoughtless (but loyal and naive) warrior; and a conciliatory, manipulative, and elusive king who concedes rather than fights for his principles and values. Gunther seemingly declines confrontation, preferring the comfortable and secure existence that comes with a myopic view of life. Is Gunther's position "wise," as many exegetes of the *Nibelungenlied* contend, or might it be better to define it as irresolute, even cowardly?

Siegfried's defiance and impudence, an expression of an unassimilated violent streak in his youthful psyche, blinds him. Similarly the position of the supposedly mature Gunther conceals fear and cowardice. The close relationship of these two men—the unbridled impulsive youth and the chief, or *head*, of a kingdom—will set the stage for the conflagration to come.

Kriemhild Observes Siegfried

Kriemhild, depicted in stereotypic fashion framed by her castle window, sees Siegfried for the first time in the courtyard below. She is duly impressed by the knight's dexterity and prowess as he participates in competitive sports or simply passes the time with other warriors (32).

Layers of meaning are implicit in the above window image. For example, just as the human eye is the organ of sight/insight, an orifice in a castle allows light/clarity to penetrate into the room from the outside. That Kriemhild peers at people and events below indicates her unconscious need and desire to broaden her point of view, to concern herself with the world at large, contrary to her earlier decision to pursue a reclusive existence. Her former intransigence or one-sidedness seems to be opening up to the *light of consciousness*.

In keeping with the rules of etiquette of the day, Siegfried, Kriemhild's future swain, must wait an entire year before setting eyes on the maiden. As a dutiful, proper, and passive princess, Kriemhild will repress the transgressive elements within her psyche in observance of prescribed conduct. Their meeting will occur only after Siegfried carries out his offer to Gunther to fight off an unprovoked attack on Burgundy by the Saxons and Danes. Inviting the monarch to enjoy the comforts of his castle and remain in the company of his entourage—"Stay at home, my lord King, since your knights are ready to follow me. Remain here with the ladies and be of good cheer" (36)—Siegfried asks only that he be allowed to meet Kriemhild upon his return. Gunther agrees. It takes only slight persuasion to convince Gunther to remain behind.

Despite Siegfried's victory and heroic comportment in battle, Gunther conveniently forgets his promise. His memory loss suggests a lack of integrity on his part as well as a penchant for spuriousness—characteristics that will become increasingly marked in the years to come. Reminded of his claim by Siegfried, Gunther realizes that he is bound to accede to the hero's wishes.

So anxious is Kriemhild to know the outcome of the hostilities that in complete disregard of her decision to avoid suitors because of her archetypal dream, she secretly summons a messenger to question him about the fate of all the knights except Siegfried. Perhaps suspecting her real intent, the messenger tells her that Siegfried was the noblest fighter of them all. Kriemhild's "lovely face blushe[s] red as a rose," and she gives the messenger gold and clothes as a reward (43). Thus are we made privy to her hyperemotionality or proneness to mood swings.

At the victory feast marking the couple's first meeting, Kriemhild, attired in a splendid gown, her gems highlighting the glow in her cheeks, is the incarnation of perfection. "Kriemhild emerged like the dawn from the dark clouds, freeing from much distress him who secretly cherished her and indeed long had done so" (47).

Following her presentation to Siegfried, she welcomes the noble knight and takes him by the hand—a gesture preluding their love. By the beginning of summer, she has "conveyed her liking" for him, and he, having been granted permission to exchange a ceremonial kiss, has cause for "ecstasy" (49).

The delicate subject of marriage now has to be broached to Gunther. As is frequently the case in myths, the propitious occasion will present itself fortuitously: the day Gunther decides to marry Brunhild, the queen of Iceland, a "formidable" warrior woman whose strength is as great as that of any man. Firm in her determination not to marry, Brunhild will accept betrothal only if her future husband outdoes her in such competitive sports as javelin- and boulder-throwing contests. Failing, the suitor and his retinue will be put to death.

The morally and physically weak Gunther is once again succored by the fearless—and undiscerning—Siegfried, who, always intent upon proving his valor, offers his services to the king. In return he asks for, and is granted, Kriemhild's hand.

Readying their paraphernalia—weapons, standards, horses, and clothing—Gunther, Siegfried, and the knights prepare for the long and perilous journey to Iceland in quest of Brunhild. They have to be outfitted with the finest of clothes, since wealth is equated with power. Gunther turns to his sister in recognition of her superior knowledge of garment making. "I am ready to do anything within my power for you," she replies, adding somewhat surprisingly and critically: "You must not ask so timidly but command me as my lord, since I am at your service for whatever you care to ask of me" (56). Clearly, having seen Siegfried and her brother side by side and noting the character difference between them, she wishes to express disapproval of his pusillanimity and demonstrate her own strength of character.

Taking command of the situation and bringing her organizational talents to the fore, Kriemhild instructs Gunther and Siegfried: "Silk I have myself but you get your men to fetch us jewels by the shieldful and then we shall stitch your clothes" (56). No sooner had Kriemhild chosen thirty of her most gifted seamstresses than work begins.

> They threaded precious stones into snow-white silk from Arabia or into silk from Zazamanc as green as clover, making fine robes, while noble Kriemhild cut the cloth herself. Whatever handsome linings they could lay hands on from the skins of strange water-beasts, wondrous to see, they covered with silk, just as the knights would wear them. (56)

That Kriemhild undertakes the task of cutting the fabrics herself suggests an incisive and active nature, as well as an ability to plan ahead, distinguishing the different tasks that will be required to accomplish the act of sewing. Like a sculptor, she knows how to cut and thereby modify matter; like Atropos, one the three Fates, she will, as we shall see, cut the thread of life as well.

Only seven weeks are required to produce the garments, thanks to Kriemhild's aesthetic sense, her managerial expertise, and her extraordinary efficiency. Her artistic talents come to the fore as she styles and blends brilliant colors of her own creation and groups her fabrics: Moroccan and Libyan silk, some garnished with ermine furs, others lined "with coal black brocades all spangled with brilliant stones set in Arabian gold" (57).

Although Kriemhild has been depicted physically as a vision of beauty and spiritually as a pure-minded angel, we have just been made privy some other, previously unknown, qualities: a strong sense of commitment, unflagging determination, industriousness, and organizational talent. Unlike her brother in his lack of boldness and determination, she takes charge of the clothes-fashioning project incisively and rationally. Given the visceral, cruel images projected in Kriemhild's archetypal dream, the reader may not really understand what to expect from her.

That Kriemhild is charged with the creation of sets of clothes for Gunther's army identifies her with feminine occupations and skills as well as with the domestication of women in society. Thus far she conforms to the patriarchal canon of femininity. In sharp contrast, at least at the outset of the *Nibelungenlied*, is Brunhild, the warrior queen Gunther seeks to marry.

Brunhild: Queen of Iceland

The warrior maiden Brunhild, queen of Iceland, rules her land with apparent equanimity and justice. As the governmental head of her land, she is in full command of herself, her situation, and her people. Man's defeat of this type of woman, referred to as an Amazon in patriarchal societies—be they Greek, Chinese, or medieval German—was intended to show his empowerment of women, her domestication, and her functionality as wife, mother, or daughter.

Some feminists suggest—but without factual evidence in support of their theory—that the existence of shield-bearing maidens, such as Brunhild or Hippolyta, an Amazon queen in Greek mythology, indicates the existence of matriarchal societies. The notion of the Amazon woman has fascinated humanity since ancient times. Legends revolving around this type of woman have been transmitted to us by the geographer Strabo (58 B.C.E.–24 C.E.), and by historians such as Herodotus (c. 484–420 B.C.E.), Diodorus (d. 21 B.C.E.), and Suetonius (75–160 C.E), to mention but a few. Warrior maidens, generally speaking, placed value neither on marriage nor on men. In fact, the male was either excluded entirely from their lands or simply tolerated for procreative purposes. If allowed to remain, he was held in positions of social abasement if not actual slavery, relegated to performing those commonplace household tasks usually performed by women. By forcibly crippling the arms or legs of male children, women robbed men of their ability to bear arms, thereby rendering them harmless to the feminine ruling class (just as, mutatis mutandis, foot binding was practiced in China).

The Danish historian Saxo Grammaticus considered warrior maidens a threat to Christian patriarchy, describing them as women

> who sought the clash of arms rather than the arm's embrace, fitted to weapons hands which should have been weaving, desired not the couch but the kill, and those they could have appeased with looks they attacked with lances. (Saxo Grammaticus 1979, 212ff.)

The very notion of the warrior woman violates the medieval concept of the meek, helpless, frightened, obedient virgin under the dictates of the man who was considered *the crown of all creation*. In literary works written by males, such as the *Nibelungenlied*, and, interestingly enough, among some of its exegetes even today, the warrior woman appears as a threatening, castrating, and destabilizing force. That she is a means of subverting and/or pointing up social inequalities that perpetuate the oppression of women is a truism.[4]

Iceland's Queen Brunhild, defiant of the norms for women, will become the victim of androcentric Burgundian arrogance and lust. Because Gunther has neither the vigor nor the insight to overpower this so-called man killer, as she has always been considered stereotypically in patriarchal societies, Siegfried, the great hero, will be the instrument of her psychological undoing.

As the Burgundians make their way to Brunhild's fortress, Siegfried, perhaps in an act of bravado, asks Gunther to point out the queen in the bevy of beautiful maidens standing in array at the windows. His sexually oriented answer is as follows: "the one in a snow-white gown who is so beautiful that my eyes have singled her out, so that had I the power to choose I would assuredly make her my wife" (*N*, 60).

Unwilling to remain an object of "spectacle" for strangers—or of worship or lust—the self-assured queen commands her ladies-in-waiting to move away from the windows. Obedient, they are nevertheless curious, and continue to peer at the mighty warriors through "loopholes," without being seen themselves (60). As for Brunhild, she moves into the "splendid hall of noble, grass-green marble" (61).

The weakly structured Burgundian king is somewhat uneasy about meeting a ruler so antipodal to himself. To cap it all, she is a woman! Her spirit of independence and her equation of physical strength with kingship underscores even further the dichotomy between the two. Gunther might reason that she is a counterpart of the self-assured Siegfried, who gains victories because of his prowess. The powerful impression the young knight makes on Brunhild might also spark, at least unconsciously, a pang of jealousy in Gunther.

Uneasiness is also manifested by Hagen, who, alone among all the Burgundian knights, refuses to comply with the Icelandic custom of giving up sword and corselet prior to entering the castle. Indeed, so fearsome does Hagen consider Brunhild's power that he later compares her to "a rib of the Devil himself!" (65).

The Gender Bypass

To win the queen's hand, a suitor, as previously mentioned, was required to outdo her in javelin throwing, boulder casting, and other feats of strength, and if he failed he would be summarily be killed together with his retinue. Siegfried, knowing he would have to resort to deception to achieve his end, nevertheless had to let it be known that Gunther was the overlord, and he, Siegfried, his vassal (59). Instinctively he knew that rank and status as well as brawn would serve to impress Brunhild.

Realizing that Gunther would be unable to outdo Brunhild in any competitive sport, Siegfried planned a strategy designed to subdue her. When the time came for the radiant Brunhild to make ready for the contest, Siegfried returned surreptitiously to the ship that brought him to Iceland to fetch his *tarnkappe*. Undercover—or, symbolically, in darkness—our stereotypical hero would compete with Brunhild.

His resort to the magic of the *tarnkappe*—perhaps another type of deception—would deplete Brunhild's energies and bring her under control for her new master to enjoy. Although the use of the *tarnkappe* was an avowal of Siegfried's inability to deal unaided with difficult matters, it was also a sign of his strength and discernment. By relying on dominant forces operational in both cosmic and psychological spheres, as in magic and/or religion, Siegfried was lending an apotropaic quality to the *tarnkappe*. Like a shaman, he chose to call upon spirits—unseen forces, mana, or invisible energies identified with the magic object—to help him in his struggle to protect Gunther from overwhelming odds. Such maneuvers were tantamount to an attempt to manipulate transpersonal forces to his advantage (Franz 1980b, 67, 102, 152).

The introduction of the *tarnkappe*, or persona, indicates Siegfried's desire to cloak or to hide the reality of the inner personalities participating in the event. The timorous nature of Brunhild's future husband was hidden. Siegfried performed the required feats of strength while creating the impression that it was Gunther who was doing so. Such deception may also be considered a desire to live out an unconscious fantasy on the part of both men: Gunther wanted to become a hero and to attain the unattainable; Siegfried, to parade his great strength and to demonstrate his superiority to Gunther (Donnington 1963, 94). Siegfried's self-interest played a role as well: if he served Gunther, Kriemhild would be awarded to him as a bride. Political motivations also entered into the scheme: if Gunther had conceded his inferiority as chief of state, his nation would have been degraded.

The magnificent ceremony of competition began as Brunhild was handed her broad shield of "reddest gold" and her

> great spear, both sharp and heavy, which she was accustomed to throw—
> it was strong, and of huge proportions, and dreadfully keen at its edges.
> And now listen to this extraordinary thing about the weight of that spear:
> a good three-and-a-half ingots had gone into its forging, and three of
> Brunhild's men could scarcely lift it. (*N*, 65)

At the sight of the weapon, Gunther became alarmed. Dancwart, Hagen's brother, conveyed the consensus: "[W]hat a shameful way of dying if we are to perish at the hands of women!" (65). Seeing Brunhild hurl her heavy javelin and a weighty boulder as well, Hagen disdainfully questioned the king's courting of such a woman: "What sort of a lover has the King got here? Rather should she be the Devil's drab in Hell!" (66)

Readying herself for the match, Brunhild "furled her sleeves over her dazzling white arms, took a grip on her shield, snatched her spear aloft, and the contest was on!" (66) As planned, Gunther went through the motions, while Siegfried, invisible in his cloak and wielding the king's shield and javelin, vied with his female counterpart. Steel javelins shot through space;

flames flared; sparks leaped upward, carried by the wind. Siegfried/Gunther having won the round, Brunhild expressed her esteem to our hero acting in the Burgundian king's stead: "My compliments on that throw, Gunther, noble knight!" (67). And Gunther, as an impostor, accepted the praise.

Now taking an exceptionally heavy boulder and flinging it twenty-four yards, Brunhild leaped an even further distance, only to be exceeded in her extraordinary feat by Siegfried/Gunther. Although flushed with anger, she had the strength of character to concede failure. "Come forward at once, my kinsmen and vassals! You must do homage to King Gunther" (68).

Brunhild's humiliation sealed her fate. That Siegfried, to her knowledge, was Gunther's vassal exacerbated her sense of disgrace: "I am delighted to hear that your pride has been lowered in this way . . . and that there is someone alive who can master you. You must come to the Rhine with us now, noble maiden" (68).

Brunhild intuited that a dismal future was in store for her. Not only to follow a husband's dictates but to share his bed with him left her alienated from herself—morally and psychologically destitute. Robbed of her identity by an oppressive and duplicitous patriarchal system, Brunhild was to face her psychological divestiture in stages that began at the moment she left her land, never to return.

Prior to her departure for Worms, she made over her territories to her maternal uncle and dispensed gifts to her faithful people. With two thousand retainers and several coffers filled with precious stones, she faced what she sensed would be her dismal, if not despairing, future.

She and her entourage were received by the Burgundians, and especially by Kriemhild, with great "elegance and breeding," as well as warmth. "The ladies embraced and embraced again, and, indeed, you never heard of a welcome so affectionate as that Queen Uote and her daughter extended to the bride, for they kissed her sweet mouth many, many times" (83).

Following the crowning of Brunhild as queen of Burgundy, Siegfried reminded Gunther of his pledge to grant him his sister's hand. Having appropriated, on a psychological level, Siegfried's heroic acts as his own, might Gunther perhaps want to disavow his word? To save face, however, he was compelled to fulfill his promise.

Something strange and perhaps inexplicable occurred at dinner that very night. As Brunhild and the king took their seats opposite Siegfried and Kriemhild, "never had she [Brunhild] suffered such torment—she began to weep so that the hot tears fell down her radiant cheeks" (86). Gunther, lacking insight into his own psyche and that of others, and failing to understand the cause of Brunhild's sorrow, questioned her, only to be told: "It wounds me to the heart to see your sister sitting beside a liegeman, and if she is to be degraded in this fashion I shall never cease to lament it!" (86)

Undoubtedly Brunhild was projecting her own sense of degradation onto the newly affianced maiden, making an analogy in her mind between her own sharing of Gunther's bed that night—the "sexual ordeal"—and the Princess Kriemhild's wedding to a vassal. Brunhild abhorred the position into which society's deprecation of the feminine principle had cast them both.

In keeping with the traditions of the time, once couples were affianced, lord and lady could lie together. In Siegfried's case, "he lay with the young lady [Kriemhild] and inured her so tenderly to his noble loves, she became as dear to him as life, and he would not have exchanged her for a thousand others" (87).

Gunther and Brunhild's first night was no seduction scene. Although she may have sensed Gunther's fecklessness despite his exterior show of strength, the warrior maiden felt physical revulsion for him as well as for the marriage bed per se. Self-serving and too self-involved to have any idea of Brunhild's feelings, the timorous Gunther had great expectations for his first night with his bride. After dimming the lights, he made ready to take his joy.

Impotence and Rape

The shock effects of the scene in which Brunhild repulses Gunther's every caress and word of endearment are perhaps unique in medieval literature. Brunhild warns: "Sir . . . you must give up the thing you have set your hopes on, for it will not come to pass. Take good note of this: I intend to stay a maiden till I have learned the truth about Siegfried" (88).

Such stereotypically unfeminine conduct—a woman's rejection of a husband's advances—reveals a state of psychological independence and leads to Gunther's wrathful but unsuccessful attempts to take Brunhild by force. His abuse of her body was not only a "misuse of sexuality" but a failure to understand the "connectivity of body and psyche," the one working in close community with the other (Reis 1991, 113).

Anger, often a cover-up for failure, was for Gunther a means of hiding his emotional impotence. Such an upsurge of affects, as in temper tantrums, is deceptive, inasmuch as the outburst of concentrated energy may be interpreted as a sign of power. Brunhild was not to be duped. Unexpectedly

the haughty girl reached for the girdle of stout silk cord that she wore
about her waist, and subjected him to great suffering and shame: for in
return for being baulked of her sleep, she bound him hand and foot, carried him to a nail, and hung him on the wall. She had put a stop to his
love-making! As to him, he all but died, such strength had she exerted.
(88)

Anger gave way to shame. Resorting to pleas and promises revealing his
utter impotence, he begged Brunhild to loosen his bonds. In vain. Not only
did he remain hanging until dawn, but she taunted him still further: "Would
you mind it if your chamberlains were to find you, bound by a woman's
hand?" (88). Finally, and only after extracting his word that he would not
touch her, she freed him.

The following day at mass, Gunther apprised Siegfried of his humiliation. Again the knight took up the king's cause—the "taming" of Brunhild.
As required in their rite of passage, heroes are frequently called upon to
rectify difficult and dangerous situations. In this instance Siegfried demonstrated the same bravura and self-confidence he had displayed in fighting the
Saxons and Danes and in practicing competitive sports in Iceland. Gunther
had only one admonition: "[Y]ou must not make love to my dear lady in
any way. Do anything else you like" (90).

Siegfried donned the *tarnkappe* before entering the king's nuptial chamber. So offended and outraged was Brunhild at what she thought was Gunther's
second attempt to deflower her that she fought even more valiantly than
before. Even Siegfried had difficulty taming her. In fact, after pinning him
down, she "flung him out of the bed against a stool nearby so that his head
struck it with a mighty crack!" (90). After more contention, she "carried
him with irresistible force and rammed him between the wall and a coffer"
(92). Because Siegfried's manhood was at stake, he, like Gunther, grew even
more fearsome in his rage. No longer did he view himself simply as an
individual male helping a friend, but rather as the defender of his own gender. A war of the male against the female sex was now being waged, in
which Siegfried summoned all his strength to brutally assault his adversary.
"If I now lose my life to a girl, the whole sex will grow uppish with their
husbands for ever after, though they would otherwise never behave so" (92).
With great effort, he finally subdued her—raped her would be the better
term—although he did not penetrate her. Shortly thereafter "she submitted
to the real Gunther" (92).

But from his intimacy she grew somewhat pale, for at love's coming her vast strength fled so that now she was no stronger than any other woman. Gunther had his delight of her lovely body, and had she renewed her resistance what good could it have done her? His loving had reduced her to this. (93)

In terms of male projection, the bridling of the bride Brunhild may be understood as an affirmation of masculine rule over the female with the intent of depotentiating her energies and minimizing her capacities. Because woman is identified with mystery—her genitals are hidden while the man's are exposed—some psychologists and feminists partly explain "rape" in terms of strong male desire to "unveil" and understand the great enigma: the secret of creation. The rapist unconsciously believes he must divest the woman of her chthonian darkness, which evidently is a source of perplexity and vexation to him. His assault is "on the unreachable omnipotence of woman and nature"—her *temenos* (Paglia 1991, 22).

In demonstration of his sexual mastery, Siegfried purloined Brunhild's belt—reminiscent of Hercules' theft of the belt Ares had given to Hippolyta, the Amazon queen. Although he did not slay his victim, as had Hercules, he destroyed her psychologically; the theft of the belt symbolized the demise of the once virile, powerful, and independent woman. To compound the symbolic mutilation, he gave the girdle he had removed from Brunhild's body (and a ring he had taken from her finger) to Kriemhild.

The girdle Brunhild wore around her waist—an identity icon—bound her to her credo and established her personality. It served as both a protective and offensive device, much like the warrior's belt to which are attached sword, dagger, and other identifying objects. The tendering of one's belt—a soldier's, a magistrate's, or a young lady's—was the equivalent of disarming or of surrendering one's function, one's self. In medieval times the removal of a maiden's girdle contrary to her will was an act designed to degrade and or rape her. Siegfried's forcible removal of Brunhild's "sacred" belt indicated a divestiture of her values, her way of life, and her psychological balance.

As for Brunhild's ring, a circle without beginning or end, it is evocative of the Gnostics' image of the serpent biting its own tail, the Ouroboros. Psychologically it represents, on the one hand, the most primitive experience of the undifferentiated union of opposites in the unconscious; and, on the other hand, the highly differentiated union of opposites that, through effort, increases consciousness. Brunhild made a conscious exertion to live her own life and determine her own future. Her ring having been snatched from her finger, she was reduced to her lowest components: primitiveness and stuntedness.

By ravishing Brunhild's girdle and ring, symbols of her wholeness and well-being, the unthinking, childlike Siegfried is transformed into a plunderer and rapist. His arrogance in stealing the ring and girdle and then presenting them to Kriemhild may also suggest an attempt on his part to further enhance her image of him—the image, that is, of his masculinity and machismo. His violence may have been instrumental as well in arousing him sexually, as is frequently the case in combat per se, and in sadomasochistic acts performed in extramarital relationships.

Kriemhild's Clear Thinking

Following the two-week-long marriage celebrations of Siegfried/Kriemhild and Gunther/Brunhild, the prince of the Netherlands and his bride prepared to return to his homeland.

According to the law of the land, upon Kriemhild's marriage one-fourth of the kingdom of Burgundy should have devolved on her, but her husband as her legal guardian renounced her inheritance in favor of her brothers without her permission, claiming that his own holdings were vast enough for both of them. His seeming indifference to a woman's wishes and rights (which had already been displayed by his theft of Brunhild's girdle and ring and his gift of these to his wife) was perhaps an unconscious attempt on his part to prove his political and economic power. It certainly must have irked Kriemhild, who was ever vigilant in protecting her own rights and refusing to be dominated.

> "You may well renounce my inheritance . . . but it will not be so easy where knights of Burgundy are concerned. They are such as a king may gladly take home to his country and I request my dear brothers to make division of them with me." (*N*, 96)

Prior to the couple's departure for the Netherlands, Kriemhild assembled a retinue of thirty-two maidens and five hundred vassals to accompany her to her new home. Although she had chosen Hagen to be her liege man, he refused to identify himself with any king but Gunther, nor any land but Burgundy (96).

Kriemhild and Siegfried Return to the Netherlands

The crowning of their son and daughter-in-law by Siegfried's parents was accomplished with all the pomp and circumstance of the day.

> Marvels could be told of the Netherlanders' wealth, as they sat in their glory and abundance. The sight of all the gussets agleam with gold which their followers wore, embroidered on golden wire with pearls and jewels—so well did noble Queen Sieglind care for them! (97)

By accepting the kingship of this powerful land, Siegfried became dispenser of justice, and he exercised his functions with felicity. That he had conquered the land of the Nibelungs, their warriors, and their treasure in single battle prior to his journey to Burgundy made him one of the most powerful rulers of the time. After he had been happily married for ten years, a son was born and was baptized Gunther, after Kriemhild's brother. Following Queen Sieglind's death, on Kriemhild was bestowed the power "which such great ladies are entitled to wield over their territories" (98).

Almost concurrently, a son was born to Gunther and Brunhild, whom they named Siegfried. Brunhild, still intent on learning the truth of Siegfried's relationship to her husband, and no longer the forthright and wholesome person she had once been, manipulated Gunther to her advantage. "If you wish to please me, help me to get Siegfried and your sister to visit us—I assure you nothing would make me happier" (100). Although he was averse to her proposal, since Siegfried's presence was a constant reminder of his own failures, Gunther once again chose the easy path. He yielded to his wife's request for the sake of peace and harmony.

The Queens' Quarrel

Kriemhild, Siegfried, and his father, Siegmund, accepted the invitation to visit Brunhild and Gunther. Following a royal reception, eleven days of festivities ensued. "The mighty queens," preoccupied with thoughts of their husbands, engaged in verbal dueling, each seeking to establish the superiority of her spouse. To Kriemhild's "I have a husband of such merit that he might rule over all the kingdoms of this region," Brunhild countered: "How could that be? If there were no others alive but you and he, all these kingdoms might well subserve him, but as long as Gunther lives it could never come about." Kriemhild, observing her husband admiringly, parried: "See how magnificently he bears himself, and with what splendour he stands out from the other knights, like the moon against the stars. . . . It is not for nothing that I am so happy" (111).

Brunhild's thrust: "However splendid and handsome and valiant your husband may be . . . you must nevertheless give your noble brother the advantage. Let me tell you truly: Gunther must take precedence over all kings." Kriemhild stood firm: "My husband is a man of such worth . . . that I have not praised him vainly. His honour stands high on very many counts. Believe me, Brunhild, he is fully Gunther's equal" (111).

Brunhild, who had been told from the very outset that Siegfried was the declared liege man of Gunther, was completely destabilized upon hearing Kriemhild blurt out the impossible: "You will have to renounce your claim to him and to his attending you with services of any kind! He ranks above my noble brother Gunther, and you must spare me such things as I have had to hear" (112). Kriemhild further challenged her rival: "You must see visible proof this day that I am a free noblewoman, and that my husband is a better man than yours" (112).

The height of their dispute was reached as Kriemhild with her retinue approached the cathedral. Brunhild, with understandable malice, ordered Kriemhild to halt: "A liege woman may not enter before a Queen!" By way of retort, Kriemhild called Brunhild "a vassal's paramour" who could never wed a king (114). Preceding Brunhild into the cathedral, she revealed to her rival:

> My dear husband Siegfried was the first to enjoy your lovely body, since it was not my brother who took your maidenhead. Where were your poor wits?—It was a vile trick.—Seeing that he is your vassal, why did you let him love you? Your complaints have no foundation. (114)

Perhaps aware of the deception she had been living as Gunther's wife and experiencing as never before the utter abjectness of her situation, Brunhild let her tears flow. During the service she conveyed helplessness and rage in an interior monologue, swearing that should Siegfried boast of his act in public, it would cost him his life. Once outside the cathedral, Brunhild demanded proof of Kriemhild's allegation. Only then was she shown the gold ring Kriemhild wore on her finger, the one "which my sweetheart brought me when he first slept with you" (114). Arguing that the ring could have been stolen from her, Brunhild demanded further confirmation. Kriemhild's response was devastating: "As proof that I am not lying, see this girdle which I have round me—you shared my Siegfried's bed!" (115)

Faced with this irrefutable evidence, a tearful Brunhild demanded that Gunther clear her of "this monstrous infamy" (115). Called in, Siegfried emphatically denied having told his wife that he had been the first to enjoy Brunhild's body. As he raised his hand to swear to this, however, Gunther, perhaps trying to avoid a confrontation or unwilling to allow him to perjure himself, stopped him: "Your great innocence is so well known to me that I acquit you of my sister's allegation and accept that you are not guilty of the deed." Thus both he and the great hero Siegfried took the coward's way out. Exchanging "meaningful glances," they followed the well-known dictum—the best defense is a good offense—and blamed the women for the misunderstanding. Siegfried went so far as to suggest that "women should be trained to avoid irresponsible chatter" and, turning to his accomplice, admonished him to "forbid your wife to indulge in it," adding, "I shall do the same with mine. I am truly ashamed at her unseemly behaviour" (116).

Strangely enough, yet much to Kriemhild's admiration, Siegfried, a man of his word in this case, punished her for her indiscretion. Elated, she recounted to Hagen that "Siegfried has beaten me soundly and taken ample vengeance for my having said anything that vexed" Brunhild (120).

Kriemhild should have been aware of Hagen's profound allegiance to Gunther, inasmuch as he had refused to be her liege man and accompany her to the Netherlands following her marriage to Siegfried. Yet she failed to understand his determination to rectify the wrong done to his humiliated queen, Brunhild, and by extension to his king.

Hagen's decision to seek revenge against Siegfried may have also been motivated by his jealousy of this hero's growing power in Burgundy, his wealth, reputation, and most importantly, his influence over Gunther. Victimized by his own drive for control, Hagen may have reasoned that his defense of the queen would also enhance his prestige with the king and the court. He swore that "Kriemhild's man should pay for it" (116). With this in mind, he convinced the court dignitaries to begin plotting the death of Siegfried, despite Gunther's feeble attempts to protect his erstwhile friend: "He has done us nothing but good" (117). Hagen persisted in his murderous scheme, assuring the timorous king that the planning and perpetrating of the murder would take place in "secret"—the shadowy realm where both Gunther and Hagen, to be sure, functioned most successfully (118).

Four days later Siegfried was deceitfully told that war had again been declared on Burgundy by the Saxons and Danes. Instinctively the fearless hero offered his services to the king: "I shall make your enemies suffer!" (120).

Kriemhild again failed to detect Hagen's machinations. She protested to him that Siegfried "must not be made to pay for any wrong that I may have done to Brunhild" (120). Like Iago in the tragedy *Othello*, he graciously offered his help. He said to the concerned Kriemhild: "If you have any apprehension that a weapon might wound him [Siegfried] tell me by what means I can prevent it, and I shall always guard him, riding or walking" (121).

Duped by these comforting words, Kriemhild not only commended Siegfried to Hagen's guard but also confided her fears for her husband's welfare. Her anxieties were not about his strength in battle, but rather about his "rashness," his lack of judgment, his inability to discern danger. Imprudently, she revealed to Hagen the long-guarded secret of her husband's vulnerability.

> My husband is very brave and very strong. . . .When he slew the dragon at the foot of the mountain the gallant knight bathed in its blood, as a result of which no weapon has pierced him in battle ever since. Nevertheless, when he is at the wars in the midst of all the javelins that warriors hurl, I fear I may lose my dear husband. . . . Now I shall reveal this to you in confidence, dearest kinsman, so that you may keep faith with me, and I shall tell you trusting utterly in you, where my dear husband can be harmed. When the hot blood flowed from the dragon's wound and the good knight was bathing in it, a broad leaf fell from the linden between his shoulder-blades. It is there that he can be wounded, and this is why I am so anxious. (121)

Foolishly heeding Hagen's suggestion, Kriemhild sewed a mark on Siegfried's clothing that identified the vulnerable spot on his back. Once apprised of the place, Hagen would know where to "protect" her husband in battle. Thus did Kriemhild become the instrument of Siegfried's death.

Kriemhild: Instrument of Death

Now disabused with regard to the enemy's intention to make war, Siegfried, deprived of yet another occasion to flaunt his might, accepted Gunther's carefully worded invitation to hunt boar and bear in the Vosges forest.

Meanwhile, Kriemhild's agony over what she now recognized as a crucial lack of judgment on her part triggered another archetypal dream, which she related to her husband. "I dreamt last night—and an ill-omened dream it was—that two boars chased you over the heath and the flowers were dyed with blood!" (124)

In ancient hyperborean, Celtic, and Viking cults, the boar, a powerful male hog, was identified with the spirit; the bear, with temporal matters. The forest, the habitat of both these animals, was also a place to which the Druid priests withdrew to worship. Hunting parties of men, so popular in medieval times, concluded frequently with the killing of the boar and the bear, and were viewed as tests for humankind: the attempt of the spirit (boar) to dominate the temporal (bear), or the replacement of one order by another. Venerated for its ability to ward off disaster, the sacred boar was imaged on amulets, votive offerings, and standards (Webster 1986, 118). Unlike the Druids, Christians looked upon the boar as an evil force, perhaps because they saw this animal as lubricious, impetuous, and passionate, or as a ravager of fields, orchards, and vineyards.

The hunting of the boar in Kriemhild's dream syncretizes Celtic, Nordic, and Christian beliefs. It indicates a reversal of the hunter's quest: Siegfried was not killing the boar, but was being killed by this sacred animal. As representative of spiritual factors for the Celts and Nordics, the boar, symbol of transcendent power, was chosen to mete out divine punishment; but this animal's ferocity, according to Christian standards, suggests the onslaught of irrational and devastating forces—foretelling an impending reign of chaos, of fatal ruination, and of death. That two boars were featured in the dream symbolizes duality: an intense conflict between spirituality and temporality, or between light and darkness.

Kriemhild's inauspicious dream also reveals the depth of her own projection onto the two boars. That she identified with them may prelude her own proclivities for destruction. Her sense of guilt for having disclosed Siegfried's vulnerable spot to Hagen was also instrumental in increasing the burden of her despair. Only by withdrawing into the shadowy world of the forest—of the Great Mother—would she perhaps find a way to deal with her feelings of culpability. New perspectives might be gained within this maternal shelter, considered by psychologists as paralleling the most primitive level of the psyche.

Although she admonished her husband to stay clear of Hagen during the hunting trip, she failed to reveal that single factor which would have protected him: her disclosure to Hagen of his vulnerable spot. To do so would have been damaging to her. Fearful of her husband's wrath, self-interest took primacy. In this regard for self-interest, she and her timorous brother were alike.

In a second sinister dream, Kriemhild saw "how two mountains fell upon [Siegfried] and hid [him] from [her] sight!" (*N,* 125).

The hunt began. Siegfried rode into the forest with Gunther, Hagen, and other brave knights and proved his unparalleled skills in this domain, too. Regal dishes were served the party following their sport. Notably absent were wine and water. Those tormented by thirst, Hagen proposed, could repair to a cool spring nearby. Siegfried raced Gunther and Hagen to the spot. Out of courtesy, he allowed the Burgundian king to drink first. Then, as Siegfried bent over to imbibe the cool waters, Hagen hurled his spear at the spot marked with the cross that Kriemhild had sewn onto his shirt. Blood spurted and Hagen fled. Although he was mortally wounded, Siegfried took his shield, followed Hagen, and dealt him a blow that made him reel.

After Siegfried's death, Gunther, concealing Hagen's guilt and lying to the disconsolate Kriemhild, asserted that her husband had been killed by robbers. Insidiously, and in keeping with his character, Hagen ordered that Siegfried's corpse be carried to Kriemhild's apartment and placed on the threshold of her room so that she would see it when she set out to matins at daybreak.

Kriemhild's lacerating hurt and overpowering sense of guilt turned to rage: she was determined to discover the identity of the murderer and seek retribution. When her brother and Hagen expressed regret at Siegfried's passing, she retorted forcefully, just as when she had been charged with preparing the garments for the trip to Iceland. "You have no cause to do so. . . . If you regretted it, it would never have happened. . . . Would to God it had befallen me." Interrupting their protests, she flung her challenge: "Let the man who says he is innocent prove it, let him go up to the bier in sight of all the people and we shall very soon see the truth of it!" (137).

It was believed in medieval times that when "a blood-guilty murderer" passed in front of the corpse of his victim, the wounds would bleed. And so it happened when Hagen passed before the corpse of Siegfried. Gunther reaffirmed the robbers' guilt in an attempt to exculpate Hagen, but Kriemhild stood her ground, inculpating them both: "Gunther and Hagen, it was you who did the deed!" (137).

To be beholden to anyone, as Gunther had been to Siegfried for saving his kingdom from the Saxons and Danes, and helping him win and subdue his bride, may have overwhelmed him with an already built-in but now reinforced sense of failure. Unaware perhaps of his own psychological and physical impotence, one frequently dependent on the other, the weakly structured Gunther yielded once again to another agenda: this time Hagen's suggestion to further punish his sister.

At Siegfried's graveside, Kriemhild begged that his sarcophagus be opened once more so she could gaze at her beloved for the last time: "She raised his handsome head with her white hand and kissed the noble knight in death, while her bright eyes in their sorrow wept tears of blood" (140).

Faced now with the alternatives of returning to the Netherlands with Siegmund to rejoin her son, or remaining in Burgundy with her mother and her brothers Giselher and Gernot, Kriemhild chose the latter. Why? To be near Siegfried's tomb? But how could she face abandoning her son, the living embodiment of her husband? Siegmund played on her feelings as a mother. "Come back with us, too, for the sake of your little son—you must not leave him an orphan. When he grows up he will console you. Meanwhile many brave warriors shall attend you" (142). Would remaining in Worms give her the opportunity to plan her revenge? Kriemhild's refusal to return to the Netherlands, she maintained, was because she would have no kinsmen in her father-in-law's kingdom. With full knowledge that she would never again set eyes on her son, the sorrowful widow remained in Burgundy. As for Brunhild, she "sat enthroned in her pride" and in her inflexible hatred for Kriemhild (144).

Kriemhild's Introversion

Grief would change Kriemhild. Unable to face the outside world, she withdrew into her own primeval sphere, her inner forest, the domain of the Great Mother. Scorning the joys of life and concentrating on spiritual matters, she went to church daily and sobbed at Siegfried's tomb. For the next three-and-a-half years she neither spoke to her brother Gunther nor set eyes on Hagen.

The state of introversion, or shifting of libido from outer to inner worlds, is frequently a self-regulating process engendered by the psyche. For Kriemhild, this was not the case. To have moved toward herself as subject rather than focusing on people as outer objects might have allowed her to live out her potential, or that unlived factor in her life, and might have served also to constellate those still undeveloped and unregenerative areas of her personality. Although a change of focus gave her time to indwell and thus to establish new parameters or modes of adaptation to life, it proved in her case to be negative in essence (Jung 1990, par. 567).

Repressed libido, which could have worked in her favor during her long period of introversion, remained blocked in her subliminal spheres. Rather than guide her to more enlightened modes of behavior, the imprisoned psychic energy reached explosive force. So great was the tension between inner and outer worlds that her ego-complex, or conscious personality, shattered. The potential lying dormant within the "matrix" or "womb aspect" of her subliminal domain suddenly erupted. A formerly functional ego-complex was in the process of being replaced by autonomous groupings (or a different network of electric circuits), each accountable to itself rather than to the whole. So sudden and so powerful was the change brought about by the dissociation of Kriemhild's ego-complex that her comportment henceforth became unpredictable (Franz 1980a, 19, 20, 54).

Kriemhild's blindness to Hagen's duplicity was a disclosure of her own vulnerability. Her obsessive involvement with and love for her husband had robbed her of discernment, just as Siegfried's bravado and fearless naïveté had divested him of a sense of danger. Her lack of insight was again to cause trouble for her: when Giselher broached the topic of making peace with Gunther, she not only agreed to see her brother, but having received the kiss of reconciliation, renewed her love for and confidence in him and his entourage. Her thinking processes thus subverted, she again became prone to mood swings, each of which were to dictate her actions.

Hagen, meanwhile, had set as his goal the theft of Siegfried's gift to Kriemhild: the Nibelungs' gold treasure. Her trust in her brother having been restored, she willingly agreed to have it brought to her rooms, and it was but a matter of time until Hagen secured the keys to her living quarters and stole the vast hoard, which he later sank in the Rhine. Although Gunther, Giselher, and other lords of Burgundy were, at least outwardly, averse to Hagen's latest infamy, not one had the courage to punish him.

Treasures (as, for example, the Argonauts' Golden Fleece) symbolize not only knowledge, spirituality, and power, but life's energy as well. They are "symbolic carriers of immaterial value"—such as "the water of life, the healing herb, the elixir of immortality, the philosopher's stone, miracle rings"—each symbolizing in its own way "the treasure hard to attain," unless a hero or heroine completes certain arduous tasks or rites of passage. A treasure consisting of purely material gold, such as the hoard featured in the *Nibelungenlied*, "is a late and degenerate form of the original motif." In ancient myths, gold was a concretization of a centralizing agent identified by the individual or by the collective with their highest values or ideas (Jung 1976, 1:103). Kriemhild was now robbed of both her material treasure (given to her by Siegfried as part of her dowry) and her human treasure (her husband). Accordingly, her sense of authority, governance, and influence over herself and others was paradigmatically depleted.

Kriemhild's Remarriage

When Etzel, king of the Huns, became widowed, he was urged by his advisors for political reasons to marry Kriemhild, renowned for her beauty and virtue. The fact that Etzel was a Muslim and Kriemhild a Christian posed no problem, for in the former's lands "the Christian life and the heathen existed side by side" (170).

Hagen alone opposed Kriemhild's marriage to Etzel, fearing that new power and wealth would prompt her to seek vengeance on the Burgundians—and on him in particular. But despite Hagen's warnings, Gunther and his council accepted Etzel's marriage offer. According to the laws of the time, however, a widow's consent was required before contracting a second marriage. Kriemhild's brother could not, then, dispose of her person as he had when she was a maiden. The still-grieving Kriemhild at first resisted the proposal, accepting it only after Etzel's ambassador let it be known that on her would devolve crown, wealth, and great political power.

King and queen lived in great entente for seven years, during which a son, Ortlieb, was born to them, and Kriemhild proved herself to be an extraordinary queen beloved by the Huns. Her second marriage, nevertheless, had never been emotionally consummated.

Kriemhild: Persona versus Shadow

Despite the power and wealth Kriemhild enjoyed with Etzel, whose kindness and thoughtfulness toward his queen were quite unusual for the time, Kriemhild could not help brooding over her great loss and the wrongs perpetrated against her. More than ever Hagen was her bête noire!

The more virtuous her actions as queen and wife—or psychologically, the greater her identification with her persona (that is, her social face)—the darker became her shadow, or the "other," unconscious side of her personality. Rage and thirst for vengeance—identified with the shadow—were alien to her persona and had to remain hermetically sealed in her unconscious. Those social traits identified with consciousness or reason—such as generosity and affability—were exhibited for all to see, so as not to erode the balance in her relationship with Etzel and his court (Sharp 1987, 94).

The more restrained her thirst for revenge, the greater the build-up of undirected libido in her subliminal spheres, and concomitantly, the power of the shadow. The increasing dichotomy between her persona and her insalubrious, unregenerate darkened realm served as an imminent threat to her ego-consciousness and dashed any hope for the future formation of a different mode of behavior. As Jung posited, "With what irresistible persuasion and force the libido streams within or without, with what unshakable tenacity an introverted or extraverted attitude can take root" (Jung 1990, par. 256).

Blinded by the momentum of inner pulsations, Kriemhild became the victim of what was called in medieval times (and even today, in some milieux) demonic possession, but which in psychological terminology is alluded to as obsession and/or idée fixe (Jung, 6, 156). Henceforth, Kriemhild's irrational or shadow factors would direct her in matters of state and personal relationships, her affects emerging, paradoxically, as evolved, detailed, and differentiated thought processes. Thus she gave an impression of capacity to adapt to the world at large. Indeed, the pulsations brought into consciousness were received by her rational thinking factor as finely tuned and sharply edged perceptions (par. 182).

In that everything in the outer sphere would be determined from the point of view of an inner necessity, Kriemhild's acutely honed intuitions focused exclusively on the attainment of her goal: Hagen would have to journey to Hungary to suit her plan.

Whenever Kriemhild reached a crossroads in her life, the tension experienced in her subliminal world was conveyed, as we know, in dream form: "[S]he dreamt that she was walking with her brother Giselher, hand in hand, repeatedly, and that she kissed him time and time [again]. . . ." (*N,* 177).

Giselher, in the guise of the helpful and loving brother, had encouraged his sister to marry Etzel and promised he would come to her aid should she suffer any "annoyance" in her new land (166). Symptomatic of his behavior throughout life, he had not forcefully attempted to prevent Siegfried's murder, pleading his youthfulness, weakness, and lethargy, or perhaps fear of Gunther and Hagen. Kriemhild's passion for revenge had, in any case, taken on such proportions that it blocked out any objective assessment of Gilselher's weaknesses.

Etzel, cleverly duped into believing that his wife loved him and his people, became one of the earliest objects of Kriemhild's astute machinations. Choosing the propitious moment—when "he held her in his arms and caressed her as was his wont"—she coaxed him into inviting her brother and his entourage to Hungary (178). The invitation would not only put to rest rumors suggesting that she was "a friendless foreigner" in Hungary, but would also warm her heart. A thoughtful and gallant man, Etzel understood his wife's loneliness and complied with her wishes. Gunther and his kinsmen were invited to Etzel's summer festival.

Prior to the departure of Etzel's two messengers for Burgundy, Kriemhild summoned them in secret to her apartments, charging them to inform her brother Giselher that she "was never made to suffer through any fault of his" and that she would be happy to see him "because of the great love he bears me" (180). She also instructed the messenger to assure that Hagen make the journey as well, since, she claimed, he was the only one to know the roads leading to Hungary.[5]

Upon their arrival at Worms, Etzel's envoys delivered Kriemhild's messages. Gunther and his intimates were very well disposed to making the journey, while Hagen, Siegfried's killer, warned that Kriemhild must ever be feared. Fully convinced that his sister's kiss of reconciliation was given in sign of forgiveness, Gunther failed to grasp the true nature of Kriemhild's intent, just as she had failed to see through his own deception. Giselher, intervening in what we might characterize as an unusual show of strength, said to Hagen: "Since you are so conscious of your guilt, Uncle Hagen, you stay here in safety and let *those that dare* come with us to see my sister" (185). His pride piqued, Hagen decided to join the group, if only to prove his courage.

When finally the Burgundians arrived in Hungary, Etzel rejoiced. Kriemhild's mood, as she stood at the palace *window*, reminiscent of the first time she had seen Siegfried, was vastly different now. Expressing her real intent obliquely, she said to Etzel: "How happy am I! My kinsmen are bringing new shields and dazzling hauberks here in plenty. Whoever is willing to take gold, let him remember my grief and I shall always show myself grateful" (213).

With the keenness of a military strategist, she ordered Gunther's train—including Hagen and his brother, Dancwart—to be lodged in different quarters from the rest of the armed Burgundian knights. "With perfidy in her heart," writes the author of the *Nibelungenlied*, siding obviously against Kriemhild, she welcomed her kinsmen. Only Giselher did she kiss and lead away by the hand. To Hagen she spoke the following words: "But I shall not greet you for any love between you and me. Tell me what you bring me from Worms beyond the Rhine, that you should be so very welcome to me" (216). Not the least embarrassed, he retorted: "Had I but known that knights were meant to bring you gifts, I am not so poor that I could not have brought you some present here—had I given it more thought." Nor did Kriemhild blanch as she broached a delicate subject: "Tell me further: what have you done with the treasure of the Nibelungs?—It was mine, as you well know. *That* is what you should bring me here to Etzel's country" (216). Annoyed, Hagen responded in kind: "I have brought you nothing and be damned to you! My shield, my corselet, and my bright helmet are burden enough for me. As to this sword in my hand, it is not for you that I bring it" (217).

Cleverly Kriemhild resorted to the law of the land, just as Brunhild had done when the Burgundians arrived in Iceland. In both countries it was forbidden to carry weapons into the fortress and into the king's hall, and Kriemhild demanded that Hagen give his up. Since Hagen refused to comply, the queen realized that he must have been forewarned of possible danger. Indeed, King Dietrich (Theodoric the Great, a favorite hero of the Germans), who was in exile at Etzel's court and whom Kriemhild feared, was the author of the warning to Hagen and of the appellation "she-devil" applied to the queen. Realizing that discretion was the better part of valor, Kriemhild sealed her lips for the moment (217).

Downcast, she again went to her window, this time weeping from frustration. Only after Kriemhild revealed to Etzel's brave warriors that Hagen was responsible for her great sorrow did they begin to fathom her consternation. In chivalrous manner, they kneeled before her, listened to her words— "Avenge me and kill Hagen!"—and complied (220).

The Dismemberment

Obsessions, as previously mentioned, indicate an unconscious one-sidedness, an inability to objectify the components and ramifications of a problem within a broad frame of reference. Losing sight of the whole in the face of a problematic situation, one focuses exclusively on a single angle, closing off all else to consciousness. The obsessed and enraged Kriemhild, therefore, unable to hold down the onslaught of her libido, became an overt destroyer—a Medusa force. The breaking out of "daemonical compulsion" irremediably quashed Kriemhild's former beauty, spirit of harmony, and composure (Jung 1990, par. 256).

Medusa is in one myth a beautiful young girl who had grown so proud of her hair that Athena transformed it into serpents. In another, she is transformed by Athena into a monster as punishment for her affair with Poseidon. The terror inspired by her gaze, it is said, so petrifies observers that they are turned into stone. To rid the world of her destructive force, the hero Perseus, following Athena's instructions not to look at Medusa directly but at her image reflected in a mirror, decapitates her.

Kriemhild, too, had suffered the sin of pride, boasting of her strength and power as Siegfried's wife, even going so far as to identify with his characteristics, which she opposed to Gunther's. Like the transformed Medusa, the once beautiful and charming Kriemhild turned into her monstrous opposite. No barriers could block the blood-orgy that followed.

Kriemhild donned her crown and in regal attire descended the stairs to meet the four hundred knights who had gathered before her. By apprising them of Hagen's guilt, she aroused their ire against her enemy. Her wrath was exacerbated by Hagen's utter disregard of courtly etiquette: he not only failed to rise to honor her presence; even worse, he had placed Siegfried's "sacred" sword on his knees. Her violent and uncontrolled anger had turned her into a veritable Medusa—a devouring dragon.

In the presence of all, she accused Hagen of having murdered Siegfried. His blithe retort was: "There is no denying it, mighty Queen, I bear the entire guilt of your ruinous loss. Now let anyone who likes avenge it, be he man or woman. Unless I were minded to lie to you, I must admit that I have wronged you greatly!" (*N*, 222). Kriemhild's poisons were being decanted even as she summoned Ortlieb, her son by Etzel, into the dining hall, counting on the psychological effects of his presence: "Do you hear, you knights! He does not deny that he is the cause of all my sorrows. Whatever fate were to overtake him in consequence, it would not trouble me" (222).

As the valiant Huns began their attack on Hagen and his men, Dancwart, Hagen's brother, dealt such blows to Etzel's brother Bloedelin that his head lay at his feet. No sooner had his decapitation taken place than Bloedelin's men attacked Dancwart. Hagen rose and "struck Ortlieb so that the blood washed along the sword to his hands and the boy's head fell into the Queen's lap" (243). That Kriemhild was instrumental in her son's death—just as she had been in her husband's—elicited from the author of the *Nibelungenlied* a comment tinged with androcentrism: "How could a woman ever do a more dreadful thing in pursuance of her revenge?" (236). But no moral condemnation of Hagen's nefarious act was forthcoming.

Kriemhild's shadow projected darkness throughout her world. Her blood lust was unrelenting. Thousands perished. Hagen emerged unscathed. After perpetrating the most ignominious deed of all—the killing of a child—he taunted King Etzel: Why should Etzel fight to redress Siegfried's death, when Siegfried had "had his pleasure of Kriemhild long before she met you! So why, you dastardly King, do you plot against my life?" Within earshot of these words of abuse, the incandescent Kriemhild goaded Etzel's men on (250).

All calls for pardon and mercy were repulsed by Kriemhild. From the depths of her being, she articulated for the first time the polarization that had taken place within her psyche.

I cannot show you mercy—my heart has none to show! Hagen of Troneck has done me such wrong that there can be no reconciliation as long as I live! You must all pay for it together. Yet if you will give me Hagen alone as my prisoner I will not deny that I may let you live—for are you not my brothers, and sons of the same mother?—and I will discuss the matter of a settlement with these warriors standing here." (260)

The Burgundians refused. Kriemhild now addressed the Huns:

You gallant warriors, close in on the stairs and avenge my wrongs, and I shall always seek to reward you, as indeed I should be bound. I shall pay back Hagen's arrogance in full. Do not let a man leave the building anywhere, while I have the hall fired at all four corners. Thus shall all my sorrows be utterly avenged! (261)

Etzel's men drove the Burgundians back into the hall, which had now been torched in obedience to Kriemhild. Bodies were bloodied, then consumed by the flames. Yet fighting went on. The men were like Berserkers— Odin's redoubtable warriors who donned the skins of bears and wolves during their battles and conveyed their passion for their deity by howling like frenzied beasts (Davidson 1969, 38).

Only when Hagen was overcome, bound, and brought to Kriemhild did the slaughter abate. To Hagen in his dungeon Kriemhild gave her ultimatum: "If you will give me back what you have robbed me of, you may still return to Burgundy alive!" (*N*, 290). His reply: "Your words are wasted, most noble Queen. I have sworn as long as any of my lords remain alive never to reveal the treasure or yield it to anyone!" Whereupon, she ordered Gunther's decapitation and herself held his head by the hair before the eyes of Hagen, whose final words were: "Now none knows of the treasure but God and I! You she-devil, it shall stay hidden from you for ever!" (290). And to this day it has never been found.

Without hope of restitution, Kriemhild spoke her last words to her enemy. "You have repaid me in base coin, but Siegfried's sword I shall have and hold! My fair lover was wearing it when last I saw him through whom I suffered mortal sorrow at your hands" (290). Consumed with rage and diseased by her passion for retribution, Kriemhild, who had taken Siegfried's sword from Hagen after his imprisonment, now drew it from its sheath, raised it with both hands, and struck off Hagen's head.

Etzel, adding a strange androcentric twist to the scene, lamented the fact "that the best knight who ever bore shield to battle should now lie slain by a woman!" (291).

Old Hildebrand, the exiled King Dietrich's tutor and master-at-arms, leaped toward Kriemhild and hewed her to pieces for having killed Hagen. And so, "The King's high festival had ended in sorrow, as joy must ever turn to sorrow in the end" (291).

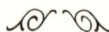

The gender bias in the *Nibelungenlied* has been exacerbated by the negative press Kriemhild has received at the hands of many exegetes. Had she been a man, her conduct might have been considered acceptable—even heroic, just as were Hagen's murderous deeds in the eyes of his male admirers. Kriemhild's blood orgy has been looked upon as paradigmatic of the devouring feminine principle—namely, the dragon motif—so terrifying yet so popular during the Middle Ages. Brunhild, too, endowed as she is with enormous physical strength, has been considered a threat to manliness. Both Kriemhild and Brunhild dared to confront and challenge the dominant zeitgeist: the prevailing "valorous, well-armored masculinity of the conscious ego." Indeed, the stereotypical image of the male—powerful, aggressive, warlike, and bloodthirsty—is never called into question on moral or psychological grounds. Hagen has even been elevated by some of the protagonists and exegetes of the *Nibelungenlied* to the supreme post of hero. Perhaps he is just that. It depends on one's point of view.

Kriemhild and Brunhild were both negativized for having dared to step out of the habitual role imposed upon women during thousands of years of patriarchal dominion: that of meek, withdrawn, and passive females. Only when the female was imprisoned in a tightly corseted, contained existence did the male feel safe. With stunning lack of discernment, the author of the *Nibelungenlied* places the onus for Siegfried's betrayal and the ensuing bloodshed squarely on the women: "[T]hanks to the wrangling of two women, countless warriors met their doom" (118).

It may be suggested that feminine principles as well as their equally sordid male counterparts were symptomatic of a degenerate and disintegrating society. The fall of the once powerful kingdom of Burgundy, as depicted in the *Nibelungenlied* and concluding with the dismemberment of its people and kingship, did not narrate a twilight of gods, but, rather, of mortals.

4 The Quiché Mayan *Popol Vuh:*
Mother Participates in the Creation

Unlike the biblical Genesis, in which the male God was solely responsible for the creation of humankind, in the *Popol Vuh* (Council book), the sacred book of the patriarchal Quiché Mayas, a primordial couple ("mother-father") actively participated. Together, they were

> the Maker, the Modeler,
> mother–father of life, of humankind,
> giver of breath, giver of heart,
> bearer, upbringer in the light that lasts
> of those born in the light, begotten in the light.
>
> (*PV,* 72)[1]

In the *Popol Vuh* creation "divine women exist from the beginning, while human women, rather than being derived from men, are created separately, and they are never made to carry the stigmas that God inflicts upon Eve" (Tedlock 1986, 80).

The origin of the *Popol Vuh* is, like that of many religious myths, bathed in mystery. The extant document is not the original text written in Maya hieroglyphics, but a sixteenth-century transliteration into European script composed by someone said to be a Quiché nobleman. The Spanish friar Francisco Ximénez, having discovered the existence of the *Popol Vuh* in Chichicastenango, copied it and then translated it into Spanish in 1701–3 (*PV,* 28).

The extant *Popol Vuh,* seemingly a fragment of the original sacred text, narrates the cosmogony, history, and traditions of the mighty Quiché Mayas prior to the Spanish conquest in 1541. An ethnic group living in Guatemala,

117

the Quiché were Mayas who spoke the Quiché language. In pre-Columbian days, the Mayas occupied lands in what is today referred to as Mesoamerica, which includes *grosso modo* the Yucatan Peninsula, Copan, Honduras, Campeche, Palenque, Tabasco, part of Chiapas, El Salvador, Belize, and most of Guatemala.

During the so-called Classical times (200–900 C.E.), the Mayas, extending their reach from the highlands into the lowland rainforest area, built enormous pyramidal structures, palaces, ball courts, plazas, stelae, and altars, all decorated with sculptures of divine, human, and animal forms. Hieroglyphic texts describing Gods and kings and the events marking their reigns were cut into rock and stucco. The complex decorative patterns and figures of the carvings had symbolic ramifications, while even painted pottery designs served to enhance aesthetically what otherwise would have been simple mundane articles. Official documents and almanacs, which were recorded in images inked on long strips of bark or deerskin and then folded, resembled our books in many ways. It is believed that the original *Popol Vuh* was inscribed on either bark or deerskin.

Mayan cities, which may at first appear to be simply groupings of rambling structures, are actually examples of expert organizational and technological city-planning systems. Indeed, together with Maya philosophical, religious, architectural, and artistic accomplishments, as well as outstanding achievements in mathematics (the Mayas are said to have invented the zero) and in astronomy (their Long Count calendar), these attainments attest to the greatness of this once-flourishing culture. For unknown reasons, perhaps overpopulation, starvation, disease, or environmental factors—many of the great Mayan cities were abandoned around 900 C.E. Some, however, underwent renewal, emerging as a new Mayan culture based on the military state, which lapsed into anonymity following the ignominious bloodbath perpetrated by Spaniards intent upon lucre, conquest, and conversion.

Ectypal Analysis

Most contemporary scholars divide Maya history into three general periods, the first being the Preclassic (1500 B.C.E. to 200 C.E.) which may be further subdivided into Early Preclassic (2000–900 B.C.E.), Middle Preclassic (900–300 B.C.E.), and Late Preclassic (300 B.C.E. to 200 C.E.). The following era, the Classic period (200–900 C.E.), comprises Early Classic (200–600 C.E.)

and Late Classic (600–900 C.E.). The Postclassic years date from 900 to the conquest of the Mayas by the Spanish in 1541 (Schele and Miller 1986, 11).

Far ahead of the Mayan culture during the Early Preclassic period was the highly developed Olmec civilization. Deeply impressive are the latter's gigantic basalt sculptures (1200 B.C.E.) at San Lorenzo (Vera Cruz), the site inexplicably destroyed around 900 B.C.E.; the huge thrones (altars) found at La Venta, from which the lords of the lands had ruled; the first pyramidal form; and unusual jade carvings and figurines (Coe 1984, 36). Because trade routes had been established by the energetic and highly innovative Olmec peoples, who traveled widely throughout Mesoamerica to western Mexico, it is believed that by 900 B.C.E. the ceramics and jade carvings of the early Mayan civilization at Copan indicated Olmec influence (Miller and Taube 1993, 16). Indeed, Olmec-style petroglyphs have been discovered on the cliffs of highland Guatemala and Chiapas, confirming the linkage between the Olmecs and the Mayas. Understandably, many scholars consider the Olmecs to be the seminal culture of Mesoamerica—inventors of the Long Count calendar, of writing, and of other marvels—the "mother culture" of Mesoamerica, which spurred the growth of Mayan cultural achievements (Coe 1984, 37).

During the Middle Preclassic period, small communities were established in the Mayan lowlands and highlands. In time increasingly sophisticated agricultural and engineering works (such as raised fields, water drainage, and scenic causeways) appeared, as well as complex religious and political rituals, as attested to by the platform (400 B.C.E.) at Cuello, where sacrifice and dismemberment were practiced (Schele and Miller 1986, 26).

By the Late Preclassic era (300 B.C.E.–300 C.E.) Mayan culture had grown at a rapid pace, leading to large population centers. Rulership by elitist groups was on the ascent, while construction of stelae featuring Long Count calendar images, rulers, deities, jaguar masks, and so on could be found at El Mirador and Kaminaljuyu, to mention but two sites.

The city-states of the Classic period, looked upon as the Mayas' golden age (200–900 C.E.), rose and fell, as had those of the Olmecs before. The Early Classic saw the construction and growth of Tikal, Uaxactun (in the Peten region), and other cities, as well as the rise of perhaps 350 independent states, such as Copan, Palenque, and Tonia. Temple pyramids and palaces made of limestone masonry with vaulted rooms were erected; polychrome pottery, bas-reliefs, wall paintings, and sculptures of all types were created; and stelae found at such sites as Tikal, Uaxactun, Palenque, and Caracol recorded historical events and dynastic histories. By 810, the classical Mayan sloping foreheads and stepped haircuts characterized the figures engraved on monuments (28).

As city-states grew in power and wealth, competition between them increased in ferocity, resulting in frequent wars. One of the most important, a six-year struggle between Tikal and Caracol, concluded in 562 with the defeat of the former. Tikal made a remarkable comeback in the eighth century, only to suffer military defeat once again and total collapse by 869. Virtually simultaneously (and mysteriously) sites such as Palenque, Yaxchilan, and Copan (c. 800) as well as Naranjo and Quirigua (820) were abandoned, thus ending the glories that were Maya.

During the Postclassic period, dating from 900 to the conquest by the Spaniards in 1541, a different kind of Mayan culture developed, based on confederation-type governing units: Chichen Itza, Mayapan, Cakchiquel, and Quiché, the latter two claiming descent from the legendary Toltecs. Whereas the Classic Maya communities had bestowed power on the individual king and his lineage, and observed his religious cult, after 900, in Chichen Itza and Tula, for example, rulership was invested in a warrior-king. Personal portraits that eternalized the people's rulers were replaced by collective images, such as that of a carved throne upon which anyone worthy of the office could sit. Blood sacrifices, although practiced prior to 900, assumed greater importance and popularity in the Postclassic period. Chichen Itza and Tula suffered decline by the twelfth century, while the rulers of Mayapan, having built a wall around their city, continued to exercise power for two more centuries. Because of the vacuums created by the rise and fall of city-states, quarrels and internecine warfare erupted. The Spaniards, taking advantage of the disarray, allied themselves in 1524 with the Cakchiquels at Iximché, defeating the Quiché Mayas at Utatlan (Miller and Taube 1993, 24).

Post-Spanish Conquest: Book Burnings

In 1524 Pedro Alvarado was sent by Hernán Cortés to subdue the tribes of Guatemala. One of the most bloodthirsty of military men, he not only destroyed lives but leveled the Quiché capital as well. Once the Spaniards had gained control of Mérida in 1542, Catholic priests and missionaries, adamant in their desire to bring the spirit of the Inquisition to the new land, destroyed whatever "heathen" hieroglyphic books they could find.

The books of Chilam Balam, works sacred to the Mayas of Yucatan, were used by their priests to eternalize their ancient prophecies, histories, ceremonies, and chants. These books were named after their "last and greatest prophet," Balam (late-fifteenth century to early-sixteenth century), the word *balam* (jaguar) being a common family name in the region, while *chilam*, or *chilan*, the prophet's title, was translated as "the mouthpiece or interpreter of the Gods." Nearly every town and village of northern Yucatan had its own *Book of Chilam Balam*, which bore the name of the town to which it belonged. In *The Book of Chilam Balam of Chumayel*, the prophet unequivocally foretold the arrival of peoples from the east who would bring with them a new religion (Roys 1967, 3).[2]

> It was only because these [seventy-nine] priests of ours were to come to an end when misery was introduced, when Christianity was introduced by the real Christians. Then with the true God, the true *Dios*, came the beginning of our misery. It was the beginning of tribute, the beginning of church dues, the beginning of strife with purse snatching, the beginning of strife with blow guns, the beginning of strife by trampling on people, the beginning of robbery with violence, the beginning of forced debts, the beginning of debts enforced by false testimony, the beginning of individual strife, a beginning of vexation, a beginning of robbery with violence. This was the origin of service to the Spaniards, of service to the local chiefs, of service to the public prosecutors by the boys, the youths of the town, while the poor people were harassed. (79)

The perseverance of Friar Diego de Landa, Antonio de Cuidal de Real, and Friar Luis de Villalpando in uprooting native religion led to the burning of innumerable Mayan religious books, documents, and other cultural marvels. Landa held an auto-da-fé in Mani (July 1562) in which were burned twenty-seven hieroglyphic rolls as well as codices made up of strips of pounded bark or deer hide coated on both sides with white lime gesso. The surfaces of these works were garnished with hieroglyphics and colored with vegetable and mineral dyes, after which they were folded and placed between wooden or leather covers (Gallenkamp 1959, 22).

> We found a large number of books in these characters [hieroglyphs], and as they contained nothing in which there were not to be seen superstition and lies of the devil, we burned them all, which they [the people] regretted to an amazing degree, and which caused them much affliction. (Gallenkamp 1979, xiv)

Manuscripts that were not destroyed in the auto-da-fé were immediately hidden by the natives, and still have not been found. After the fact, Friar Diego de Landa was tried and condemned in Spain by the Council of the Indies. Because his case was committed to the "learned" Tomás López, however, the "learned friar Diego" not only was absolved of any criminal act but by 1572 returned to the Yucatan as bishop (Landa 1978, xii–xiii).

Book-burning ceremonies were only the initial phase of Spain's cruel and repressive policy, which included the burning, hanging, and torturing of "heretics." Wherever Landa traveled, he applied the spirit of the Inquisition, making certain that the "cleansing" process was carried out as thoroughly as possible. In his *Yucatan Before and After the Conquest*, he describes the difficulties facing the Spaniards during their campaign of conversion and subjugation of the Mayan population of the Yucatan.

> Information being laid against the people of Yobain, a town of the Chels, they took the leading men, put them in stocks in a building and then set fire to the house, burning them alive with the greatest inhumanity in the world. I, Diego de Landa, say that I saw a great tree near the village upon the branches of which a captain had hung many women, with their infant children hung from their feet. At this town, and another . . . Verey, they hung two Indian women, one a maiden and the other recently married, for no other crime than their beauty, and because of fearing a disturbance among the soldiers on their account. . . . Unheard-of cruelties were inflicted, cutting off their noses, hands, arms and legs, and the breasts of their women; throwing them into deep water with gourds tied to their feet, thrusting the children with spears because they could not go as fast as their mothers. (25)

As a result of the Spanish conquest and conversion policy, the Mayas "were never completely conquered, but their civilization and spirit were broken (Coe 1984, 142). In the *Chilam Balam of Tizimin*, it is written:

> Eat, eat, thou hast bread;
> Drink, drink, thou has water;
> On that day, dust possesses the earth;
> On that day, a blight is on the face of the earth,
> On that day, a cloud rises,
> On that day, a mountain rises,
> On that day, a strong man seizes the land,

On that day, things fall to ruin,
On that day, the tender leaf is destroyed,
On that day, the dying eyes are closed,
On that day, three signs are on the tree,
On that day, three generations hang there,
On that day, the battle flag is raised,
And they are scattered afar in the forest.

(Craine and Reindorp 1979, 116)

Women and Mayan Social Structures

The Classic society of the Mayas was many-layered. At the top of the pyramidal sociopolitical structure, authority was vested in the ruler, who wielded
power over the common people and peasants at the base. Evidence gathered
by archaeologists at Tikal, Seibal, and Dzibilchaltun reveals extended family
units rather than households based on a nuclear family. These households
were patrilocal as well: the just-married groom brought his bride home to
live with his parents (Hammond 1982, 180–82).

That the male enjoyed a preeminent position in Mayan society is evident from the expenditures for men's tombs and the importance of the buildings chosen for their burial. Women were rarely, if ever, accorded such
lavish and honored treatment. With few exceptions, the tradition of primogeniture, believed to date to the first century B.C.E., perpetuated a patrilineal
succession of rulers. However, it is believed that the women of Tikal, in
view of the "greater parity of grave goods," attained nearly equal status with
men in the Late Preclassic period (183).

The artifacts that have been unearthed have led scholars to suggest that
women's activities, as in other societies, consisted of grinding corn, cooking,
and taking care of babies, which they carried, swaddled, on their backs. That
males hunted was normal, but that musicianship should be exclusively theirs
is surprising. It has been surmised that pottery (such as large jars for storing
liquids and/or grain, bowls for serving food, and highly decorated polychrome vessels) was crafted by women and painted by men during the Classic period (193). Women wore long skirts and a loose, usually decorated
blouse *(huipil),* while men donned long loincloths *(maxtli).* Sexes could be
distinguished in Mayan art by the dress and hair style, sometimes by a woman's
breasts (185).

Women as Rulers

Kingship was hereditary within the Maya primogeniture framework. Although the culture was patriarchal, women were awarded significant titles: lady *ahau* (lord) or lady *cahal* (also indicative of high rank). There is no evidence that women ever bore the title of *mah k'ina* (great sun), given only to a king, but according to a deciphered inscription at Palenque, twice had a woman become the chief ruler and fulfilled the office traditionally held by a male king. It was possible, then, for a female to exercise real power as a head of state (Schele and Miller 1986, 28).

In the sarcophagus text commemorating the dynasty of King Pacal ("Shield"), one of the best known rulers of Palenque, the names of two women appear: those of his mother, Lady Zac-Kuk, and his great-grand-mother, Lady Kanal-Ikal, the only women who were neither consorts nor regents, but who ruled as kings (Schele, Freidel, and Parker 1990, 221). Since kingship was inherited through the father, Lady Zac-Kuk's son could not rule. Power, then, would be passed on through the father's lineage, thereby confirming and perpetuating patrilineality. By astute maneuvering on Pacal's part, his kingship was legitimized by his claiming descent from Bahlum-Kuk, the founder of the first lineage. Following Lady Kanal-Ikal's rulership, inheritance was once again claimed through the father's royal lineage. In the latter instance, dynastic succession proved to be more important than patrilineality (222).

To further assure the dynastic sequence at Palenque, King Pacal held that his mother, Lady Zac-Kuk, occupied a position parallel to that of the First Mother of Gods and Kings. (Archaeologists called her Lady Beastie, and the human analogue of this divine figure is as recorded on tablets in The Temple of Inscriptions.) By bestowing this status on his mother, Pacal invested his own position, and that of future progeny as well, with divine essence. Thus the claim to the kingship of Pacal's son, Chan-Bahlum, was legitimized (223–28, 245). Because divine elements could be transmitted by females or by males, the concept of patrilineality eroded in Palenque. (Similar patternings also occur, as will become evident, in the *Popol Vuh*.)

Pacal began his rule at the age of twelve, after Lady Zac-Kuk had been the reigning power for three years. During the next twenty-five years, she and her consort, Kan-Bahlum-Mo, created politically correct alliances that worked in her son's favor. Indeed, it is thought that until her death in 640, by replicating the talents of her grandmother, Kanal-Ikal, she masterminded the successful political strategies that subverted rival claims both in and out-side of Palenque (Schele, Freidel, and Parker 1990, 225).

Lady Zac-kuk was the first female to be depicted on a monument: stela 23 was dedicated to her and on stela 25 she was featured standing in the place of honor, to the right of her husband. Archaeologists believe that not only was her tomb concurrent with her husband's but that it was one of the most elaborate of those for any Mayan woman. It contained such valued items as the skeleton of a spider monkey and shells of the spondylus (spiny oyster), an import from the Caribbean coast that was usually found in burial sites of great men (Hammond 1982, 209).

Another interesting example of a woman's role in government comes from Tikal. Although succession here could pass through a female, the "Woman of Tikal," the well-known daughter of King Kan Boar, did not rule. To make certain, however, that his line would continue, the king adopted his daughter's husband. Thus the husband became a kind of son to the Woman of Tikal, while the ruler became his legal father. As a result, power remained in the family rather than passing on to another dynasty (209).

A second woman in Tikal's history remains mysterious to us. The nobles of Tikal early in the seventh century grieved over the death of this highly placed lady and accorded her a unique burial ceremony. That her mortuary chamber, located in the suburbs of the city, had been cut into "living rock," then vaulted with great honor, was the prerogative usually accorded to a great ancestor. In her tomb was placed a beautiful polychrome bowl on which replicas of the Celestial Bird had been painted; its rim was garnished with a text indicating that its first owner had been Ruler I of Naranjo. Questions revolving around this high-ranking lady abound. Who was she? Why was she worthy of the gift entombed with her? Was she married to or the lover of a ruler from Naranjo? (Schele, Freidel, and Parker 1990, 177).

Names of noblewomen were recorded on stelae, tombs, and pottery. For example, to enhance his power, Flint-Sky-God K, the king of Dos Pilas, a fierce warrior and brilliant military strategist, not only arranged for marriages with women from neighboring kingdoms but also required that those of his house marry exogamously. To guarantee an alliance with the kingdom of Naranjo, thereby assuring the reestablishment of its royal house after its destruc-tion by the Caracols, he contracted a marriage between his daughter, Lady Wac-Chanil-Ahau (Sixth Celestial Lord), and Naranjo, a nobleman. Although she was accompanied by a retinue of guards, travel through the Petén penin-sula was dangerous. Her journey has been imaginatively depicted as follows:

[She was seated] in her sedan chair of dark polished wood upon royal pillows of stuffed jaguar skin, veiled from the prying eyes of village spies by a canopy of fine cotton gossamer. A company of sturdy bearers surrounded the four sweating men who carried the long poles of the sedan chair on their shoulders, ready to relieve them in the work of relaying their precious burden to its final destination. Behind came more bearers with bundles of cotton and bark cloth laden with gifts of jade, painted pottery, embroidered textiles, perfumed wooden boxes, and carved-shell diadems. (184)

Upon her arrival in Naranjo territory in August 682, Lady Wac-Chanil-Ahau stood on a high pyramid to perform a sacred bloodletting ritual.[3] Ecstatically she addressed her ancestors, thereby establishing the importance of the power she brought to Naranjo. On the large plaza below, the inhabitants, through dance, song, and drum beating, conveyed their joy and pride in celebration of the new dynasty to come. Dedicating the pyramid three days after her marriage, Lady Wac-Chanil-Ahau entered into a trance state, which enabled her to gain access to the Otherworld (Xibalba), the domain of the dead, and communicate with her ancestors. That she had succeeded in ushering into the world of the living such important presences, blocked for years following Naranjo's military defeat, was deeply meaningful to the people. Thus was her prestige further enhanced, and by extension, that of the future rulers (184–85).

Although her name does not appear in Naranjo's historical texts, it is believed that on 6 January 688, Lady Wac-Chanil-Ahau gave birth to Smoking Squirrel, thereby assuring the continuity of the royal family. The monuments that her son later erected to commemorate his accession to the throne at the age of five were combined with ones dedicated not to his father, perhaps a man of little importance, but to his mother, the daughter of his maternal grandfather, the famous Flint-Sky-God K of Dos Pilas. Perhaps he felt the need to advertise his illustrious heritage in order to help prove the legitimacy of his kingship (187).

Since Smoking Squirrel was too young upon accession to the throne to lead the army, it was his mother—featured standing on an enemy's bruised body on stela 24—who was credited with the defeat of Kinichil-Cab of Ucanal, a small border community between Naranjo and Tikal (190).

Another prominent woman among the Mayas was Lady Xoc, the principal wife of Shield-Jaguar, one of the best known rulers of Yaxchilan.[4] She wielded such political power that her husband, to maintain her support, honored her by inviting her to commission and dedicate a temple. Unlike Lady Zac-Kuk of Palenque, however, she never ruled the kingdom. She became famous for her performance of excoriatingly painful acts of piety in bloodletting rituals. Narrative scenes sculpted on lintels of Temple 23 feature her in a perhaps trancelike state perforating her tongue with a stingray spine, then pulling a thorn-laden rope through her mutilated tongue. She is also delineated with a materialization of "the Vision Serpent rearing over her head as she calls forth the founder of the lineage." (The image of the Vision Serpent symbolizes "the path out of Xibalba through which the ancestral dead and the gods enter the world when they are called in a blood letting rite" [417].) Lady Xoc's apparent grandeur and great courage marked her— a woman—as the protagonist in a sacred ritual, a distinction unheard of at Yaxchilán and virtually unknown in Mayan monumental art (266–72).

Archetypal Analysis

The *Popol Vuh* narration, although underscoring mainly a patrilineal, patriarchal, and patrilocal society, invites the feminine principle or primordial Mother to participate in the creation of humankind, and endows an important figure called the Maiden with courage and a spirit of independence.

The legends and chronicles of the *Popol Vuh*—concerning the Creation, the adventures of the Maiden, and the Hero Twins—are embedded in a complex animistic cosmogony in which concepts such as sacrifice, good and evil, and victory and defeat are revealed in Mayan terms.

The Mayas' Cosmic View

Within the Mayas' cosmos existed three dynamic and interdependent living spheres. Heaven above, also referred to as the Otherworld, included a sky, imaged as a celestial or cosmic monster: an enormous bicephalic crocodile that shed its blood in order to bring rain to humans, thereby fecundating the land. Inhabited by a pantheon of mainly male gods and ancestors of reborn mortals, the Otherworld had a population that subsisted on the food offered to them by humans in earthly sacrificial blood rituals. Understandably, then, bloodletting ceremonies were held on what was considered sacred space: pyramids and plazas, that is, the summit of the Middleworld.

The Middleworld, or earth, sphere was luxuriant with greenery, animals, humans, and other living things. Shaped in some myths like the back of a turtle or of a caiman, the earth was conceived as a living entity floating in the primordial sea. When inhabitants of the Otherworld were invoked into the human domain, they might become hierophanies: concretizations in ritual objects, landscape configurations, or living human beings (70). In that the king was held responsible for the health and well-being of his people, his primordial sacrifice "was to Maya propitiation of the divine what wine and wafers are in the Christian communion" (90). Bloodletting ceremonies allowed humans to integrate a collective past into a present reality, and thus to participate in God's sacred cosmological act.

During the sacrificial rituals, the king and those who took part in these ceremonies, weakened perhaps by the loss of blood, experienced moments of expanded consciousness. During these time spans, the king was able to penetrate transcendent or Otherworld spheres where the mysteries of time-lessness and the perception of future happenings opened to him. As seer or shaman, it was incumbent upon him to clarify the secrets to which he had been made privy by explaining these to his people in terms they could un-derstand: planting and harvesting, sickness and health, peace and war, and so on. The recording in imagistic configurations of the acts of the king or his nobles must not be understood simply as the narration of events of his reign, but rather as examples of sacred happenings. Daily activities became embed-ded in the cyclicity of eternal cosmic time schemes.

The Underworld (Xibalba), also referred to as the Otherworld, while located in dark waters below the earth by day, became sky at night. Like the Middleworld, it enjoyed human, animal, and plant populations. The doors leading to Xibalba opened for kings, shamans, and those who participated in prolonged blood rituals. Humans could not only transcend the workaday do-main during periods of ecstatic trance, as has been mentioned, but, it was be-lieved, could even manipulate the inhabitants of the Underworld (65–66, 87).

So rooted is sacrifice in the human psyche that it appears in one form or another in almost all faiths. For the Mayas it was one of the most important religious rituals. The ritual slaying (or sacrifice) of a king in many cultures assured fertility and prosperity at a time when either crops were failing or society itself revealed signs of impotence. Human sacrifice, including dis-memberment, was looked upon as pleasing to deities, serving to revivify them and solidify their harmonious rapport with humankind. In this con-nection, C. G. Jung writes: "It is clear, then, that in Christ's sacrifice and the Communion one of the deepest chords in the human psyche is struck: hu-man sacrifice and ritual anthropophagy" (Jung 1963, par. 339).

Within a larger frame of reference, one may suggest that the perpetra-tion of violence against oneself may be taken as an appeasement of the gods, but it also replicates an atemporal deed marked by symbolic cruelty: the Creation itself, or any creative act. Innovation in art, architecture, literature, science, or religion may be viewed as a "cruelty," since it implies the destruction of the old or of the status quo, and the bringing forth of the new and the different (par. 206).

The Creation

The *Popol Vuh* thus depicts the primordial world prior to Creation: "Now it still ripples, now it still murmurs, ripples, it still sighs, still hums, and it is empty under the sky" (*PV,* 72). An undifferentiated, unclear, and unnamed universe existed prior to the creation of humanity. Unmanifested potential lived in a state of limitless nebulosity, in a paradoxical condition of motionless activity, in endless soft soundings and ripplings beyond a world of silence, within the hiddenness of dimensionless darkness.

To plan such a gigantic enterprise as the Creation required dialogue and consultation among the gods. The unarticulated "murmurs" and "ripples" of the cosmos became the conversations between the deities inhabiting the primordial sea: Maker, Modeler, Bearer, Begetter, Heart of the Lake, Heart of the Sea, and Sovereign Plumed Serpent. They dialogued with Heart of Sky, Heart of Earth, Newborn Thunderbolt, Raw Thunderbolt, and Hurricane, who descended from the primordial sky. Together did these architects, masons, and sculptors—"great knowers, great thinkers in their very being"—verbalize their thoughts in planning the deliverance of the Cosmic Womb of its unmanifested riches (73).

"For the forming of the earth they said 'Earth'"; thus was it conceptualized in the name, and rose from the primordial sea by means of speech: "their word brought it forth." Actively and cogently did the Deities participate, both individually and collectively, in the birth process. They negotiated as to the how and why, the "sowing, the dawning of the sky-earth." From nothingness developed the differentiation of cloud, mist, mountain, flatlands, water, greenery, and so on (73). The interrelatedness of phenomena was called into being through words.

The Mayas' intriguing emphasis on measurement, mathematical concepts, and numbers, also evident in Hindu, Chinese, Judeo-Christian, and other creation myths, is underscored in the *Popol Vuh*. The importance accorded to digits, and especially the number *four*, is evident at the outset of the Creation process:

> the fourfold siding, fourfold cornering,
> measuring, fourfold staking,
> halving the cord, stretching the cord
> in the sky, on the earth,
> the four sides, the four corners.
>
> (*PV*, 72)

The quotation reveals the gods busying themselves in "measuring" and "stretching the cord," perfecting their architectural work, linking elements of disparateness. Such focus indicates a unity of purpose among the deities.

Such frequent recourse to numbers also discloses a psychological need for order and balance. Numbers serve to fix the unpredictable and to arrest disquieting interrogation of imponderables.

It has been posited that numbers, psychologically, are not invented by the conscious mind, but emerge from the unconscious spontaneously, as archetypal images, when the need arises. Juxtaposing a rational cosmic order with an irrational or inexplicable terrestrial condition, they unconsciously compensate for a chaotic inner state. Numbers, as ordering devices, are one of the most ancient representations of humanity's spirit and intellect.

The number *four*, identified in the above quotation with the cardinal points, may be considered as the archetypal structure of the Mayan cosmos and community. As such, it takes on a numinous quality. Each of the four directions was associated in the *Popol Vuh* with a color, a tree, birds, gods, and rituals. The east, the most significant directional point in that it gives birth to the sun, was identified with red. The north, the harbinger of refreshing winter rains and related to the North Star, around which the heavens turn, was white. The west, attending to the sun's daily demise, was black. As for the south, the sun's "great side" was yellow (Schele, Freidel, and Parker 1990, 66).

The cardinal points, as these appeared in the Mayas' concentric/quadrangular format, had their own individual centers in the form of a tree, also oriented to a specific direction. The most important tree of all was located in the center of the world, and was alluded to as the great or world tree. The roots of this fifth tree, which plays such a significant role in the events depicted in the *Popol Vuh*, penetrated the earth, reaching down into the watery depths of Xibal-ba, while its branches soared high up to the heavenly Otherworld, thus connecting the various cosmic planes (Schele, Freidel, and Parker 1990, 67).

The Archetypal Couple

The existence of an archetypal couple in the creation motif—the "mother-father of life, of humankind"—is all the more striking because the female (Xmucane) is named first and then the male (Xpiyacoc). These divine parents, older than the other gods, it is believed, worked in consort with the younger ones to bring life into existence. "Now they planned the animals of the mountains, all the guardians of the forests, creatures of the mountains: the deer, birds, pumas, jaguars, serpents, rattlesnakes, yellowbites, guardians of the bushes" (*PV*, 76).

The enormous effort expended by the couple and the other gods was, however, largely unrewarded, because the animals' speech was incomprehensible and they were unable to render homage to their creators. "Talk, speak out. Don't moan, don't cry out. Please talk," said the Maker, Modeler, Bearer, Begetter. Impatiently, the gods commanded: "Name now our names, praise us. We are your mother, we are your father" (78). But the animals only chattered, squawked, and howled.

The Mayas did not look upon creation as a gratuitous act. The archetypal couple and the other Deities who had brought life into existence demanded not only reverence from the creatures but also recognition of their dependence on the gods for their well-being (Girard 1977, 33). Able neither to fulfill the deities' expectations, nor to celebrate their feast days by verbalizing in prayer their gratitude, adoration, and homage, the creatures were destroyed (*PV*, 79).

A second creation followed. "How else can we be invoked and remembered on the face of the earth," the gods questioned, if not through speech? Just as Adam had been shaped of earth, so the second creation was also made of "earth and mud." Unlike Adam, however, the Mayan construct was more mud than earth. Soft and lopsided, these new entities were unable to stand. They talked a bit, but "senselessly." Finally, they dissolved into nothing. Existing as "merely a thought," they were summarily "dismantled" as physical entities (*PV*, 79).

Once again the primordial parents, Xmucane and Xpiyacoc, worked together in active participation with mason, sculptor, and mathematician. Together the "mother-father" dialogued in consort with the other deities to bring forth the unmanifest: "to construct a person again" (*PV*, 80).

In time, further epithets were appended to the archetypal mother-father couple, or unit: "Grandmother of Day," referring to Xmucane, and "Grandmother of Light," identified with Xpiyacoc, inviting some scholars to consider them androgynous. Nevertheless, each had her and his specific function, and thus they were paradoxically divided. A paradigm of the coexistence of antithetical attributes, this primordial couple worked as a cohesive whole in the creation of humankind.

> Midwife, matchmaker,
> our grandmother, our grandfather,
> Xpiyacoc, Xmucane,
> let there be planting, let there be the dawning
> of our invocation, our sustenance, our recognition
> by the human work, the human design,
> the human figure, the human mass.
>
> (*PV,* 80)

As *midwife,* Xmucane assisted at childbirth, bringing newborns—the unmanifested—into the world. As such, she was considered a healer and shaman (72). The appellations "Grandmother of Day" and "Grandmother of Light," in contrast to night, indicated numerical divisions (in a twenty-four-hour cycle) and visual dichotomies (blackness and lightness) implicit in night and day, and thus an ability to differentiate between the hours that were propitious to plantings and those that were not.

Xpiyacoc, referred to as *matchmaker,* consolidated what was separate, sewed together what was disparate. A planter, he became the earth's inseminator.

Xmucane, alluded to as "the daykeeper, diviner," had the capacity to prognosticate, and thus to bring the unmanifest into being (83). Endowed with mathematical, astronomical, spiritual, and shamanistic knowledge, she was well versed "in performing calendrical divination for the gods." As the one "who stands behind others," she was experienced as the catalytic element that symbolizes potential.

Xpiyacoc (the archetypal Father) was called "the master of the coral seeds." He was identified with an aquatic tree, and thus associated with the world axis and also the ocean or lower waters.[5] Because the roots penetrated into Xibalba and the trunk inhabited the Middleworld, Xpiyacoc represented harvest and planting. As such, he existed in a physical, material dimension rather than in a strictly spiritual sphere. The wood of the coral tree was to be used to fashion a male figure: "to gouge a mouth, a face in wood," and thus sculpt his proper configurations (81, 332).

Work on the third Creation was again followed by failure. This population consisted of "manikins" carved out of wood. Although articulate, they were rigid, without memory, and oblivious to the needs of the gods for gratitude and worship. They were unable to convey their gratitude—that is, to create a religious cult. Nor had they any "blood" or "lymph. Their complexions were dry, their faces were crusty. They flailed their legs and arms, their bodies were deformed" (84). They were flooded out of existence.

Just like the creatures of mud, those of wood were *sacrificed* as inferior types, regressive beings who could only stunt the deities' powerful urge to create a dynamic population for the earth.

Because the Great Mystery that had existed prior to the cosmogonic act had to be sacrificed or destroyed for differentiation to come into being, sacrifice of the unfit implies the destruction of a past condition that no longer meets present needs. Conveyed psychologically, such a transformatory process indicates the freeing of libido (psychic energy) from possible domination by "unconscious compulsions," inviting it to focus on higher matters. The gods, who had sacrificed their previous creations and comfortable condition of oneness, or unconsciousness, sought once again to put thought to work. Releasing themselves from their previous relatively peaceful state, and opting for consciousness—the rational principle—they turned to mind-oriented matters that would, however, lead to disparity, and thus disagreement and conflict (Jung 1956, paras. 644ff.).

As is the norm in the miraculous world of myth, linear time schemes disappear. For this reason, the fourth and last creation does not follow the third, but is recorded in part 4 of the *Popol Vuh,* following the activities of Xmucane, Xpiyacoc, the Maiden, the Hero Twins, Hunahpu and Xbalanque, and others.

The Archetypal Grandmother: "Great White Tapir"

Untold time has elapsed since the last sequence. The primordial couple have been invoked by their twin grandsons, Hunahpu and Xbalanque, future culture heroes, to redress a wrong. Old now, the primordial couple are "a truly white-haired grandfather, and a grandmother, a truly humble grandmother—just bent-over, elderly people. Great White Peccary is the name of the grandfather, and Great White Tapir is the name of the grandmother (92).

The names awarded the primordial couple are revelatory of both their actions and their character traits. Instead of being identified with the Central American nocturnal tapir, which is brownish-black, the grandmother is identified with the white tapir, a breed of mammals (unknown to the Mayas) living in the Malay Peninsula. Her whiteness associates her with the moon. Thus she serves to link celestial and terrestrial spheres. Like the tapir, she may be large in stature, suggesting both outer and inner strength. That she is ungulate and stout of limb may indicate an ability on her part to come to speedy decisions. The grandfather, as the "Great White Peccary," may, like this musk-secreting mammal, work in unison or in conjunction with his wife. He is—one could say—glued to his job.

The twins have asked their grandparents to lead a mission for the recovery of Hunahpu's severed arm, lost in his battle with the giant bird Seven Macaw. Claiming to be both sun and moon, Seven Macaw was so inflated by his sense of self-worth, so proud of his sparkling metallic eyes and his glittering jewel-like teeth, that he considered the brilliance emanating from every part of him sufficient to light the world (86). His sons, Zipacna, the maker of mountains, and Earthquake, the mover of mountains, had inherited their father's arrogance.

Hubris, which destabilizes the harmony and balance of the three cosmic spheres, is considered evil in the *Popol Vuh*. The task of annihilating it had fallen upon Hunahpu and Xbalanque (87–89). Although during Hunahpu's first skirmish with his enemy he succeeded in dislocating his jaw, he, in turn, suffered the loss of an arm. The twins sought to retrieve it, having learned that Seven Macaw had hung the arm on the wall of his home.

Having assessed the situation, Hunahpu and Xbalanque understood that the task was too complex for them to accomplish alone. Such reasoning indicated both an objective approach to their problem and an awareness of their limitations.

The primordial couple acquiesced to their grandsons' petition, thereby becoming instrumental in the death—or sacrifice—of Seven Macaw and of his sons. Both Xmucane and Xpiyacoc participated in redressing a cosmic imbalance that, although originating in the earthly domain, affected the entire universe; theirs was a holistic approach to life. Their intervention in time of need also revealed a highly developed sense of justice and an acceptance of a pragmatic view of life. Love was also implicit in the grandparents' response to the twins, family ties determining their decision. Neither intransigent nor set in their ways, as is frequently characteristic of *senex* figures, Xmucane and Xpiyacoc were malleable and succeeded in recovering the severed arm. "The genius of the grandmother, the genius of the grandfather did its work when they took back their arm: it was implanted and the break got well again (94).

The Archetypal Grandmother as Moon Figure

The archetypal Grandmother demonstrated her emotional involvement with her family on other occasions as well—for example, in the vengeance for the killings of her twin sons: One Hunahpu, father of Hunahpu and Xbalanque, and their uncle, Seven Hunahpu (105).

Although described as seers, "great thinkers," and possessors of "great knowledge," One Hunahpu and Seven Hunahpu had been called to Xibalba (the Underworld) as punishment for "stomping and shouting" while playing on the ball court of the "Great Abyss." Since ball courts in Mesoamerica were constructed on a lower level than plazas and courtyards, they were believed to be located "on the road to Xibalba" (113). The importance of ball playing for the Quiché Maya, and the mathematical precision with which the four-cornered ball courts were constructed, cannot be overemphasized. In this regard, analogies between earthly and celestial spheres are in order: the center of the ball court, considered sacred space, corresponded to the center of the world axis or tree. Specific areas in ball courts were considered as doors or openings leading to the Underworld. Games, therefore, were not viewed simply as contests between mortals, but between mortals and gods. Thus they were metaphors of life, death, and regeneration. Since the Xibalbans had interpreted the noise made by One Hunahpu and Seven Hunahpu as a "lack of respect" for the Lords of Death, they took offense and decided, as we shall see, to trick, defeat, and sacrifice the brothers (106).

Prior to their departure on their dangerous mission to Xibalba One Hunahpu and Seven Hunahpu returned home to their mother, Xmucane, their father having died during the interim. They informed her most tenderly of the perils such a journey to the land of the dead entailed (as it always does in myth). They then told their sons—One Monkey and One Artisan—how to entertain and show love to their grandmother during their absence. It must be noted that One Monkey and One Artisan had been well taught by their father, One Hunahpu, and uncle, Seven Hunahpu. Both were skilled flautists, singers, writers, carvers, jewelers, and metalworkers.

The feeling world prevailed in the admonitions given by One Hunahpu and Seven Hunahpu to the lads: "[J]ust play and just sing, write and carve to warm our house and to warm the heart of your grandmother" (110).

Despite the tender and reassuring words spoken by One Hunahpu and Seven Hunahpu to their mother prior to their departure—"We're going, we're not dying. Don't be sad"—nothing could assuage her sorrow. Xmucane "sobbed, she had to weep" (110).

The Grandmother's tears, associated with water, liken her once again to the moon, in its capacity to influence tides and rains. That she could not control her emotions indicates not only the depth of her *feeling* function, but another aspect of her makeup: her openheartedness. No longer detached or guided by reason, as when participating in the collective cosmogonic event, she now acted sincerely—from the center of her being. Her heart, which beat with love for her offspring, dominated her actions. The pain she experienced on this occasion also reveals another aspect of her psyche: that of the seer with a highly intuitive nature. Rather than heeding the reasonable declarations made to her by her sons—assuring her of their return—as diviner, she *saw* into the reality of the matter and knew they would not come back to her.

And so it happened. One Hunahpu's head was cut off and hung on the fork of a calabash tree. Immediately—and miraculously—the tree bore gourdlike fruit. His body was buried in the ground next to that of Seven Hunahpu, beneath the Place of Ball Game Sacrifice (113).[6]

The fruit miraculously born from One Hunahpu's head suggests the sacrifice of his earthly existence for the benefit of humankind and its rebirth in the plenitude of the gourdlike fruit. Thus we may look upon the sacrifice as a metaphor for the eternal mystery of nature's regenerative processes. In that the fruit burgeoning on what we may consider to be the Tree of Life emanated from Hunahpu's head, it points to the world of the mind. He had not used his "head" during his earthly trajectory—only his emotions. What he represented—the instinctual rather than the thinking function—had to be sacrificed. That his body and his twin brother's were buried in the ground suggests that a more evolved and balanced personality might come into being.

The twins' knowing surrender of their lives, approached psychologically, may be considered as a demise, but if it is understood as a response to society's conscious yearning for a world in which higher (supernal) values predominate, it may be viewed as a gain for the collective. Deleterious personality traits inherent to individuals (the visceral comportment of the twins on the ball court) are banished, that is, sacrificed in favor of the group (Jung 1963, paras. 390, 257).

Xmucane, nevertheless, was not yet prepared, either emotionally or intellectually, to lose her two sons. Both archetypal and very human, she sought to preserve their adolescence, their temperamental dispositions, their deep devotion to her. But Xmucane had to release her sons, whom she sought to keep enfolded within what could have become a progressively regressive state. By seeking to tie them to childhood, she overlooked the necessity for transformation and regeneration, or perpetual sacrifice of past states and past connections for the purpose of personal and collective growth.

A Maiden's Impregnation

No sooner had the Maiden, Blood Woman, the daughter of Blood Gatherer, the fourth-ranking god of Xibalba, heard about the growth of miraculous fruit from the Tree of Life than she, like Eve, experienced immense curiosity.

Understandably, the Maiden was intrigued by the Tree of Life as world axis. Not only did she seek to discover and to learn, but she wanted to enter fully into the *life experience*. No longer did she want to live within a patriarchal fold, which denied her liberty of expression and freedom of action. Her desire to escape her father's compound indicated independence of mind and of person, and great courage as well. She was fully aware of her father's interdict: to pick the fruit of the tree or to walk beneath it was strictly forbidden— and severe punishment was meted out to those who failed to obey (113).

The determined Maiden nonetheless went alone to the Place of Ball Game Sacrifice, where the Tree of Life was located. Amazed at the sight of such a marvel, she spoke truthfully and openly to this living and dynamic entity—and with all the naïveté of an unworldly girl:

> "What? Well! What's the fruit of this tree? Should this tree bear something sweet? They shouldn't die, they be wasted. Should I pick one?" said the maiden.
>
> And then the bone spoke; it was here in the fork of the tree:
>
> "Why do you want a mere bone, a round thing in the branches of a tree?" said the head of One Hunahpu when it spoke to the maiden. "You don't want it," she was told.
>
> "I do want it," said the maiden.
>
> "Very well. Stretch out your right hand here, so I can see it," said the bone.
>
> "Yes," said the maiden. She stretched out her right hand, up there in front of the bone.
>
> And then the bone spit out its saliva, which landed squarely in the hand of the maiden.
>
> And then she looked in her hand, she inspected it right away, but the bone's saliva wasn't in her hand.
>
> "It is just a sign I have given you, my saliva, my spittle. This, my head, has nothing on it—just bone, nothing of meat. It's just the same with the

head of a great lord: it's just the flesh that makes his face look good. And when he dies, people get frightened by his bones. After that, his son is like his saliva, his spittle, in his being, whether it be the son of a lord or the son of a craftsman, an orator. The father does not disappear, but goes on being fulfilled. Neither dimmed nor destroyed is the face of a lord, a warrior, craftsman, orator. Rather, he will leave his daughter and sons. So it is that I have done likewise through you. Now go up there on the face of the earth; you will not die. Keep the word. (114, 115)

The bone—in this instance a symbol of the body's inner structure or architecture—is not only its most durable part, but also contains marrow or pith. Thus One Hunahpu's bone represents vigor, energy, and substance in concentrated and material form.

Sensitive to all aspects of nature, both human and nonhuman, Blood Woman immediately understood as well as felt the message given her by One Hunahpu's head. Its placement in the fork of the tree, that is, above the earth and pointing toward the heavens, identified it with moral and spiritual values, as well as with the Quiché Mayas' upper classes—lords, priests, and orators. That the head was attached to the tree's branches as well as to its trunk associated it with the phallus. Blood Woman was also drawn to its roots beneath the earth, where the bodies of One Hunahpu and Seven Hunahpu had been buried—that is, to the visceral world of instinct and sexuality. Just as the dead were undergoing the transformatory process—rotting first, then absorbing the surrounding nourishment to be born again in some other form—Blood Woman, although still living within the earth under her father's rulership, also experienced the biocosmic fecundating power of One Hunahpu and Seven Hunahpu.

The saliva/semen that the head spat into Blood Woman's hand symbolizes nature's regenerative principle: the creative and/or destructive power that is handed down from one generation to the next. Bodily secretions have always been endowed with magic and supernal powers: Job spoke of his enemies spitting in his face (17:6), Jesus cured a blind man with his saliva (John 9:6), and other examples abound. Such emanations, however, are double-edged: they serve to unite and to dissolve, to cure and to corrupt. Because saliva is identified with speech, that is with the mind—in this case born from the fruit of One Hunahpu's head—it is considered a seminal fluid enabling those gods and heroes born from it to accomplish their supernatural deeds. Parallels may be drawn between spiritual and physical rebirth: human procreation is symbolized by One Hunahpu's head, and germination by earthly plant life (Girard 1977, 91).

The hand that Blood Woman extended to One Hunahpu's head revealed an inner dynamism motivated by a psychological urge toward independence, as well as by a natural sexual urge. Her openhandedness suggests her desire and need to accept the role allotted to her: recipient as well as partner. The five-fingered hand has been analogized to the body (four extremities and the head), and is thus identified with an emotional realm, including feelings of love and relatedness. It may also be looked upon as the vehicle for the exchange of energy between bodies. The fecundator, namely One Hunahpu's head, was so sexually aroused by the Maiden that he emitted his fertilizing saliva.

The coitus between the two was traumatic for Blood Woman, and upon returning home she was aware that something had been "generated in her belly." Six months later, when her father, Blood Gatherer, discovered that she was carrying what he called "a bastard," he and the Xibalban lords sought to discover the father's name. She spoke the truth when replying: "There is no child, my father, sir; there is no man whose face I have known" (*PV,* 115). Inasmuch as Maya custom forbade unmarried women to look upon the face of a man prior to marriage, Blood Woman had obeyed the social code, extending her hand but not looking up at the head.

Because this woman of independent mind stood firm and refused to name the father of her future child, Blood Gatherer ordered his military keepers to kill her and bring him her heart in a bowl. The keepers obediently left with the Maiden, the bowl, and the white dagger—"the instrument of sacrifice" (115).

Reasoning with her guards not to sacrifice her, the Maiden maintained that hers was an immaculate conception: "What's in my belly generated all by itself when I went to marvel at the head of One Hunahpu" (116). She was successful in persuading her would-be murderers to spare her life, but the keepers asked her what they could bring back to her father in lieu of her heart. She cleverly channeled a croton tree's red sap into the bowl; the glistening bloodlike substance congealed, taking on the round configuration of the bowl. The owls, who had befriended Blood Woman during her ordeal, guided her up to earth. During the trajectory they asked her to walk ahead while they delivered the duplicate heart to the lords of Xibalba.

After examining the blood and reassuring themselves that it was the Maiden's, they put it over a fire to dry it out. During the process they savored its aroma, later to be called incense by the Quiché Mayas. "They found the smoke of the blood to be truly sweet!" (117).[7] So sweet, indeed, that the Underworld deities were dazed and dazzled by its power, and thus were "defeated by a maiden" (117). The Maiden's thinking principle had prevailed over the instinctive nature of the Underworld Deities. As a blend of instinct (sperm) and mind (head), she was conscious of what she said and did, and thus earned the light of day (Girard 1977, 107).

Blood Woman as Waxing Moon

Having escaped her martyrdom by relying on her own wisdom and intelligence, Blood Woman, or the Maiden, demonstrated her intent to carve out her own way in life. Considered psychologically, the Maiden's upward journey, from Xibalba to earth, may be regarded as the fulfillment of her deepest yearning. By desiring a departure from an implicitly unconscious way of life, she experienced a concomitant increase in consciousness that permitted her to leave the patriarchal fold—a first step in transforming her way of life. As a conscious individual, she sacrificed the security that she had enjoyed as her father's docile daughter and opted for a new, dangerous, and perhaps painful existence on earth or in the Middleworld.

Strong-minded, she chose to live in a matrilocal/matrilineal family situation. Blood Woman's full belly, viewed as a personification of the continuously altering full moon, suggests an altering attitude on her part. After rising from the Underworld into the Middleworld, she, like the moon, was also to pass through various phases in her physical and psychological development. Like the earth's only known satellite, she too would become the harbinger of light in darkness, setting her behavioral patterns in keeping with nature's own cyclicity. Both light (consciousness) and darkness (unconsciousness) became instrumental in guiding her actions and making her accountable for her fate.

Upon reaching the Middleworld, Blood Woman went directly to Xmucane, the primordial Mother/Grandmother. It was she, let us recall, who, after the demise of her twin sons, One Hunahpu and Seven Hunahpu, had been caring for her grandchildren, One Monkey and One Artisan. Until Blood Woman's arrival, One Monkey and One Artisan had spent their days entertaining the Grandmother with their singing, flute playing, writing, and sculpting. Yet, by dint of their art, their "genius," they knew they would experience pain and grief as future culture heroes. Such was and is the lot of superior people—"great knowers," who intuit future events. Born ahead of their time, they are frequently doomed to suffer: "In their hearts they [One Monkey and One Artisan] already realized everything when their younger brothers came into being, but they didn't reveal their insights because of their jealousy" (*PV*, 120).

Naively, perhaps, the Maiden introduced herself to Xmucane as her daughter-in-law. She was summarily rejected by the all-powerful Grandmother, who believed not a single word of her tale of woe. She was carrying "bastards," Xmucane declared, and not her deceased son's progeny. "Get out," she commanded the pregnant Maiden (117). Blood Woman responded in kind:

> Even so, I really am your daughter-in-law. I am already his, I belong to One Hunahpu. What I carry is his. One Hunahpu and Seven Hunahpu are alive, they are not dead. They have merely made a way for the light to show itself, madam mother-in-law, as you will see when you look at the faces of what I carry. (118)

The Grandmother finally decided to put the Maiden to the test, ordering her to go to the garden and fetch a "a big netful of corn" for One Monkey and One Artisan—the planting and the production of food and the replenishment of the earth's womb paralleling the gestation in Blood Woman's own belly. The Maiden having acquiesced, she discovered much to her despair that in the garden grew only one clump that had already borne its ears. Her emotivity displacing her rationality, she suddenly saw herself as a "sinner," thereby giving credence to her father's and to the Grandmother's judgments of her.

The Maiden immediately called upon the Guardians of Food for help. Nature's feminine principles responded:

> "Come thou, rise up, come thou, stand up:
> Generous Woman, Harvest Woman,
> Cacao Woman, Cornmeal Woman,
> thou guardian of the food of One Monkey, One Artisan"
> (*PV*, 118)

That the pregnant Maiden had recourse to female deities in her hour of need is understandable both emotionally and rationally. She is associated by them with bounty, as in a "harvest"; with the cosmic tree as world axis; with "cacao" and with "cornmeal," which, when blended with cacao, becomes a sacred brew. These attributes and beneficial properties of plants may be seen as paradigms for cosmic harmony.

Miraculously the single ear of corn reproduced itself and made food enough to fill the net. The disbelieving Grandmother, having gone to the garden to assure herself that the "one clump was still there," welcomed into her household the Maiden, who now took her rightful place as the gestating and fecundating Mother figure in an agrarian society (119).

The unexpected birth in the mountains of Blood Woman's twin boys, Hunahpu and Xbalanque, perhaps reflects ancient Mayan mores. As in China, a mother was considered impure at the time she was to give birth, and thus was sent away from the home during parturition. Upon Blood Woman's return home, the Grandmother, overwhelmed and unable to sleep because of the noisy newborns (the twin sons of One Hunahpu and Blood Woman), labeled them "loudmouths" and cast them from the house (119).

Thus began the ordeals of the culture heroes Hunahpu and Xbalanque. During the course of their travails, by transforming their elder brothers One Monkey and One Artisan into monkeys, they gained release from their power (121).

The time had now come for Hunahpu and Xbalanque to put the Grandmother to a test. They informed her that One Monkey and One Artisan were behaving shamelessly, like animals (they had been changed into monkeys). She replied that to harm them would be tantamount to knocking her down headfirst. Protesting that they would never harm their elder brothers unless she laughed at the sight of them, Hunahpu and Xbalanque brought them into her presence. Seeing their ugly faces and their outlandish antics, the Grandmother "could not hold back her laughter" (122). Three times did the same drama unfold; three times did the Grandmother laugh uncontrollably at the sight of the monkeys' ridiculous prancings.

Then they vanished, beyond recall. Hunahpu and Xbalanque consoled the Grandmother: "We're here—we, your grandchildren. Just love our mother, dear grandmother." Sibling rivalry and jealousy were transformed by Hunahpu and Xbalanque into love and harmony. Their words "Just love our mother, dear grandmother" revealed the powerful maternal feelings implicit in a matrilocal, even matrilineal society (124).

The House as Sacred Space

To fill in the emptiness in the Grandmother's life, Hunahpu and Xbalanque dedicated themselves to her and the Mother. The Grandmother responded in kind. With the love and spirit of harmony that now reigned in the household, the once authoritarian matriarchal figure had become a pliable and understanding one:

We'll do some gardening, our dear grandmother and mother. . . . Don't worry. We're here, we're your grand-children, we're the successors of our elder brothers." (124)

Whereas the custom in Quiché Mayan society was to bury the dead under the dirt floor in the center of the house, to the accompaniment of dirges, Hunahpu and Xbalanque would instead plant maize in the center of the home. The Mayas' houses, like their pyramids and citadels, were built for the gods. A microcosm, its roof resembled a celestial vault; the rest of the home symbolized the heart of the telluric domain; and the area beneath the floors represented the Xibalbian sphere. Hunahpu and Xbalanque opened a passageway from Xibalba to the Middleworld, thereby evoking a more joyful understanding of nature's death/rebirth ritual.

A descent into Xibalba, the most harrowing of all rites of passage, was required of Hunahpu and Xbalanque in order to become culture heroes (133). But unlike One Hunahpu and Seven Hunahpu, who had died during their trajectory to Xibalba, the younger generation of twins, conceived in the Underworld, were better equipped for the ordeal. Their familiarity with the Underworld's geography, understood psychologically as the unconscious, and their understanding of the Middleworld, or consciousness, had enabled them to expand their perceptive and intuitive faculties. Not only did they intuitively *know* the proper strategies to use in difficult situations; they also had learned, as previously mentioned, how the feeling principle functions when relating to loved ones. The consideration they showed the Grandmother and Mother before their departure for Xibalba gives evidence of a further broadening of their understanding. They consoled the women maturely and with poise:

> "So here is the sign of our word. We'll leave it with you. Each of us will plant an ear of corn. We'll plant them in the center of our house. When the corn dries up, this will be a sign of our death:
> "Perhaps they died," you'll say, when it dries up. And when the sprouting comes:
> "Perhaps they live," you'll say, our dear grandmother and mother. From now on, this is the sign of our word. We're leaving it with you," they said, then they left. (133)

And so it happened that when the corn ears dried up, the primordial Grandmother, the Mother-of-all-Mothers, wept. But when she burned "copal before the corn as a memorial" to Hunahpu and Xbalanque, she saw the corn plants sprout, and her heart was joyous. A parallel was thus created between human and plant life, which would give rise to the cult of maize.[8]

> Then the ears were deified by their grandmother, and she gave them names: Middle of the House, Middle of the Harvest, Living Corn, Earthen Floor became their names.
>
> And she named the ears Middle of the House, Middle of the Harvest, because they had planted them right in the middle of the inside of their home.
>
> And she further named them Earthen Floor, Living Corn, since the corn ears had been placed up above an earthen floor.
>
> And she also named them Living Corn, because the corn plants had grown again. So they were named by Xmucane. They had been left behind, planted by Hunahpu and Xbalanque, simply as a way for their grandmother to remember them. (158–59)

During the twins' fierce ordeals among the Xibalbans, not only was Hunahpu's head cut off and then restored, but both he and his brother submitted to the sacrifice of their bodies, including the grinding of their bones, only to reappear whole five days later. After outwitting the Lords of Death, reducing "their greatness and brilliance" to naught, Hunahpu and Xbalanque dug up the bodies of One Hunahpu and Seven Hunahpu. They revived them, but incompletely.

> He [Seven Hunahpu] had wanted his face to become just as it was, but when he was asked to name everything, and once he had found the name of the mouth, the nose, the eyes of his face, there was very little else to be said. Although his mouth could not name the names of each of his former parts, he had at least spoken again. (159)

Although they left their father at the Place of Ball Game Sacrifice, they had been "respectful of their father's heart." They told him, "You will be prayed to here," and the father's "heart was comforted" (159).

> Once their mission was completed, the Twin Heroes "ascended . . . into the middle of the light, and they ascended straight on into the sky, and the sun belongs to one and the moon to the other. When it became light within the sky, on the face of the earth, they were there in the sky. (160)

Having been born in Xibalba, or in the psychological condition of non- or unconsciousness, having lived their existence in earthly spheres where they developed their consciousness, Hunahpu and Xbalanque now ascended to the Otherworld: the supernal domain of the spirit. Having completed their tripartite trajectory, as culture heroes they were awarded knowledge in such matters as religious rituals and astronomy. Understandably they became paradigms for humanity of everything that was wise and great.

The maize planted by the twins in the center of the house represented their living bodies; the aridification of the plants, their death; the replantings, their rebirth and ascension. Thus they were immortalized as plants above the earth and as deities incorporated into the sun and moon.

The Fourth Creation: The Primordial Mother/Ancestress as Fashioner

Assiduously did the gods "search for the ingredients of the human body," finally fashioning humans out of staple food. White and yellow corn became "the flesh of the human work, the human design, and the water for the blood" (163).

As a lunar deity identified with water and plant growth, the Grandmother now reigned virtually supreme, for it was she who was responsible for the maintaining of sustenance. It was she, Xmucane, as primordial Ancestress and Mother, in consultation with her husband Xpiyacoc, who participated in the creative act. Not only did she grind the colorful yellow and white corn nine times, but she blended the mixture with water to make nine drinks. From this mixture came the blood, flesh, fat, muscle, bone, and strength of humankind (Goetz and Morley 1983, 167).[9]

From the "staples alone that made up their flesh" did the first "mother-father"—or archetypal couple—model and bring into being four great men: Jaguar Quitze, Jaguar Night, Mahucutah, and True Jaguar, who became the four heads of Quiché patrilineages (*PV,* 165).

As in the Judeo-Christian and so many other myths, the notion of miraculous or spontaneous birth is here present: the fourth creation was deprived of personal or even collective human parents.

> They were simply made and modeled . . . they had no mother and no father. We have named the men by themselves. No woman gave birth to them, nor were they begotten by the builder, sculptor, Bearer, Begetter. By sacrifice alone, by genius alone were they made, they were modeled by the Maker, Modeler, Bearer, Begetter, Sovereign Plumed Serpent. And when they came to fruition, they came out human. (165)

The deities could not, however, cope with the perfection of the four lords now walking the face of the earth, who "saw everything under the sky perfectly. . . . They understood everything perfectly, they sighted the four sides, the four corners in the sky, on the earth" (165–66). Despite the gratitude the lords conveyed verbally to their creators, they who were possessed of infinite understanding and sight—able to see "through trees, through lakes, through seas, through mountains, through plains"—posed a threat to those in power. Nonetheless their creators did not seek to destroy them. They altered them instead.

> And when they changed the nature of their works, their designs, it was enough that the eyes be marred by the Heart of the Sky. They were blinded as the face of a mirror is breathed upon. Their eyes were weakened. Now it was only when they looked nearby that things were clear.
> And such was the loss of the means of understanding, along with the means of knowing everything, by the four humans. The root was implanted. (167)

Despite its limitations, civilization was a triumph, and it was ushered in with the advent of humankind.

> The dawn has approached, preparations have been made, and morning has come for the provider, nurturer, born in the light, begotten in the light. Morning has come for humankind, for the people of the face of the earth. . . . It all came together as they went on thinking in the darkness, in the night, as they searched and they sifted, they thought and they wondered. (163)

Although women came into being after men (as in Genesis), in this increasingly patriarchal society what is of interest to us is that "With their women there they became wider awake. Right away they were happy at heart again, because of their wives (167).

Beautiful wives were indeed created for Jaguar Quitze, Jaguar Night, Mahucutah, and True Jaguar. From these couples emerged the powerful Quiché tribes, who always tendered respect and reverence for those who had given them life. But human beings needed something more than mere sentient existence, and though they sacrificed, prayed, and fasted, yearning for dawn and the emergence of the sun, the morning star, a "sign" that would guide and enlighten them, it was not yet to be.

Jaguar Quitze, Jaguar Night, Mahucutah, and True Jaguar went to the eastern city of Tulan (Place of Reeds, identified today with Teotihuacan) in search of their patron Deities—the three most prominent of which were

Tohil, Auilix, and Hacauitz—who might award them sun/enlightenment. Happiness reigned; hope abounded. Their populations grew. But so did frustration and linguistic diversity. Climatic changes were also drastic as intense cold, hail, and rain descended upon the land.

Tohil, giver of fire, would provide the tribes with warmth if they rendered proper homage to him: allowing him to "suckle" them. "Isn't it their hearts' desire to embrace me? I, who am Tohil? But if there is no desire, then I'll not give them their fire. . . . When the time comes, not right now, they'll be suckled on their sides under their arms." To "suckle" means to sacrifice the penitents' hearts by cutting them out of their bodies "through their sides, under their arms," in order to give blood to their god. In ecstatic frenzy, other sacrificers "bled their ears," passed a cord through their elbows, fasted, made burnt offerings (incense), and sang "The Blame is Ours" (174–75).

The surviving penitents and sacrificers left Tulan at the instigation of Tohil. During their long march, which may have led them across seas and mountains, they suffered cold and virtual starvation. Thus they began their seemingly endless migration—hoping beyond hope to *see* the first dawn! Finally, on the summit of a mountain, known today as Hacauitz (Place of Advice), they witnessed the coming of light: the emerging of a radiant sun. Weeping with joy, they danced and burned incense in honor of this nourishing fireball.

In the differentiating world, however, extremes become intolerable. When the sun rose "like a man," so intense was the heat that Tohil, Auilix, and Hacauitz, as well as such animals as pumas, jaguars, and snakes, were turned into stone (182). Let us note, however, that in the animistic culture of the Quiché, stone was a living and dynamic entity. Petrification of the deities did not indicate a diminution of their power; they continued to appear and to speak to their worshipers.

In time, the Quiché built a citadel on Hacauitz mountain and multiplied, always rendering homage to their trinity of most important deities. At first Tohil told them that the sacrifice of animal rather than human blood would be acceptable to him. Later, because this form of oblation was considered insufficient, he asked to be suckled by his faithful. Sacrifices to Tohil, Auilix, and Hacauitz intensified: "They spilled their blood, they poured gourdfuls into the mouths of the stones" (187).

Tribal killings and abductions for sacrificial purposes became so rampant as to create dissension among the faithful. Those opposed to the practice of human sacrifice were determined to defeat the religious fanatics demanding the suckling ritual. A council was held to determine a means of releasing the people from the grip of the trinity of deities. What better way to achieve this end, in patriarchal societies, than by seduction?

The Hierodules

Two maidens were chosen to seduce and thereby vanquish Tohil, Auilix, and Hacauitz, thus putting an end to their stranglehold over the people.

The hierodules, identified with courtesans, court priestesses, sacred prostitutes, and temptresses in myths, were perfect vehicles to bring about change.[10] Although their function was mainly to confuse men and lure them from their preoccupations, paving the way for catastrophe, hierodules also enlarged the outlook of the males by bringing them to consciousness after leading them into temptation. When these maidens were identified with fertility and the nourishing Mother archetype, they helped steer the devout away from their extreme asceticism, even masochism. Thus the more moderate thinkers—the antifanatic factions—in Quiché society attempted to liberate their people from religious enslavement (Kluger 1991, 35–37).

The council members sent two of their beautiful daughters—Xtah and Xpuch—to seduce what appeared to be adolescent boys who bathed daily at the river bank. "Let them be in full blossom, maidens who radiate preconsciousness, so that when they go they'll be desirable" (*PV*, 189). The maidens were instructed as follows: "You must go, our dear daughters. Go wash clothes at the river, and if you should see three boys [Tohil, Auilix, and Hacauitz], undress yourselves in front of them. And if their hearts should desire you, you will titillate them" (190). If they were pleasing to the boys and if they should be asked where they came from, the maidens were to answer:

> "'We are the daughters of lords, so let a sign be forthcoming from you.'
> Then they should give you something. If they like your faces you must
> really give yourselves up to them. And if you do not give yourselves up,
> then we shall kill you. We'll feel satisfied when you bring back a sign, since
> we'll think of it as proof that they came after you," said the lords, instruct-
> ing the two maidens. (190)

Although the gods did not lust for the maidens as the nonsacrificers had expected, they did give them the "signs," or gifts, that had been requested of them. These took the form of three magic cloaks: on the inside of these, Jaguar Quitze was told by the deities to paint the image of a jaguar; Jaguar Night, an eagle; and Mahucutah, swarms of yellow jackets and wasps.

No sooner had Xtah and Xpuch delivered the cloaks to the antifanatical lords than they, believing these gifts to be proof of the maidens' sin, tried them on. Although pleasure was experienced by the first two, the third lord discovered too late that the yellow jackets and wasps were real and not painted. So badly was he stung that he could barely endure the pain. Accused of being "tricksters," the girls were "reprimanded." As punishment for failing to defeat the opposition, they were ordered to follow the profession of "bark shins," or prostitutes.

Their defeat by the divine trinity (Tohil, Auilix, and Hacauitz) and by their worshipers (Jaguar Quitze, Jaguar Night, and Mahucutah) did not diminish the will of the antisacrificers to attack their opponents on their turf: the citadel built on the summit of Hacauitz mountain. So powerful was the zeal of its defenders that "even their wives became killers" (192–96).

Predictably, the moderates were defeated. Those who escaped death begged the lords of the land to spare their lives. Although their plea was heard, they were required to pay the victors tribute. In time a highly organized Quiché society emerged. Their progeny multiplied. When the great lords—Jaguar Quitze, Jaguar Night, Mahucutah, and True Jaguar—prepared for their deaths, they bequeathed "enlightened words, enlightened advice" to their sons, after which they returned to the place of their origin.

Jaguar Quitze "left a sign of his being, the Bundle of Flames, as it was called." Although no one knew what it was, it was depicted as follows: "It was wound about with coverings. It was never unwrapped. Its sewing wasn't clear because no one looked on while it was being wrapped" (198).

Never again were the Quiché lords seen by their wives or children. Only the legacy of the Quiché Lords, that precious bundle, remained as proof of their earthly trajectory: "a memorial to their fathers . . . the first people to come across the sea, from the east" (198). Their descendants, in keeping with the instructions given them by their departed fathers, undertook a pilgrimage to the east, to the lowlands on the other side of the sea, which their fathers had crossed prior to their journey to the highlands. After settling in a variety of areas, and building a new capital packed with enormous, mathematically conceived monuments, temples, palaces, ball courts, and extraordinary works of art, their power was recognized by neighboring tribes. Although a plethora of births ensued, so, too, did wars that drained the communities of their strength. Thus the way was paved for their ruthless conquest by the Spanish.

The *Popol Vuh* concludes with a listing of the names of generations of Quiché lords, their descendants, and the deities whose supernal wisdom became the people's guiding principle.

> This is enough about the being of Quiché, given that there is no longer a place to see it. There is the original book and ancient writings owned by the lords, now lost, but even so, everything has been completed here concerning Quiché. (227)

5 Racine's *Phaedra:*
"The Horror of Remorse"

Swept up by a raging passion for the young and handsome Hippolytus, Phaedra suffered self-torture, a sense of culpability, and "the horror of remorse," which drove her to suicide. Racine's tragic heroine was the daughter of Minos, king of Crete, and Pasiphae. As the wife of Theseus, ruler of Athens, she was Hippolytus's stepmother as well.

In his preface to *Phaedra,* Jean Racine (1639–99) declared that Euripides' *Hippolytus* (428 B.C.E.) had been the source of his inspiration.[1] While retaining in his work vestiges of the ancient Greek myth, Euripides dramatized problems of interest to him and to his contemporaries. Unlike Racine, he highlighted the dismal fate of illegitimate children, of which Hippolytus was one—the bastard son of Theseus and an Amazon queen, Hippolyta. Since this young man, the product of illegitimate love and sex, was rejected by Greek society, it was natural that he despise women. Religion also preoccupied Euripides, as it had Racine, but for different reasons. The former considered the existence of gods a fact of life and a tragic burden that humanity had to bear. Because they did not function rationally, Euripides considered their acts gratuitous and incomprehensible, and their influence on people inexplicable. He warned humankind to be *aware* of the actions of deities, and take whatever steps necessary—albeit without effect—to prevent disaster from befalling them.[2]

Unlike the Greek tragedy, in which Hippolytus was the hero and Phaedra a secondary character, Racine's version of the myth places Phaedra in the center of the drama, all else radiating outward from her. Racine's play, converging on the excoriating struggle within a woman whose highly developed conscience probes such eternal problems as good and evil, is a projection of the dramatist's own pain onto Phaedra's love experience. He was plagued by feelings of culpability for his supposedly heinous comportment as

151

a youth toward the Jansenist fathers of Port-Royal. Like his heroine, he yearned for redemption.

Racine's *Phaedra* takes place in Troezen in the Peloponnesus, about fifty miles southwest of Athens. Its plot is relatively uncomplicated. While Theseus is away from Athens on a military mission, Phaedra tells her confidante, Oenone, that she is in love with Hippolytus. Shortly thereafter an announcement is made at court that Theseus has been killed. Oenone now encourages the newly widowed queen to reveal her love to Hippolytus. Phaedra does so and is scorned by the young man. Again at Oenone's instigation, Phaedra tries to win Hippolytus's affection by offering him the crown. Theseus's sudden and unexpected return produces an explosive triangular confrontation. Guilt, shame, and despair encourage Phaedra to harbor thoughts of suicide. To relieve her, Oenone suggests that Hippolytus be accused of trying to win her favors. Indignant at first, Phaedra finally accedes, and Oenone makes the accusation. Infuriated, Theseus banishes his son and calls down upon him one of the three curses his father Neptune has granted him. Although the innocent Hippolytus discloses to his father his love for the young Aricia, his sense of integrity seals his lips with regard to Phaedra. Theseus then reveals to Phaedra Hippolytus's love for Aricia, whereupon, in rage and humiliation, she poisons herself. Learning that his wife is dying and that Oenone has thrown herself into the sea, Theseus begs Neptune to retract the punishment to be meted out to his son. It is too late. A monster thrust up from the sea seizes Hippolytus, who fends him off. The struggle and the monster's howlings frighten Hippolytus's horses, and they drag their master to his death. Phaedra appears and blames Oenone for her undoing, but confesses the truth and dies onstage. Theseus despairs.

Racine's *Phaedra* opened on 1 January 1677 at the Hôtel de Bourgogne; a similarly titled drama was performed by the second-rate playwright Jacques Pradon two days later at the Hôtel Guénégaud. Racine's earned failure; his rival's, success.[3] The competition between the two was stirred by a concerted and ruthless effort on the part of Racine's enemies to destroy the famous playwright's reputation. By March, however, a reversal occurred and Racine's *Phaedra* had won the day.

Ectypal Analysis

Why had Phaedra—a creature of conscience—emerged raw from Racine's subliminal world? What had motivated him to project his abrasive religious struggle onto her experience of unrequited love? What was the nature of his ideological and psychological dilemma?

Early Life

Racine's birth in Ferté-Milon, seventy-six kilometers from Paris, into an upper-bourgeois family did not augur anything out of the ordinary. But the soothing pattern of normalcy of his early years concluded with his mother's death after the birth of a daughter, Marie, in 1641 and his father's demise the following year. Orphaned and penniless, Jean was taken to live in the home of his paternal grandparents, the Desmoulins, righteous, kind, and highly moral people. They were so poor, however, that when their daughter (the future Mother Agnès de Sainte-Thècle) chose to enter a convent, they were unable to pay the customary dowry. As Racine grew older, other deprivations accentuated for him the stigma of poverty. His sister, Marie, was brought up under more favorable conditions by her maternal grandparents, the Sconins.

Further misfortune befell the barely ten-year-old Racine when in 1649 his grandfather, whom he had grown to love, died. His grandmother, perhaps unable to meet the expenses of maintaining a private home, retired with her grandson to the Jansenist convent-monastery at Port-Royal des Champs. Befriended by the deeply religious Jansenists, who were known for the excellence of their schools, Racine would live and be educated under their influence.

Jansenism

To better understand the role that Jansenism played in Racine's life and the religious torment it provoked in his psyche, a brief excursus on this sect, on the role played by the fathers of Port-Royal, and on their persecution by the Jesuits and the pope (Innocent X) is in order.

Jansenism was introduced into Port-Royal in 1636 by the priest Saint-Cyran. Officially, the doctrine of Jansenism came into existence with the publication in 1640 of the *Augustinus* by Cornelius Jansen (called Jansenius), bishop of Ypres. In this religious work he declared that the ideas of Saint Augustine concerning grace had been misinterpreted and that his present explication was the correct one. After Adam's fall, according to Jansenius, humans lost their free will, either becoming subject to God's grace or falling victim to *concupiscentia*. If God were to grant humans eternal grace, then they would veer toward good. Since this is not always the case, many are drawn to evil. On the other hand, God endows certain people with what is called "efficacious grace"—attracting them toward Good and ultimate salvation. An individual's salvation or damnation is predetermined and depends on God rather than on any human intermediary. Whereas the Jansenist credo denies free will, Jesuit thinking and papal decree awarded it to human beings. Because Jansenist doctrine, which preached the "all-powerful" nature of grace, ran counter to the Catholic Church and to Jesuit dicta, it was declared a heresy. Louis XIV, his ministers, and the Sorbonne theologians, made up largely of Jesuits, were unfavorably disposed toward the Jansenists. Indeed, the Jesuits had good cause to frown upon their rigor. The Jesuits had been accused of laxity of morals, of casuistry, and of having transformed the holiest of sacraments, Communion, into a hypocritical ritual and confession into a parody because of its frequency and the penitent's lack of sincerity. Sins, the Jansenists felt, could not be adjusted with facility, nor could they be remedied through senseless verbiage. Penitence, prayer, and pain must be part of pardon and purification.

In time, relations between the Jansenists and the highly influential Jesuits grew stormy. Several dates mark the extremes of their antagonism: 1638, when the Solitaires, as the fathers of Port-Royal were called, were forced to disperse and leave Port-Royal; 1642, when the *Augustinus* was condemned by Pope Urban VIII; 1653, when Pope Innocent X condemned the Five Propositions extracted from the *Augustinus,* which had been appealed by the Jansenists in the ecclesiastical courts; 1656, when Blaise Pascal, the Jansenist mathematician and philosopher, unmercifully satirized the Jesuit ideas of grace, and the fragility of their mores and precepts, in the form of eighteen sardonic writings entitled *The Provincial Letters*; and 1661, when the Petites Ecoles—known to be one of the finest educational institutions in France— was closed. Seven years later, by 1668, the struggle between the Jansenists and the Jesuits seems to have subsided—on the surface at least. On that date the so-called Paix de l'Eglise (or of Clement IX) was proclaimed, and the Jansenists signed the act of faith offered them by Pope Alexander VII. The battle, however, raged again a year later, after it was decreed that one-third of the revenue accruing to the Jansenists was to be placed under Jesuit management. By 1706 no more novices were permitted to enter Port-Royal. A year later the Jansenists were denied the sacraments. In 1709 the Solitaires were dispersed; in 1710 the buildings at Port-Royal were leveled; and in 1711 the three thousand corpses buried at Port-Royal were disinterred and removed to other areas.

Jansenism for the Solitaires living at Port-Royal des Champs was not only a religious doctrine but a unique way of life characterized by austerity, honor, and fervor. Among the Solitaires were many brilliant minds: specialists in letters, philosophy, logic, law, language, science, and mathematics. Antoine Le Maître (1608–58) was a successful lawyer in Paris prior to leaving the city for Port-Royal in 1638. Had Cicero and Demosthenes known him, claimed the popular writer Guez de Balzac, they would have been jealous of his extraordinary rhetorical capacity. Le Maître worked in the peace and quiet of Port-Royal with his brother, Le Maître de Sacy, on the *Translation of the New Testament* and a new version of the *Lives of the Saints*, among other works. Antoine Arnauld, known as Le Grand Arnauld, one of the most exceptional minds of the century and author of *The Frequency of Communion*, criticized Jesuit doctrine even while spreading Jansenist philosophy. It was this work which caused him to be censured by the Sorbonne and excluded from the faculty of theology in 1656. Dom Claude Lancelot (1615–95), with whom Arnauld wrote the *General Grammar*, was one of the founders of the Petites Ecoles (1645), which was located first in Paris in the Faubourg St. Jacques and later transferred to the Granges at Port-Royal des Champs. Pierre Nicole (1625–95) was one of the most distinguished teachers at the Petites Ecoles and perhaps the true director of Port-Royal. It was he who wrote ten anonymous letters, *Letters on Imaginary Heresy*, in which he defended Jansenist views, and stinging diatribes against such "evil" dramatists as Desmarets de Saint-Sorlin, author of the comedy *The Visionaries*.

Under Jansenist tutelage Racine developed a veritable passion for study. He read and annotated texts from Plato, Plutarch, and other Greek masters. He translated Plato's *Symposium*, composed essays on Pindar and Homer, and had a special affinity for Sophocles and Euripides, who must have mirrored his feelings and answered an unknown need within him.[4] Antoine Le Maître was so impressed by his "lively" mind and astonishing facility for learning that he decided to train him for the law, spending long hours with the lad inculcating him with logic, astuteness, and mental dexterity. His affection for Racine went beyond the intellect, however; Antoine Le Maître, treating Racine as his own son, showed great tenderness and warmth, and called him "mon fils" in his letters. When away from Port-Royal on a brief trip, he wrote to Racine admonishing him to "detach himself from the world," the enemy of piety, and added that "youth must always let itself be guided; it must not be emancipated" (Racine 1950, 1:11).[5] Such advice must have dug deep within Racine's fiber.

Following Le Maître's death in 1658, Racine was drawn toward a very kindly doctor, Jean Hamon (1618–87), who thereafter guided his studies.

Once associated with the medical faculty of Paris, Hamon had withdrawn to Port-Royal at the age of thirty-three. When, years later, Racine dictated his will, he allegedly asked to be buried at the doctor's feet.

Racine was a many-sided individual, difficult to know and still more puzzling to assess. Just as he was an inveterate reader of Greek literature, so was he a devotee of nature in all its aspects. Wandering through the woods and fields surrounding Port-Royal, he communed with nature—those sublime forces which he could "feel" but perhaps could not yet analyze: the trees, stocky yet graceful; the bushes, stumpy yet delicate; the many hues orchestrating certain scenes—reds, browns, and golden colors of autumn and the deep greens of summer. These colorations would later be transposed in his dramas. Whatever emerged from Mother Earth fixed itself in his mind's eye—starkly, sternly, and stormily. So moved was he by the beauty of his surroundings that he began composing verses on prairies, on woods, and even on the monastery buildings—everything he had come to know so well. All in nature, in life, began to feed his inner world and then his pen.

The moments of solace and comfort that Racine drew from nature were of short duration. A sensitive youth, he must have shared the Solitaires' anguish during their persecution. To the feelings of divestiture Racine had known upon being orphaned and the financial difficulties he had witnessed when living with his grandparents were added the suffering he shared with those he looked upon as "his" fathers at Port-Royal. Living through monstrous and fabulous days—a time when men fought harshly for ideas and for principles, when they expressed in moving and profound terms their belief in the divine—Racine must have experienced ambivalent emotions toward both religion and life in general. On the one hand, militancy would plunge him into the turbulent forces of the world; on the other hand, feelings of detachment, inwardness, and meditation enticed him into his own resplendent inner realm.

The Solitaires were adept at facing dangers courageously and astutely. During a crisis hovering over Port-Royal, in January 1656, they acted with quiet determination. Fearing for their own lives, they sent Racine to safety at the Château de Vaumurier of the duc de Luynes, not far from the Jansenist convent-monastery.

In the impressive milieu of the adroit and affable duc de Luynes and of the duc de Chevreuse, minister to Louis XIII, Racine found himself in a different type of society—one of wealth and success. It was here perhaps that he felt a need to succeed in life, that a desire to ingratiate himself became apparent. The months Racine spent at the castle of the duke de Luynes allowed him to renew his acquaintance with his father's cousin, Nicholas Vitart, a former student at Port-Royal and now wealthy and powerful as manager of the duke de Luynes's estates. Their ensuing friendship was to play an important role in Racine's future activities.

Upon his return to Port-Royal in 1657, broader in his outlook and more courtly in his ways, Racine resumed for a brief period his studies with Antoine Le Maître and with the other Solitaires. When the time arrived for him to further his education elsewhere, he was sent to one of Paris's finest schools, the Collège d'Arcourt, to study philosophy. Racine thus began his creative pursuits in the city that had always been a source of inspiration for the intelligentsia and would now become a land of enchantment for the future playwright.

Paris

Having completed his studies at the Collège d'Arcourt in 1659, the twenty-four-year-old Racine did not have prospects that could be considered especially bright. Although brilliant, handsome, and certainly poised, he lacked fortune and social position—so necessary in seventeenth-century society. Fortunately Vitart came to his aid, assuring the young man's entry into the duke's household to help manage one of his estates. Such prosaic and routine activity was not stimulating to Racine. Indeed, he frequently complained of frightful boredom. Clearly, he wanted to return to Paris—a city of excitement, growth, and hope.

The Dramatist

Racine's experience in estate management reinforced his determination to follow a literary career. Although he wrote pastoral poems, odes, songs, letters, hymns, sonnets, and elegies, his particular love was for the theater, as evidenced in a letter to a friend, the Abbé Le Vasseur (Racine 1950, 2:379). More than talent and a love for the written word were needed, however, to pursue the career of a playwright. A pension from King Louis XIV was required. To win his royal favor, Racine approached Vitart, who introduced him, *inter alios*, to the pedantic Jean Chapelain, patriarch of poets. Diplomatically he spoke favorably of Racine's talent to the king's prime minister, Jean-Baptiste Colbert. Not surprisingly, Racine was awarded one hundred louis in the name of the monarch. Further introductions and subsidies led to greater encouragement—all of which were decisive in Racine's choice of a career, a career that would incur the wrath of the entire religious community at Port-Royal, including his aunt, Mother Agnès de Sainte-Thècle. Theater was "sinful," she declared; anything connected with this "artificial" art was evil. Speaking in the name of the whole Jansenist community, she threatened Racine outright with excommunication if he pursued his theatrical endeavors.

But Racine was fired with a will to succeed and an inner frenzy that made him seemingly impervious to the imprecations leveled at him by the Jansenists. His passion for the theater far outweighed his scruples. His play *La Thébaïde* (The Theban brothers), presented in 1664, is a living monument to his rebellion and to the inner rage he was then experiencing. The drama depicts the hatred between Jocasta's and Oedipus's two sons, Polyneices and Eteocles, in their dispute for possession of the throne. The two young men may be understood as symbols of two opposing forces within the playwright's psyche. The one represented the way of life inculcated in him by the fathers at Port-Royal—self-abnegation, pursuit of arduous disciplines, meditation, and solitude; the other, the offerings of the beguiling city of Paris, with all its creativity, joy, and gregariousness.

A terrible price must be paid for rebellion. The hero or creator who attempts to carve out his or her own future independently must break out of society's straitjackets. To gain victory over oneself and one's origins eventually invites a backlash of remorse, guilt, and shame. In Racine's words:

> Not always is your victory so sweet;
> She's often followed by remorse and shame.
>
> (*CP*, 14)[6]

Mother Agnès de Sainte-Thècle and the Jansenist fathers repudiated him. Still, there was no overt rift with Port-Royal. The tenor began to alter when Pierre Nicole wrote ten anonymous letters, *Letters on Imaginary Heresy*, in which he defended Jansenist views. That same year, the popular dramatist Desmarets de Saint-Sorlin wrote *The Holy Ghost's Advice to the King* (1665) and shortly thereafter an *Apology to the Nuns at Port-Royal*, in which he assaulted Jansenist doctrine as well as Nicole's poor writing style. Nicole retaliated with a second series of letters, *The Visionaries*, in which he attacked Desmarets de Saint-Sorlin, author of the comedy *The Visionaries*, in stinging terms, labeling such novelists and dramatic poets as "public poisoners"(Racine 1950, 1:24).

Racine considered the above statement, intended for Desmarets de Saint-Sorlin, as a personal attack. One wonders why he reacted in this manner when there was no mention of his name. He must have felt extreme guilt vis-à-vis Port Royal and his former fathers, who had nurtured him during so many difficult years. To rid himself of these unpleasant sentiments, Racine perhaps countered unconsciously with rising feelings of hatred against his benefactors. How else can one explain the violent *Letter to the Author of the Imaginary Heresies and the Two Visionaries* (January 1666), which devastated his former teachers and spiritual guides? In this missive, the young man expressed his conviction that Jansenism was on the decline, that Nicole's writing was pedantic, and that he was jealous of the worldly success of others. Racine added that since Nicole's morality was so austere, his condemnation of poets in general was understandable, but not his determination to divest others of the right of "honoring them" (Jasinski 1958, 159; Racine 1950, 1:24).

Bitterness and pain spread through Jansenist circles; the fathers of Port-Royal were seemingly unable to comprehend or to accept the vicious assault by one of their sons. Two anonymous pro-Jansenist letters that circulated at the time—*Answer to the Letter against the "Imaginary Heresies" and the "Visionaries"* (January 1966) and *Answer Addressed to the Author of the "Imaginary Heresies"* (April 1666)—accused Racine of speaking with the vanity of a pagan and of ridiculing humility, virtue, and penitence, the saintliest of actions and the most Christian of qualities (Jasinski 1958, 170).

Racine's reply, *Letter to the two Apologists of the Author of the "Imaginary Heresies"* (May 1666), was so vitriolic that his friends, so it is surmised, prevailed upon him not to have it published, although copies of it circulated in Paris. Meanwhile, Racine had acquired such a formidable reputation as a polemicist that the archbishop of Paris offered him a canonry if he would continue his attacks on Port-Royal (Picard 1961, 23).

Despite his repudiation by the Jansenist fathers, Racine enjoyed a momentous and stormy career as both womanizer and dramatist. In each successive play—his works, in order, were *Andromache, Britannicus, Bérénice, Bajazet, Mithridates, Iphigenia,* and *Phaedra*—he explored a variety of emotions, ranging from the most sublime to the most insidiously destructive. His output must have helped him work through his anxieties, hatreds, and jealousies, as well as his spiritual aspirations and drive for liberation.

With the writing and production of *Phaedra* in 1677, the pent-up poisons within his psyche had seemingly been ejected, cleansing his mind and body and bringing him a sense of balance. Abandoning the theater, he became officially reconciled with his Jansenist masters, whose counsel he henceforth followed assiduously. When they suggested a marriage to the pious, placid (and, strangely enough, unlettered) Catherine de Romanet, he acquiesced. She was a perfect mate for the superemotional playwright.

Turning from the creation of plays to that of progeny, Racine fathered seven children. He was named advisor to Louis XIV and became official court historiographer. His bourgeois existence and repudiation of the theater calmed his tempestuous emotions, his life became orderly, and he achieved a sense of harmony and well-being. The divine assumed a primary role in his life; God became the frame of reference from which all else seemed to emerge.

Twelve years following the production of *Phaedra*, Racine acquiesced to the request of the devout Madame de Maintenon, the wife of Louis XIV, to write "edifying" plays for the pupils of Saint-Cyr, a school for young ladies of impoverished noble families that she had founded. To conform to her desire, Racine wrote *Esther* and *Athaliah*.

It would appear, then, that prior to and during the creation of *Phaedra* Racine had undergone an intense inner illumination. His faith glowed within him like a cool blue flame.

Archetypal Analysis

Phaedra

A quotation from Saint Matthew best synthesizes Phaedra's own beliefs. "I say to you that everyone who looks at a woman lustfully has already committed adultery with her in his heart" (5:28). By assimilation, *Phaedra* signals Racine's own overt return to the Jansenist credo.

His reborn spirituality aroused in him such compassion for Phaedra's desperate lovesickness that he drew her in "a little less odious" manner, he noted in his preface, than had Euripides. Rather than highlighting this protagonist's tragic but murderous jealousy, he stressed the nobility of her character: her integrity and virtue. In defense of Phaedra's actions and reactions, Racine's two other avowals concerning his heroine revealed his own emotional needs at this time.

> Phaedra is neither altogether guilty nor altogether innocent. She is committed by her destiny, and by the anger of the gods, to an illegitimate

passion which she is the first to abominate. She tries her best to vanquish it. She prefers to let herself die rather than reveal it to anyone. And when she is compelled to disclose it, she speaks of it with an agitation which clearly indicates that her crime is rather a punishment of the gods than of her own volition. (*CP*, 2:233)

The author thus made a point of insisting on the drama's utterly moral nature.

The least faults are severely punished in it. The mere thought of crime is here regarded with as much horror as crime itself. The weaknesses of love are shown here as true weaknesses. The passions are only portrayed to expose all the chaos of which they are the cause, and vice is here throughout painted in colors which make its hideousness known and hated. Such is the proper aim that any man who works for the public should cherish. (2:235)

Her mind already troubled, Phaedra suffered further through the extremes of her highly moral standards. The outside world, aware only of her physical and mental deterioration, was not privy to her increasingly corrosive sense of culpability. She still remained free of censure. Like the man in Saint Matthew's admonition, she assumed responsibility for her thoughts, feelings, and acts, thereby becoming her own executioner.

Guilty of harboring an incestuous passion for her stepson, Hippolytus, she did not yet feel entrapped and crushed, because as long as her crime lay buried within her and remained nonverbalized, it lived as an abstract notion of the mind. Despair, as well as the urgency of having to reveal her gnawing secret, served to constrict her speech—as does a metastasizing throat cancer. Comparable to the surgeon who attempts to excise all malignant cells, Phaedra would meticulously cut out her pain through confession. Ablation through disclosure, she believed, would be curative. She also knew that excruciating pain awaited her—whether her passion remained secreted within her soul/ psyche or whether it was revealed to the world at large.

One of her earliest attempts to deal with her anguish was to exile Hippolytus from the court, erroneously believing that by so doing she would cut him from her mind and encourage a more salubrious inflow of preoccupations. Her perfectly reasonable system of healing her psychosis was to no avail. The use of logic and rational methodology to clarify her irrational disorders simply increased the acuteness of her torment.

Phaedra's Fall and Redemption

Phaedra's fall and, by the same token, her redemption unfolded in three successive stages: her confession first to Oenone; her confession then to Hippolytus; and finally, the handling of her illicit love in the world of *reality*.

Because Phaedra's sickness—her secret guilt—seems to be all-consuming at the outset of the play, she is pictured as a prey to mental derangement and close to death. Only she, however, is cognizant of the feelings of mortification that are slowly devouring her being. Not only is she unable to sleep; she feels that "eternal chaos broods within her mind." That havoc manifests itself physically is evident from her own description of the extreme weakness that overcomes her body and her vision. Her "eyes" are dazzled and blinded by the light of day, which she both despises and longs for (*CP*, 2:24).

Phaedra's ambivalent attitudes toward day and night (act 1, scene 3) mirror an inner turmoil caused by her passion for Hippolytus and her moral determination to banish it from her psyche. Racine conveys her extreme agitation in flamboyant color tones: although she is enticed by the dark chthonic powers corroding her being, she flees them in her yearning for the brilliance of purity.

Similarly, an antithetical interplay of light and dark expresses Hippolytus's devotion to his deity, Diana/Artemis. Although Phaedra despises blackness, she forever searches for "the shadow of the forest"—that is, for Hippolytus, whose domain as hunter and worshiper of an aspect of Mother Nature lies in wooded areas far from cities and settlements. Phaedra's love-hate for light and dark powers, so polarized in her mind's eye, may also be considered as metaphors reflecting her emotional state.

The chthonic realm of darkness and secrecy would bury her festering wound, she reasons. But is she longing for secrecy? or does she yearn to be with her would-be lover?

> How sweet to sit amid the shaded woods!
> When might I follow through the noble dust
> A chariot driven breakneck in the track?
>
> (*CP*, 2:14)

In her blind turmoil, her aimless wandering entraps her still further. Her attempt to control her secret by imposing her imperious will upon her mouth, her annihilation of the word and the thought, serves only to increase her passion. As a fungus thrives in dark, damp realms, so does her obsession take on energy.

If we glance at Phaedra's heritage, we better understand why images of night and day are basic to her psychology. She is the granddaughter of Helios, the sun. Her mother, Pasiphae, fell in love with a white bull that Neptune had presented to her husband, Minos, king of Crete. The offspring of this union was the Minotaur, the monster for whom the labyrinth was constructed and who became the vehicle for the Nature Goddess to impose her will in the Cretan myth. (It must be noted in connection with this legend that the Creto-Mycenean culture was a patriarchate in its earliest days, but was transformed into a partial matriarchate—a land in which the Great Mother archetype prevailed.)

The adored Nature Goddess inhabited caves and forests. Her consort, the bull, a symbol of fertility, was looked upon as both a youthful god (her son-lover) and as the Nature Goddess's victim (Neumann 1970, 77).

The responsibility for sending "Aphrodite mania," or "Venus mania," to the goddess's enemy Phaedra lay with the Great Mother, as manifested in Venus/Aphrodite. (Racine refers to Aphrodite as Venus throughout the play, and we will do likewise.) The madness, verging on the psychotic in the case of both Pasiphae and her daughter, Phaedra, consisted of unbridled sexuality and uncontrollable hysteria.

Phaedra's relegation of the mania to the depths of her unconscious had the same effect as starving a hungry animal, which then grows vicious and uncontrollable. On the contrary, by feeding the so-called beast within a person, however, that person may gain release from a mania through a process of understanding.

Phaedra's obsessions surge forth in all their excess and fury during the course of the play, causing her to be identified with an aspect of the Great Mother, of whom she is a victim. She is neither a suprapersonal power like Venus nor a depersonalized being like the suffering Pasiphae. What sets Phaedra apart and increases her fascination for modern audiences is Racine's reevaluation of the feminine principle in terms of this legendary figure.

As the daughter of Pasiphae and the granddaughter of Helios, Phaedra possesses characteristics of both instinctuality and lucidity. From her mother, a mortal woman, Phaedra had inherited a propensity for lustful passion; from her grandfather, an incisive eye—consciousness. It was Helios, let us recall, who indiscreetly shed light in the skies, dispersing the cloud that hid Venus and Mars as they were making love. Venus, in retaliation, cursed all of Helios's descendants, including Phaedra.

Confession: Undoing? or Salvation?

Oenone, Phaedra's beloved confidante, prods her mistress into disclosing the source of her pain. Her confession is the first step in what may be viewed as either her *undoing* or as her *salvation*.

Blaming Venus for her "fatal anger," Phaedra reveals to Oenone that the source of her passion is divine and therefore uncontrollable. "My pain [evil] goes back further," she cries out (*CP*, 2:251). That her sickness has been divinely sent may be understood in Greek and in Jansenist terms as having been predestined—she is fated to be tossed between the dictates of her conscience (originating in the solar principle, or in God for the Jansenist) and her human instinct. No effort can stymie the continuous course of her illicit love. Yet she continues to fight this frenzied power within her. Greatly weakened by her attempt to excise it, she nonetheless moves from darkness toward semiclarity. But the light of day, or the light of consciousness, finds her increasingly enfeebled. Because she can no longer sleep or eat, with Oenone's encouragement she allows what she considers to be her inner pollution to ooze forth, like pus from a boil.

> I saw, I blushed, I paled at sight of him;
> A strange disquiet seized my stricken soul;
> My eyes could see no more, I could not speak;
> I felt my body burn and freeze in turn;
> I recognized the fearful sting of Venus,
> The destined torments of the blood she hunts.
>
> (2:250)

Phaedra informs Oenone how with method, order, and good intent she prayed to and honored Venus, lighting fires, erecting altars, and sacrificing to the goddess. In her prayers to Venus, she asks paradoxically for the obliteration of love and sexuality—the very forces for which this deity stands. Unable or unwilling to understand the "blood" price demanded by Venus for redemption, Phaedra fights an ineffective battle to subjugate her sensuality.

With the intrusion of daylight into her darkness, her increasing self-knowledge serves only to accentuate the abrasiveness of her conflict. No longer, she realizes, is she in a position to obliterate what her ego (center of consciousness, or religious attitude) finds so distasteful. Thus has her entire existence turned into a prolonged flagellation.

At once my wound, still open, gushed afresh,
It's no mere passion tingling in my veins;
It's Venus tense extended on her prey!

                                   (*CP*, 2:251)

Her speech, still constellated with sun imagery—fire, torch, blood, illumination, brilliance, day, eye—represents the smarting, flaying, abrading sensations aroused by the light of consciousness flowing through shaded inner space. Because Phaedra is unable to assimilate the insights provided by her vision, she becomes, ironically, the sun's victim, deluded by the very knowledge she believes it imparts to her.

Images such as veils, jewels, and baubles of all types are introduced into the text by Racine to indicate Phaedra's craving to throw off the weight of her burden. She finds her queenly garments and accoutrements difficult to bear. Considered symbolically, these objects may be viewed as masks serving to hide her pain and as veils to obscure the evil that gnaws at her vitals.

And heavy are these veils, these baubles vain.
And whose unwelcomed hand, with all these knots,
Has on my brow with care arranged my hair?
Oh, all of you pursue and persecute me!

                                   (*CP*, 2:245)

The above lines refer also to the role played by Helios in revealing Venus's escapade with Mars. The sun had dispersed the cloud that hid the lovers, snatching their veil-like coverings from them and disclosing their lustful antics. Venus and Mars reacted angrily; unlike them, Phaedra desires her grandfather's light to shine on her and reveal her corrosive guilt. Once her dismal veil would be snatched from her, she would be free to earn her redemption via humiliation—an ordeal, like any rite of passage, that is difficult and often requires the experience of death.

The drama's entire frame of reference suddenly changes with the false announcement of Theseus's demise (act 1, scene 4). No longer is it a question of deceiving Theseus or of committing so-called incest, but simply of confessing what was considered in patriarchal societies the "shameful" love an older woman bears for a virgin boy.

Phaedra fantasizes about Hippolytus, the immaculate hunter who roams the woods, whose strength is unparalleled, whose youth is extraordinary in its freshness. He is par excellence the young male fully attuned to nature, living out a *participation mystique* with earthly forces, reveling in the paradise of the Ouroboric state. So distant from Phaedra's polluted self-image is this realm of pristine cleanliness, of untouched, unlived, undeveloped, and un–differentiated wholeness, that union with it would cleanse her soul of its detritus.

To have a son as a lover, however, is contrary to nature. According to traditional seventeenth-century views, the mother (like the father, in Judeo-Christian societies), representative of past and worn concepts, must be su-perseded by a girl who is either younger than or the same age as the son. Youth, a time of intense activity and burgeoning creativity, is crucial to the growth of nations and cultures. Thus two worlds or two generations must not meld, but follow in succession. So long as Phaedra's love remains unspo-ken, her secret is safe. Once it is divulged, she will be transformed in Hip-polytus's eyes into a vitriolic power ready to crush and mutilate her beautiful prey.

Following the news of Theseus's death, Oenone, considered by some critics an evil force, attempts to diminish Phaedra's misery and convinces her to reveal her love to Hippolytus. In reality, Oenone, the instigator of action, plays a role similar to that of the Serpent in the Adam and Eve myth. Just as no development would have occurred had Eve not yearned for wisdom—the fruit of the Tree of Knowledge—so would there have been no drama, no action, and no redemption had Oenone's suggestion not been acted upon. Let us note that Oenone, who had given up her own personal life as a young girl to care for Phaedra, is motivated by love and not evil. Nevertheless she serves as a sort of agent provocateur, injecting motility into what would otherwise have remained stagnant.

Phaedra's confession to Oenone suffices only to increase her torment. Her speech becomes confused, even aphasic, and she lapses into irrational modulations, losing her train of thought, her verbal direction, and her iden-tity. "Now I have forgotten what I came to say" (*CP*, 2:262). Momentary speechlessness generally indicates an unconscious desire to guard one's secret and reveals the emergence from within of an uncontrollable will or suprapersonal force seeking to protect one from the dangerous unknown.

> I seem to see my husband still before me.
> I see, I speak, my heart. . . . Where am I straying?
> My lord, my raving love breaks out despite me.
>
> (2:263)

A startling sequence—one of the most extraordinary in all French theater—then unfolds as Phaedra, diving ever more deeply into her own abyss, lapses into yet another irrational mode, her words cascading into what seems to be senseless obscurity and ambiguity. Linear space/time concepts are obliterated from her mind; past and present are fused in nontime. Phaedra looks upon Hippolytus, not as he is in actuality, but as she had once gazed upon the young and brave Theseus: "Engaging, young, bewitching every heart" (2:264). Father and son have become one in her mind, each a mirror image of the other. Hippolytus having been transformed into Theseus, she sees herself as Ariadne and relives the entire Minotaur legend, not as an onlooker but as a participant. No longer limp and weak, she assumes the stature of a visionary, a Delphic oracle, declaring that Theseus, having visited the "marshes of the dead," will never return. Phaedra feels an affinity with the labyrinth, from which the Athenian hero had escaped thanks to Ariadne's love and the skein she provided him. Indeed, Phaedra had always been jealous of her sister, whose role in Theseus's life had made her a savior figure. The transference of identities that has been effected indicates a rejection of herself as Phaedra. As a premonitory image, it suggests an unconscious longing on her part for death.

Accompanying her identification with the Virgin Princess Ariadne, Phaedra withdraws so deeply into her labyrinthian, or chthonic, domain, that she experiences a total eclipse of reality—of the world she cannot face.

> I, Prince, alone, my vital help alone
> Would have taught you the Labyrinth's twists and turns.
> How many cares your dear head would have cost me.
> A thread would not have satisfied your lover.
> Companion in the risk you have to brave,
> I would myself have run ahead of you;
> And Phaedra, down with you in the Labyrinth,
> Would have returned with you or with you perished.
>   (2:264)

Since Phaedra is so closely associated with the labyrinth, it behooves us to examine this symbol more closely. Designed by Daedalus to house the Minotaur in Crete, the labyrinth was so complex a structure that anyone lost in it was trapped for life. Penetration into this maze symbolizes a test, an exciting journey, an initiation into another dimension of existence—a rite of passage. Theseus entered the labyrinth only temporarily, to fulfill the hero's goal: the killing of the Minotaur. Psychologically the labyrinth has been compared to the unconscious: a dark, thus visionless, inner space, where the irrational and the chaotic dominate. Phaedra's eclipse of lucidity does not, therefore, augur well. Unprepared to experience her labyrinthian test, she becomes the maze's quarry, caught in this intricate network of shadowy halls and chambers. Reliving more and more intensely her sister's experience, Phaedra sees herself leading Hippolytus/Theseus out of the labyrinth—out of chaos into the world of light. Such role reversal—regression into early behavioral levels—causes her further to lose her own identity.

The symbology of the Minotaur is, understandably, intricately connected with Phaedra's own mother's plight. The fruit of Pasiphae's love for a white bull, the Minotaur is a monster whose lower half is that of a man and whose upper half that of a bull. This inversion of the Platonic notion (the upper half of man being his godly side and the lower the beast in him) indicates that the mind has degenerated into carnivorousness and destructiveness. Phaedra's living out of her Minotaur vision suggests an animalization in her psyche, her head having regressed to an anthropoid state.

Theseus's killing of the monster was the equivalent of vanquishing instinct that, in the guise of the Minotaur, had become a tyrannical and destructive force. Phaedra's reactualization of the Ariadne-Theseus story indicates her longing to participate in it as Hippolytus's savior figure. Only the destruction of the Minotaur will cleanse her soul/psyche of its monstrous inclinations. Her vision growing increasingly clouded and her verbiage more and more incoherent, Phaedra plunges into the depths of her own mazelike darkness. A sense of entrapment and paralysis encapsulates her, as do feelings of self-hate. She yearns, as previously indicated, to do away with her despicable self.

> Well then, now Phaedra, in her naked frenzy.
> I am in love. Do not think, though I love you,
> I approve my love or deem it innocent;
> Nor that a craven self-indulgence has
> Nourished the poison of my insane passion.
> Unhappy target of the spite of Heaven,
> I loathe myself much more than you abhor me.
>   (2:266)

She begs Hippolytus, who has reacted with such revulsion to her passion, to take up his sword against her.

Come, here your hand must strike.
Impatient now to expiate its crime. . . .

(2:266)

But Hippolytus is devoid of murderous instinct, and Phaedra seizes his sword, declaring that if he cannot muster the strength, she herself will perform the deed.

No sooner does Phaedra recover from her affective onslaught than she is overcome with shame at the very thought of her confession: "I've uttered words no human ear should hear" (2:268). Urgently, she seeks to return to labyrinthine darkness. Stark dejection, abjection, and guilt overwhelm her.

Alone with Oenone again, her weakened state having divested her of all judgmental faculties, she is encouraged by her confidante to once again listen to her counsel. Now that Theseus has been declared dead, Phaedra should reign over the land of Troezen and then offer Hippolytus the crown. Phaedra rejects the shocking idea at first.

I, reign! Impose my will upon the people,
When my weak reason reigns no more o'er me!
When I have lost dominion o'er my passion!
When I can barely breathe beneath my shame!

(*CP*, 2:269)

But finally her distorted mind begins to accept Hippolytus as her husband—and then the shock of reality intrudes. Theseus is not dead after all and has returned unexpectedly. Fearful of the king's revenge upon her mistress should he discover the truth, Oenone attempts to persuade Phaedra to accuse Hippolytus of having wanted to seduce her. Again revolted at first, Phaedra withers into submission.

Your tears prevailed upon my true remorse.
I would have died this morning, winning pity;
I took your counsels and dishonoured die.

. . . .
I dare, to brand and blacken innocence.

(2:272, 273)

That Phaedra subsequently disclaims responsibility for her confession to Hippolytus in no way alleviates her excoriating feelings of shame, which are so intense that her psychological center is totally displaced and all balance is shattered. Death, as previously intimated, remains her only exit. "Let me die. May death my shame forgive!" (2:272).

Although Theseus accuses his son of a heinous crime, for the first time Hippolytus shows strength of character. By refusing to reveal the truth that would inculpate Phaedra, he hopes to spare his father pain. By way of defending his innocence, however, Hippolytus reveals that he has countered one of his father's interdicts by cherishing a love for Aricia, whose entire "race" Theseus had condemned to annihilation. So fraught with anger is Theseus that he not only curses his son but calls upon Neptune to avenge him.

Phaedra's impulse to persuade Theseus not to punish his son alters considerably when she learns of Hippolytus's love for Aricia. Unable to endure the humiliation of rejection, her pride utterly crushed, the Terrible Mother in Phaedra swells to the point of incandescence.

> Of this most sacred Sun from whom I've sprung?
> My forebear is father, master of the gods;
> The sky, the whole world's full of my forefathers.
> Where may I hide? Flee to infernal night.
> How? There my father holds the urn of doom;
> Fate placed it, so they say, in his stern hands.
>
> (2:288)

As the waters of her unconscious swirl, she is affected with hallucinations: before her, stands Minos, her father, in his guise of judge in the Underworld, before whom she, one of the "pale" humans, passes. She perceives him shuddering as he listens to her ghastly story.

> Minos in Hades judges all the shades.
> Ah, how his stricken ghost will start and shudder,
> When he beholds his daughter come before him,
> Compelled her trembling trespasses to tell,
> And crimes perhaps unheard of even in Hell!
> What will you say, my father, at this horror?
>
> (2:288)

What Phaedra is observing is her own judgmental capacity—or conscience—projected onto her father. Her sense of righteousness as manifested in patriarchal terms is an aspect of her own spirit of authority, which lives powerfully within her—as does her grandfather's clarity of mind in the sun.

The motherly Oenone again intrudes with advice designed to protect her beloved mistress. Seeking to calm her, to reason with her, to release her from her guilt and shame, she suggests that Phaedra, a mere human, must accept her guilt, for even the gods have indulged in terrifying crimes.

Turning on Oenone like a viper, Phaedra spews forth her venom, blaming her confidante for her plight. "I will not hear you more. Get out, you demon," she cries (*CP*, 2:288). Blazing with renewed fury, Phaedra unwittingly destroys the one person who loved her: Oenone will drown herself.

The Eye of God, first mentioned at the outset of the drama—Phaedra's instrument of perception and symbol of her highly developed conscience— observes her *plain*. Discerner of the blackest of intents, this Eye pursues the sinner unrelentingly—as Saint Matthew admonished—and lives out its existence as torturer. Now prepared for the ultimate sacrifice, Phaedra takes poison, and then confesses her truth to Theseus. Although she assumes the blame for her "incestuous" and "adulterous" love, she places the onus for having revealed it on the "detestable Oenone." In death, Phaedra enters the Underworld, "the earthly womb" of the ancients, thus paving the way for her eventual transformation and redemption (Neumann 1970, 77).

Hippolytus

Because Hippolytus, psychologically speaking, is the carrier of consciousness in Racine's drama, it is through his presence that Phaedra will experience her transformation.

Hippolytus typifies the mythological figure of the son as lover, experiencing the same fate as his forebears—Pentheus, Narcissus, Actaeon—except that he, like Phaedra, lives on a higher psychological level. Although devoted to Diana, the goddess of chastity and of the hunt, he is, unlike Euripides' protagonist, capable of loving a woman. He is attracted, however, not to the lascivious Phaedra, but to the spiritually oriented and moral Aricia— a choice indicating a higher (that is, a more developed) consciousness on his part, rather than a lower masculine drive based on phallic worship, and implying an affinity with the "solar" (that is, the thinking/thoughtful) principle.

From the very outset of the drama we learn that Hippolytus, although seeking to emulate his father, clearly distinguishes his *noble* from his *ignoble* deeds.

> Since no such monsters crushed by me till now
> Have given me the right to err like him!
>
> (*CP*, 2:242)

His father's "youthful errors," such as his "inconstancy," are condemnable, but his "noble exploits" admirable.

Important is Hippolytus's insight into himself. He is cognizant, for example, that he is still very much an adolescent, that he is indolent, and that he lives a shadowlike existence in the heart of the forest. His awareness of his weaknesses drives him to overcome his natural bent and go beyond his ordinary lifestyle, to become a hero.

At first Hippolytus is a dutiful son, refusing to act against his father's will, particularly since Theseus is away from home. He cannot, however, accept all of the paternal interdicts, and particularly execrable to him is his father's relentless determination to extinguish Aricia's lineage. It is Theseus, then, who unwittingly has created the conflict within Hippolytus between his desire for Aricia and the submission to authority ingrained in him. The antinomy will pave the way for Hippolytus's evolution.

Although as yet unable to articulate or assess the meaning of his love for Aricia, Hippolytus early on detects a change in himself. Psychologically, we may say that he is emerging from his Ouroboric stage, in which a child feels a participation mystique or oneness with everything around him. Hippolytus's former undifferentiated approach to life was based on a primordial identification with Diana, the goddess of the chase, whose habitat is the obscure forest, so frequently associated with the Great Mother. Now he is able to discern contrasting color tones and textures in this realm overrun with luxurious foliage and largely inaccessible to the sun, which suggests that his affinity with Diana is receding.

Theramenes, Hippolytus's tutor, also notes a change in the young man, who seemingly is not indifferent to women and penetrates the forest less frequently than before. Theramenes has also become aware of a growing feeling of independence within Hippolytus.

> Admit the change in you; for some time now
> You are less often seen, proud and untamed,
> Driving a chariot furious on the shore,
> Or expert in the art that Neptune fashioned,
> Breaking a champing, rearing charger in.
> Less often without shouts the woods re-echo;

> Charged with a hidden fire, your eyes grow heavy,
> Why, there is no mistake, you burn with love;
> You sicken with an ill you would conceal.
>
> (*CP*, 2:243)

Having reached a new stage in his psychological development, Hippolytus will struggle to liberate himself further from what is commonly termed the domination of "world parents." Ironically, it was his father, the very person from whom he sought to escape, who, as previously noted, had forced open his son's eyes. "Theseus opens your eyes, wishing to close them," notes Theramenes (2:243).

Hippolytus voices the "embarrassment" and "despair" of the sensitive adolescent who is aroused for the first time by the opposite sex. Naively and candidly he describes himself to Aricia as "rash" and as "proud," and then discloses the fight he has been waging to subdue his emotions: "I flee your presence; find you in your absence" (2:260). But just as Hippolytus remains incised in Phaedra's mind, so Aricia's image pursues him into "the forest," Diana's sanctuary.

> Your face pursues me in the deepest woods;
> The light of day, the shadows of the night
> Thrust in my eyes the loveliness I flee . . .
> My chariot, javelins, bow, all weary me;
> No more do I remember Neptune's lessons;
> My moans alone re-echo through the woods,
> My steeds stand dull and know my voice no more.
>
> (2:260)

The fact that Hippolytus carries Aricia as a mental image (a waking or sleeping dream) into the forest indicates her invasion of and dominion over both his conscious and unconscious worlds. His newly blossoming feelings born from his love for Aricia have so altered his outlook on life that he no longer understands himself. "I seek myself and find myself no more" (2:260). His transformation underscores a departure—or passage—from adolescence into maturity, as already indicated. It reveals also the burgeoning of his ego— a growing sense of identity and self-worth.

No longer ruled by undifferentiated pulsations (forest, unconscious, darkness), Hippolytus begins to seek out the world about him for the first time. He observes it with fascination but, paradoxically, with relative objectivity, and thus begins to understand his function within it. The more his love for Aricia expands his self-consciousness and concomitant understanding of his motivations, the more he opens himself up to a fuller life experience.

To complicate matters, Hippolytus, although the object of Phaedra's desire, is also a reflection of her. As is evident from Racine's imagery, he holds the same relationship to Phaedra as the moon to the sun: he worships Diana/the Moon Goddess, just as Phaedra worships her grandfather, Sun/Helios. Moreover, both are embroiled in forbidden loves, Phaedra with her husband's son and Hippolytus with the daughter of his father's enemy.

Seeking a modus vivendi with his father on his return, Hippolytus emphasizes his innocence with regard to Phaedra and says no more. His silence endows him with a new sense of dignity, a moral strength, and a nobility of intention. He reveals his love for and intention to marry Aricia, thereby rejecting his father's orders and provoking his wrath. In so doing, he does not take on the stature of a flamboyant hero in battle, but, rather, of a reasoning and reasonable man of principle—just as he chose nonaction when Phaedra seized his sword. Had he retaken possession of the shining blade, symbol of courage, he would have weakened his attempt to gain autonomy over himself.

Theseus's disbelief in his son's integrity thrusts Hippolytus into despair. "What friend will pity me when you forsake me?" (*CP*, 2:787). Exile alone awaits Hippolytus, who leaves his father's palace and city, only to be destroyed by the sea monster sent by Neptune in answer to Theseus's supplications. Symbol of cosmic forces or nonformal potentialities, the monstrous entity with horns and scales, looking like a bull, a dragon, and a horse, erupts like a volcano, without forewarning and with devastating results. A companion of the Great Mother, it emerges roaring from under the waters and lashes about on land. It makes its way toward Hippolytus, who hurls his javelin against the creature, wounding it. Writhing in pain, the animal exhales flame, and Hippolytus's horses, insane with fear, run wild, dragging Theseus's son to his death.

> Meanwhile, surged forth from the sea a mountainous wave,
> With wild sea horses lashed to furious spray;
> The flood approached us, broke and vomited
> A monster raging through the quivering spume.
> His forehead wide was bristling sharp with horns;
> And all his body nailed with tawny scales;
> Indomitable bull or dragon bold.

With fleshy haunches tortuous fold on fold.
His long-drawn bellows set the seashore trembling.
The sky with horror viewed his monstrous rumbling,
The earth was all aquiver, air infected,
The waves that spewed him forth drew back deflected. . . .
Alone Hippolytus, a hero's son,
Halted steeds and seized his javelins,
Aimed at the monster and with expert throw
Wounded him deeply, tearing wide his flank.
Leaping with rage and pain the monster now
Falls bellowing at the startled horses' feet,
Rolls on his back, thrust forth his flaming jaw,
Engulfing them in fire and blood and smoke.
Sheer panic seizes them, and deaf to all,
Nor rein nor voice restrains them any more.
Their master, powerless, tries to hold them back—
The bit runs red with dark and bloody foam.
Some even say they saw, amid the affright,
A god who pricked with spurs their dusty flanks.
Fear hurls them hurtling on across the rocks;
The axle creaks and snaps. The bold Hippolytus
Sees all his shattered chariot fly in pieces;
He falls himself entangled in the reins. . . .
Dragged by the very steeds his hands have fed.
He calls to them; his voice now frightens them;
They gallop on, with him—one gaping wound.
The plain reverberates with our mournful cries.

(*CP*, 2:298)

The horses that finally dragged Hippolytus to his death were sacred to Neptune. Any struggle against a god generally leads to the loss of one's life. Hippolytus had "dared" to scorn Phaedra, a vehicle of Venus's will. This in itself was punishable by death. Venus, called the "foam-born" and identified with water, symbolized the fertile power that nourished the sea monster within its depths. As an agent of destruction in Racine's play, it is she, in her "monstrous" and not in her "beautiful" form, who arose from the sea to cause the young hero's demise. Thus had Hippolytus's fight for autonomy been transformed into a flagellation, in punishment of his rebellious approach to life.

Theseus

Theseus, the founder of Athens and by reputation the prototype of the hero, was the son of Neptune and of Aetra, who according to some legends had been impregnated by Neptune and by King Aegeus on the same night. Still a youth, Theseus braved the world, slaying the Minotaur, the monster at Epidaurus, and the wild sow near Attica. Although raised in a patriarchate in which supposedly sterling masculine principles had been instilled in him, he succumbed to less lofty objects of desire and lusted for sexual adventure. Having fallen victim to the hubris that frequently swells so many heroes, Theseus inadvertently paved the way for the eventual victory of Venus.

Racine's Theseus has, however, few of the characteristics of the great hero of antiquity. At the beginning of the play, he is thought to be dead—and he was, psychologically, just that, having lost his energetic and visionary approach to life. Though Hippolytus sought to emulate his valor, strength, and rational personality traits, he scorned his impulsive nature, which placed him under the sway of the Great Mother. For Phaedra, Theseus the man was nonexistent. In her clouded mind, he was Hippolytus reborn—young, forceful, godlike, and the heroic killer of the Minotaur.

Thought to be dead, Theseus was really in the Underworld, suggesting a regression into an unconscious or primal state. He was said to be surrounded in Hades by phantoms: archetypes representing his fears and anguish—those very powers he had never had the courage to face during his tension-filled youth. Upon emerging from the Underworld, or from his unconscious, he found himself unable to adjust to the situation confronting him in his kingdom. His perceptions and acuity having been dulled, he had lost the ability to communicate with the outside world and to relate to past and present, or unconscious and conscious, contents.

In the face of Hippolytus's confession, he cannot equate the purity he reads on his son's face with the blackness of his crime. Rather than assess the situation analytically, he reacts affectively, allowing his anger to burgeon. In this instance, Theseus is indeed Neptune's rightful heir, stirring as he does the inner seas of his unconscious. Utterly possessed by his daemon, he pronounces his curse: "Chased by an avenging god, escape you cannot" (2:284). Once the light of reason returns, however, he sees himself—the very cause of his son's death—and suffers pain.

"The horror of remorse," guilt, self-accusation, self-deprecation, and self-flagellation are the predominant themes of Racine's play. Phaedra's agony and growing consciousness of her judgmental error led to her demise as well as to the symbolic death of the love with which she had been identified. Having faced herself, experienced her guilt as a projection onto her father Minos in Hades, and then confessed to Theseus, she earned the flaying pain accompanying her yearned-for redemption.

Identifying with Phaedra, Racine saw his protagonist's suffering and death ritual as a mirror image of his own. Just as Phaedra had earned her redemption with the sacrifice of her life, so Racine earned his by rejecting his life of playwright/philanderer—a world he now understood to be degrading and sinful—and returning to the Jansenist fold. Phaedra and Racine had both been relentlessly pursued by what the Greeks called the Furies and the Christians the "horror of remorse," against which Saint Matthew cautioned:

> And if thy right eye offend thee, pluck it out, and cast it from thee: for it is profitable for thee that one of thy members should perish, and not that thy whole body should be cast into hell.
>
> And if thy right hand offend thee, cut it off, and cast it from thee: for it is profitable for thee that one of thy members should perish, and not that thy whole body should be cast into hell. (5:28–30)

6 Yeats's *Deirdre:*
An Irish Celtic Feminist
and Heroine

In composing his play *Deirdre* (1907), Yeats turned toward a mythical past—a period in Irish/Celtic culture filled with fabulous and heroic happenings. By reactualizing for his audiences great historical, philosophical, religious, and psychological truths, Yeats succeeded in integrating bygone days into a present reality. Fleshing out energetic patterns of behavior, he expanded the consciousness of the viewers of his play.

Deirdre, as both a personal and transcendental power, is one of Ireland's national heroines. Her inner strength and fortitude is so haunting, the poetry of her words so mesmerizing, her courage in the face of death so astounding, that she gives the impression of having stepped out of another sphere. Autonomous and objective, this archetypal figure exists within and outside of linear time, in a reversible present—in a fourth dimension or space-time continuum. For this reason she responds to universal and eternal needs, depending upon the person and/or the culture projecting on her.

Although the guiding value and single passion of this solitary woman was to live a shared life with the young warrior Naoise, she nonetheless represents a woman's will for independence. The fire burning in the deepest folds of her psyche, viewed from either a masculine or feminine point of view, made a powerful impact in her time, as attested to by the popularity of legends and fairy tales surrounding and paralleling the Deirdre love motif: *The Exile of the Sons of Uisliu; The Pursuit of Diarmaid and Grainne; Trystan and Isyllt, Noisiu and Derdriu, The Nibelungenlied,* and so on. Deirdre's all-consuming passion still stirs a twentieth-century society, as evidenced by William Sharp's *House of Usna* (1900), Herbert Trench's *Deirdre Wedded* (1901), Lady Gregory's *The Fate of the Sons of Usnach* (1902), John M. Synge's *Deirdre of the Sorrows*

(1909), and James Stephens's *Deirdre* (1923), to mention but a few (Fackler 1978, 111).

Ectypal Analysis

Because the Deirdre myth is a product of Ireland's early times, our ectypal analysis will focus both on this country's beginnings and on those factors which inspired Yeats to spawn his play.

Ireland's Early Times

Although they are shrouded in mystery, the earliest inhabitants of Ireland are known to have lived in the Middle Stone Age or Mesolithic period. Archaeologists believe the objects found in Limerick and Carlow—flint instruments, probably used to skin birds and fish, and stones for smoothing and hammering—date from about 6000 B.C.E. The utensils unearthed suggest the presence of tribes that had crossed from Scandinavia to Britain, then on to Scotland, and soon after to Ireland. By 3000 B.C.E. peoples from the Middle East seeking new farmlands traveled from Mediterranean regions to Spain and France, and then sailed north to Ireland. Found in Limerick have been fragments of pottery, stone axes, burial mounds (cairns), and massive monuments to the dead with "long galleries of huge stones" including "a forecourt or central open court where ceremonies could take place." Some "great megalithic cairns" discovered in county Sligo (where Yeats spent long periods of time) revealed burial chambers into which a "passage-grave" gave entrance. Equally intriguing for what is believed to be their religious significance are the complex patternings of spirals, lozenges, and zigzags found on the stones within the tombs at Newgrange (county Meath). Some authorities consider these images to be representations of a death goddess. From 2000 to 1200 B.C.E. metalworkers and prospectors, perhaps from the Middle East, emigrated to Ireland to mine and cast copper and gold, and to fashion jewelry such as torques, gorgets, and dress fasteners (Mitchell 1967, 32ff.). By 600 B.C.E. the first of several waves of Celts (named *Keltoi* by the Greeks) emigrated from Central and Western Europe to Ireland. Other Celtic tribes remained on the continent terrorizing Italy and Greece, and sacking Rome in 390 B.C.E. The Celtic culture of the fifth century, or the Late Iron Age—called La Tène, from the archeological site in Switzerland—was brought by a later group of Celts to Ireland around the second century B.C.E. It is believed that war trumpets and sword scabbards unearthed there had been worn by the Celtic warriors featured in such famous Irish sagas as *Tain Bo Cuailnge* (Byrne 1976, 43).

By the fifth century C.E., the date assigned to the beginning of Irish history and the end of the heroic age, the various populations inhabiting Ireland had not only absorbed Celtic culture but spoke a common language: Gaelic. Nevertheless, wars were still fierce and frequent. For example, the Ulster kingdom with its center of rule at Emain Macha, one of the most important political centers, was destroyed by Connachta (Connaught, another major state) in c. 450 C.E. (44ff.).

Farmers lived on their small tracts of land or on larger homesteads surrounded by an earthen rampart, while the spacious house of the king was enclosed by a double rampart, the outer one constructed by the king's "lower-grade vassals." Despite this architectural dichotomy, the king wielded little power: he could enact laws only in times of emergency, all power having been vested in the *brehons* (judges), a group who had completed law studies based on ancient Indo-European social concepts. The king's most important function was to lead his warriors into battle and to preside over the assembly held by his *tuath* (small local kingdom). The Irish kings, and the aristocracy in general, rooted as they were in the soil and measuring their wealth in terms of cattle and sheep, were generally traditionalists and adhered to tribal law and customs (46ff.; Snyder 1976, 26ff.).

The Fili *(Poet)*—*The* Bardd, *Druid*

The ancient Irish poets *(filid,* plural of *fili)* came from an elite, learned, and frequently hereditary class. They were considered seers endowed with prophetic talents and thus not to be confused with the simple *bardd,* also a poet or versifier, but of inferior rank. As transmitters of oral prose narratives, the *filid* set the standards, until the seventh century, for the intellectual life of the people and for the rules regarding rhythmical prose and verse. Knowledge was handed down orally from one generation to another by the *filid,* and their long and arduous training, lasting, according to some scholars, from seven to twelve years, consisted to a great extent of committing hundreds of tales to memory. As the repositories of tradition, they understandably held conservative views (Chadwick 1976, 263). It has been suggested that the *filid* commanded greater power than the kings, since they reached a larger audience and were in a position to manipulate public opinion.

A Druid, frequently alluded to as *magus,* was not only a wise man endowed with prophetic talents like a *fili* but was also well versed in the art of magic. Druids were teachers of a wide variety of subjects under the rubrics of astronomy, philosophy, and religion: the heavenly course of the stars, earth matters, and knowledge of their living/immortal gods. The Druid Cathbad, a significant figure in Yeats's *Deirdre*, is featured in some early Irish tales as teaching classes of young noblemen. Thus he, too, was a transmitter of legends and myths as well as of conventional learning (Piggott 1975, 108).

The Role of Women in Irish Society

Irish women, unlike their sisters in Greece, Rome, the Middle East, and elsewhere, enjoyed a virtually unique place in their society. Although they could not possess land, which was the property of the kingdom and thus held communally, they could own, lease, and breed livestock of their own. From their advantageous cattle-leasing contracts, moneys accrued to them, giving them control of some measure of wealth (Markale 1975, 32).

Although Irish society was patriarchal, the woman enjoyed considerable legal independence. Her fiancé, for example, was required to give a right of purchase (*coibche*, a kind of bride price) to his future father-in-law prior to his marriage. The bride, unlike a bride under Roman law, did not enter her husband's family, nor was she deprived of her personal possessions and property. Although she was expected to bring a dowry *(tinnscra)* to the marriage, it consisted of presents given her by her family. If she divorced and remarried, her father received only two-thirds of the *coibche,* the rest being hers. She also kept whatever she had acquired during her marriage. If a husband divorced his wife without cause in order to marry another woman, the first wife was protected by law: not only was her *coibche* returned to her, but the "price of honour" set for the second wife was likewise prescribed for the first wife. In cases of adultery, the wife could demand dissolution of the marriage (35ff.).

The man's position as nominal head of the family did not always mean that he exercised power over household affairs. If a wife was of the same social class as her husband and her fortune equaled his, she enjoyed equal rights with him. If she had less money than her husband and if she came from a lower class, those rights were diminished. In the epic *Tain Bo Cuailnge,* Queen Medb was featured as a warrior woman who, as commander-in-chief of the army, declared war in order to gain possession of the famous brown bull of Cuailnge. After her victory, her wealth surpassed that of her husband; she became unequivocally the head of the household, and he, "the man of service" (*fer fognama* = *fer for ban thincur* = "man under the power of woman"). Because her husband, King Ailill, could not, according to law, counter her decisions, she enjoyed both independence and rulership. It was she who rode and he who walked.

In the *Tain* as well as in other epics, Medb was considered a euhemeristic goddess known for her great sexual capacities. One of her most famous lovers—and a protagonist in Yeats's *Deirdre*—was the virile Fergus mac Roich, king of Emain, until he was unseated by Conchobar (Markale 1975, 37ff.; Byrne 1973, 51).

Irish women, whether married or not, could decide upon the roles they would play in society. No proof as yet has been found demonstrating that they were Druidesses, although it is known that they were sorceresses and prophetesses and could participate in the celebration of the Mass, despite denunciation of the practice on the continent by the Roman bishops. Monasteries in Ireland were institutions for both sexes, as attested to by the one founded by Saint Bridget on the emplacement of the ancient temple at Kildare. Importantly as well, it was the nuns who, like the Roman Vestal Virgins, constantly tended a sacred flame so that it would never die (Markale 1975, 38).

The custom of fosterage had been in place since pre-Celtic times in Ireland. Children without mothers of their own were entrusted to all types of mothers—from nurturers, to Amazons, to semiwitches, who are featured in such epics as *The Education of Cu Chulainn* and *The Childhood of Finn*. These women were trainers and educators and, some, like the sacred prostitutes, initiated the male child into sex. Because sex was not identified with sin, sexual activity, including homosexuality and lesbianism, was freely practiced without onus. Nor did the concept of "virgin" imply chastity, as in Christianity. Virgin meant simply "young girl" or "unmarried woman"—whether or not she was a *virgo intacta* (Markale 1975, 38ff., 128ff.).

Yeats's Approach to the Myth and Theater

In that Yeats's *Deirdre* is imbued with mythic qualities, his work transcends linear space and time, and thus may be simultaneously experienced in both its microcosmic and macrocosmic dimensionalities. Things mystical as well as the occult sciences had interested Yeats since his early days. "The mystical life," he wrote, "is the center of all that I do and all that I think, and all that I write." As a member of the English Rosicrucian order of the Golden Dawn from 1890 to 1903, he claimed to have communicated during that time with the *anima mundi* or the Other World through certain psychic experiences (Nathan 1965, 21).

While Yeats believed strongly in experiencing what he termed "Unity of Being" through altered states of consciousness that brought him momentary relief from disunity, he did not ignore the positive side of conflict. He considered discord to be an important factor in psychological and aesthetic evolution, and opposition and contradiction essential to the strengthening of character and the firming up of artistic endeavor. In that conflictual tension increases energy, engenders passion, and activates growth, it also breaks up hardened and stereotyped attitudes, thereby preparing the individual for new ideas and fresh yields (Yeats 1973, 216). Yeats was a partisan of Heraclitean thought, according to which:

> War is the father of all and the king of all, and some he has made gods and some men, some bound and some free. . . . The immortals are mortal, the mortals are immortal, each living in the other's death and dying in the other's life. (Brun 1969, 126; translation mine)

For Yeats, as for Heraclitus, the opposing forces of life and death, of the spiritual and the physical, the abstract and the concrete, the eternal and the ephemeral, are locked in an everlasting struggle.

Haunted throughout his life by conflict and duality, Yeats nonetheless sought to heal the breach fracturing his existence by transcending the workaday world and/or the state of human consciousness, which he conceived as "a series of antinomies" (Berryman 1967, 117). Yeatsian protagonists forever seek to transcend the human condition—the differentiated, phenomenological world of consciousness—by shattering congealed outlooks, situations, attitudes, and approaches to worldly matters. Depending on the depth of one's awareness, the differentiated world of consciousness combines and recombines in a state of perpetual becoming. Nothing ends; nothing is destroyed; all is transformed in an eternal death-birth mystery.

Desiring to create an esoteric theater that would appeal to only a few, Yeats well knew that his ritualistic and hermetic plays, like the myths and mysteries of old, would be experienced only by a minority and not by the masses. "I seek, not a theatre, but the theatre's antiself. . . . an art that can appease all within us . . ." (quoted in Ellmann 1978, 217). He strove not only to create an atmosphere of metaphysical oneness by uniting word, dance, music, mood, and gesture, but also to suggest a sense of awe by keeping the staging, characters, and events at "an appropriate distance" through stylized decor, costume, gesture, and mask. Yeats's hieratic figures, stripped of specific traits and attitudes, were endowed with collective natures and mythic qualities, which combined divine and earthly spheres (Bentley 1954, 302). In "The Tragic Theater," Yeats wrote:

> If the real world is not altogether rejected, it is but touched here and there, and into the places we have left empty we summon rhythm, balance pattern, images that remind us of vast passions, the vagueness of past times, all the chimeras that haunt the edge of trance; and if we are painters, we shall express personal emotion through ideal form, a symbolism handled by generations, a mask from whose eyes the disembodied looks, a style that remembers many masters that it may escape contemporary suggestion; or we shall leave out some element of reality as in Byzantine painting, where there is no mass nothing in relief; and so it is that in the supreme moment of tragic art there comes upon that strange sensation as though the hair of one's head stood up. (Quoted in Nathan 1965, 157)

For years, the dramatist took on the function of the Druids and the *filid*, the privileged castes of Ireland during its heroic and mythic ages. In that poets and playwrights were part of a priesthood or secret society, the theater, Yeats felt, should be looked upon as a ritual—a religious ceremony steeped in magic and mysticism.

Archetypal Analysis

Yeats's *Deirdre*, intensely concentrated in its poetic vision and feeling tones, depicts one of the most intriguing heroines of all time, on a par with such figures as Iseult, Kriemhild, Alcestas, Lady Ho, and Dido. Because of Deirdre's archetypal nature, her actions prior to and during the events dramatized in the play may be considered double-edged, having both negative and positive components.

Deirdre: An Androgynous Figure

As an androgynous figure, Deirdre is a composite of what society has until now identified with feminine and masculine power. If she is identified with woman (because of her penchant for romantic entanglement), she is considered by some to be a rebellious, destructive, and castrating force intent upon changing the male-dominated status quo. Others view her as a masculine power whose mission it is to rebel against prevailing patriarchal institutions—and thus she is regarded as intuitive, energetic, and brave.

Unlike other strong-willed and determined historical Celtic figures, such as Boudicca, Cartimandua, Macha, or Medb of Connacht, Deirdre is not a warrior; nor is she power hungry. An early feminist in some ways, she seeks independence of spirit, body, and action—an ideal difficult to attain in a patriarchal or any other society. A woman at odds with the ruling consciousness of her times and of ours as well, Deirdre is intent upon asserting her needs and wants, iconoclastically attacking a system in which old men may marry nubile young girls against their will. She rejects the social and political organization that seeks to imprison her in a physically and emotionally repugnant *senex* world. Under no circumstances, therefore, will she become the queen of the once mighty and renowned high king, Conchubar of Ulster, who, in the play, is a libidinous old man.

The patriarchal system of which Deirdre is a victim, although once vibrant and fruitful and based on principles of integrity and justice, now spells decay. The passion she feels for the young and handsome Naoise suggests that immoderation forms the structural dominant of her exceptional psyche. Her pattern of behavior, characterized by extremes, infuses her with the libido (psychic energy) required to forge ahead and reach her goal. On the other hand, when her thinking function is called into play, she proceeds in a rational manner that serves her well during particularly sinister periods in her life.

Yeats's Sets and Lighting: Analogical Dramatic Vehicles

Yeats's stage sets and lighting effects, if understood as symbols, suggest mood, plotline, and the psychological condition of introversion. Sets and lighting concretize physical presences, catalyzing a fleshing out of Deirdre's secret drama through analogy. Yeats's textual images, cascading as they do onto a brilliantly lit stage, constellate Deirdre's fiery nature and/or her inner sun. Everything with which she identifies becomes an extension of the living animistic religion so powerful in the psyches of the Irish, then as now. She responds as well to cold moon power as it emerges from the blackness into which the stage space plunges. Deirdre is sublime in her strength, in her love, and in the tragedy she is about to experience.

As the play opens, audiences are cast into an occult, inaudible, and mysterious realm.

A Guest-house in a wood. It is a rough house of timber; through the doors and some of the windows one can see the great spaces of the wood, the sky dimming, night closing in. But a window to the left shows the thick leaves of a coppice; the landscape suggests silence and loneliness. There is a door to right and left, and through the side windows one can see anybody who approaches either door. (*Deirdre*, 47)[1]

An antinomy is early introduced by the frame (house/wood) and the open spaces (wood/house) before the viewer's eyes. Although other apertures are visible onstage—"a door to the right and left," and "side windows" enabling those within the house to see outside, a sense of closure and containment dominates the scene. While the house symbolizes enclosure, it may also be experienced both as the primordial image of a containing womb and as a microcosm. The surrounding trees, on the one hand, may suggest a good hiding place for one who seeks a way out of an imprisoning situation; on the other hand, the density of the foliage may foster a sense of entrapment, an airless and stifling space laden with overgrown limbs, branches, and plant life.

The "thick leaves of a coppice," Yeats writes, are visible as one looks through the window at stage left. The grove, a sanctuary for the Druids to perpetuate their faith, was also the realm of oracles and sibyls. Celtic mysteries, presided over by Druids and sibyls, were generally observed at twilight or at dawn within areas surrounded by clusters of trees. As day yielded to darkness or night opened onto day, worshipers were invited to meditate in these specially designed sacred spaces. During such unearthly hours, when the flux of colors was most pronounced, the wanderer in search of answers was encouraged to sink into his or her depths, and thus to experience multiple states of consciousness, ranging from trance, to reverie, to prophecy.

Two other objects are visible onstage, each bearing a direct influence on the happenings: a small table holding a chessboard and chessmen; a brazier containing burning coals. The former represents the domain of the rational: lucidity and strategy in combat. The chessmen (white and black) symbolize the eternal human struggle between light and darkness in a world that relentlessly constrains us to choose and reject. The art of chess, then, forces opponents to think and to function cerebrally rather than instinctually. For some, the chessboard and its squares of alternating color replicate a map of the world; the moves made by each piece disclose the polarities and conflicts on the path of the individual involved.

Indeed, chess, meaning literally, "intelligence of trees" (*fidchell*) in Celtic, was said to have been invented by the god Lugh and was played by kings during a third of each day. Parallels are made throughout Yeats's drama with chessboard sequences in other Irish myths. For example, "The Wooing of Edain," which is referred to in *Deirdre* at the outset of the play, is a very complex tale revolving around King Eochaid Airem, his wife Edain, and his rival, the god Midir (king of the Sidhe, people of mounds, hills, or underground; that Other World) (Rees 1971, 136, 273, 307ff.). It tells of a stranger who appears at King Eochaid's court, introduces himself as Midir, and invites the king to play chess. After several games, Midir intentionally losing each time, goes to great pains to carry out the tasks imposed upon him by the winner. For each additional game played, the clever Midir offers his opponent higher and higher stakes. Finally feeling compassion for his partner, the king requests that he choose the stakes for the following game. Midir does so. He asks for the king's wife, Edain. Unthinking, the king acquiesces. Needless to say, the god Midir does not lose this round. When he comes to claim Edain after a month's time, as had been agreed, the husband attempts to put obstacles in his course. To no avail. Midir ascends with Edain in his arms through a skylight in the palace (Gregory 1987, 88–96).

That the stage sets call for a brazier with a fire suggests the importance of solar symbolism. The brazier, unlike the chessboard that stands for the thoughtful cerebral sphere, spells passion, the friction of sexuality, and occult energy. Because burning coals represent contained or repressed material, or spiritual forces that warm and enlighten, they have been associated with intuition and with mastery over self—over the fire within.

Anguish mounts as each protagonist makes his or her ritualistic entry into this remote, isolated, and solitary house, which is cut off from the mainstream of life. A world of omens emerges onstage and takes on the aspect of sacred exile.

Wandering Musicians

The sense of magic and mystery permeating the introductory part (protasis) of *Deirdre* is to some extent conveyed by the three female Musicians. As collective figures, they not only sing out their lamentations and warnings, but also question and answer the protagonists at different intervals in the drama.

Perceived in the form of archetypal or primordial images, these wandering Musicians, who "have no country but the roads of the world," may be viewed as mobile psychic elements, intruding in the events and patternings when needed (*Deirdre*, 49). As potential energy emanating from the collective unconscious, these stage presences composed of universal elements transcend personal contents, which belong to the individual. Because of their archetypal nature, they live, as does Deirdre, in a space/time continuum where past, present, and future are experienced simultaneously. Having undergone cycles of soul life during their journeys, and, as a result, lived transitional existences, the Musicians are qualified to be harbingers of metaphysical mysteries. Thus are they in tune with both otherworldly and temporal happenings.

As the curtains part, two "comely" women of about forty years of age crouch around the brazier. Their musical instruments are placed next to them. A third, carrying what resembles a triangular Celtic harp, enters hurriedly.

Yeats's introduction of the musical element into his play serves to unify the disparate. Music, like chess, arouses the rational, and, like the brazier, the emotional or feeling realm. When these antinomies are resolved in music, the entire personality is called into play: thoughtfully programmed arithmetical and scientific thinking is combined with modulated wonderment and emotion. The fusion of these polarities suggests the search for harmony and an increase of eros in the human experience.

Music also elicits a cosmic dimension. Celtic harpists or violinists, using the pentatonic scale (tones arranged like major scales with fourth and seventh tones omitted), could play in three modes, thus attaining what were considered different spheres of being. The first was the earthly domain, or that of the smile; the second, that of sleep (the world of the gods, who magically enticed the living into a condition of slumber); and the third, of lamentations, calling into being the Other World (or halfway state of the Sidhe folk), between one level of existence and the next.

The three Musicians or mysterious messengers (reminiscent of the Gandharvas or celestial instrumentalists), whose divine music of the spheres charms its hearers, bind heights and depths. They divest audiences of their mortal mental boundaries, while opening them up to a transpersonal reality. Unlike such enchantresses as the Sirens, the Lorelei, and the Ondines, Yeats's Musicians do not, through their tonal emanations, bring sleep to the protagonists. By obliterating the differences between conscious and subliminal realms—between life and death, past, present, and future—the Musicians in *Deirdre* permit an expansion of vision beyond the world of appearances into the fabulous mythical sphere of mystery and magic.

Like the Greek chorus, the three Musicians interact with the protagonists as well as with the audience, singing, speaking, and miming moods and situations, while also living in their own secret and remote world. As the purveyors of premonitory happenings, these archetypal beings interweave in cryptic terms occult messages and signs from a boundless beyond. In so doing, they transfigure both the participants and the viewers.

Huddling about the brazier during the opening sequence of *Deirdre*, the Musicians speak and chant their secret utterances concerning the heroine's past, thereby bringing the audience into their confidence. They have just learned that the High King Conchubar of Ulster is making his palace ready for a wedding feast; servants are busy placing embroideries and hangings on the walls for the great event.

As the custodians of vision and prophecy, Yeats's Musicians are to be considered not as mere expository figures, but as emissaries from cosmic spheres who see into events and people, and perceive catastrophe via their senses. These messengers from the world of the living and of the dead understand the infinite modulations of the human heart and the psyche. In their tonal world, spirit and body are one. Their harmonies or cacophonies are both celestial and earthly. They enter into the dramatic unfoldings as latent powers who warn and question ominously: "Are Deirdre and her lover tired of life?" (*Deirdre*, 49).

Deirdre: A Shamanic Type

Who is Deirdre? A priestess? an oracle? a shaman? In animistic cultures, such as that of the Celts, a life force (soul or spirit) is believed to exist in all aspects of the phenomenological domain. A love of nature and a ritual preoccupation with environment, always in a state of becoming, encourages feelings of relatedness with the surrounding world, even while enhancing one's own daily existence. The deep sense of life embedded in the earthly sphere may also account in part for the importance accorded to sacred oak groves, mistletoe rites, trees, stones, animals, insects, and birds. People not only identify with spirits and natural forces but consult them, hoping to learn their fortune from them. Manifestations of supernatural phenomena and mysterious human or animal voices, either benevolent or malevolent, reflect the immense power over the living of the invisible occult world.

Deirdre was a shamanic type: priestess, poet, judge, and prophet. Within her existed latent powers that she could tap as required, either by an inner descent or through music. During times of extreme urgency, she moved toward the dream or virtual trance state—deep into her collective unconscious. Within this limitless inner sphere, differences between mortal and divine, animal and human, were obscured and obliterated.

Like the spiritual and psychological world of the Druids, the Magi, the Brahmin, or the Greek oracles, Deirdre's knows no boundaries. Her bonding with the mineral, vegetal, and insect domains, as attested to in Yeats's many nature images throughout the drama, invites her to respond emotionally to a darkening sky, forest noises, or the wind's rhythmic inferences. Better than anyone else, she knows her fate from the very outset. In this regard, she tells the First Musician:

> You mean that when a man who has loved like that
>   [Conchubar]
> Is after crossed, love drowns in its own flood,
> And that love drowned and floating is but hate;
> And that a king who hates sleeps ill at night
> Till he has killed; and that, though the day laughs,
> We shall be dead at cock-crow.
>
> (*Deirdre*, 56)

As a shamanic type, Deirdre is empowered to experience a tripartite vision that links eye, mind, and the spoken word. Through riddles, questions, and answers—the poetry of being—she transcends the human to peer into arcane domains, to penetrate the secrets taught her by supernatural masters. Underscoring the otherworldly atmosphere are the melodious and analogical qualities of her lines, spoken in nuanced sequences that reverberate with infinite tonal and rhythmic variations. The solemnity of her language serves to activate and intensify that burning nonhuman power living within her, permitting her to go beyond the limitations of the mortal.

Interspersed with Deirdre's lyrical mode are the chants of the wandering Musicians. Their tones—sweet, harsh, or enticing, depending upon the mood to be projected—are embedded in the very fabric of mythical time schemes. As shaman, Deirdre penetrates their secret symbolic language, and the words themselves take on numinousness.

Like many religious figures, mythical or historical (Horus, Dionysus, Aphrodite, Moses, Buddha, Christ, Sita, and others), whose birth was miraculous and mysterious, Deirdre, in Yeats's version of the legend, was born under unusual circumstances. Of unknown parentage, she was possibly the offspring of some supernatural being.

Wandering one day in the past in the very wood where the action now occurs, the High King Conchubar had come upon Deirdre, the child, who was being nursed by an old witch:

> And nobody to say if she were human,
> Or of the gods, or anything at all
> Of who she was or why she was hidden there,
> But that she'd too much beauty for good luck.
>
> (*Deirdre*, 48)

That she was being nursed by a "witch" may imply that she had been born to a suprapersonal figure associated with negative qualities.

Witches, priestesses, oracles, and the like are usually associated with negative female figures: unconscious masculine visualizations of hideous feminine beings or those qualities they represent. They may be seen as materializations of repressed desires, fears, and destructive tendencies not yet brought to the light of consciousness. To be sure, the witch for the male is a manifestation of everything that is incompatible with his ego. This explains his terror that he may be overwhelmed (castrated) by a power with such close ties to an all-powerful Mother Nature. But Conchubar was so captivated with the infant he had come upon by chance that despite the Druid Cathbad's dire predictions of misfortune, he took her into his palace. Cathbad's intuitions were psychologically valid, for in time Deirdre, like the Judeo-Christian Satan, would play the role of "obstructor" or "adversary," and, like Lucifer, would become a light bringer. With this in mind, we may look upon Deirdre as having been brought into being to help defeat old king Conchubar's autocracy and regressive patriarchy. As the enemy of the domineering masculine principle, Deirdre, as either descendent of or fed by the witch, bore within her what the male sees as markings of ugliness.

Externally, however, Deirdre was all beauty, and she grew daily more exquisite. Although Conchubar's men, adepts of priestly prognostications, urged their leader to do away with the infant, he was blind to her hidden destructive tendencies and remained adamant. She would be brought up in his palace, totally restricted and utterly secluded, and then he would make her his queen.

Deirdre lived the first twelve years of her life hidden from all eyes, particularly those of men. Like a novitiate, she inhabited a cloistered and closed world, within whose precincts she began her initiation into the secret regions of an infernal patriarchate. About a month prior to the date set for her marriage to old Conchubar, a handsome young warrior, Naoise, happened (perhaps miraculously) to pass into Deirdre's view. With all the dash and insouciance known to youth, Naoise wooed Deirdre, or, Yeats writes, "as some say, [was] wooed" by her, and carried her off (*Deirdre*, 48).

The ambiguity of Naoise's wooing of Deirdre, or hers of him, is in keeping with the variations of plot in this legend. In other renditions of the Deirdre myth, we are told that upon hearing Naoise's musical war cry outside the walls of the high king's domain, she became intoxicated by the sounds and convinced Naoise to effect her escape, perhaps by means of threats (Rees 1971, 280). Unaware of the ramifications of her act at the time, she consequently assumed none of the responsibilities involved. Nor was there any conscious understanding or appraisal of Naoise as an individual. She saw him not for what he was, but subjectively, unaware that he was an aspect of herself. As a projection, Naoise existed outside of Deirdre's conscious personality; similarly, Deirdre projected her negative libido onto Conchubar.

After years of isolation, repression, and obeisance to the ruling patriarchal power, Deirdre moved to the opposite extreme by suddenly following her undirected, unconscious instinct and running away from everything she knew. Without any possible way of evaluating her actions, their motivations, or their ramifications, she allowed her libido to catalyze her basically passionate nature so completely that when she first saw Naoise, she simply followed her natural inclinations. The next six or seven years spent in exile, hiding from the enraged Conchubar, were not only immensely fulfilling but also seemed to rectify an imbalance in her psyche.

As is the case in many myths, each stage of a protagonist's existence may be considered as a step in his or her spiritual and psychological development. That Deirdre preferred years of wandering, including physical discomforts, uncertainties, and dangers implicit in the nomadic existence, rather than bedding down with Conchubar, suggests her readiness to face the ordeals involved in a rite of passage. The rigors of exile, coupled with a fulfilling love experience, served to awaken Deirdre's ego (center of consciousness).

The first stage of Deirdre's evolution occurred when she eloped with Naoise, thus shedding her infantile, Ouroboros (unconscious and self-fecundating) characteristics. The naive and unthinking adolescent, whose animal nature had dictated her elopement, now savored the immense joys of visceral love. Unlike many submissive girls living in patriarchal societies, Deirdre was not willing to subvert her independence by marrying a highly placed and wealthy old man. She rejected the power that might accrue to her and the resulting security that would be offered her as compensation for the lack of passion in such a relationship. Because she instinctively refused to be the passive recipient of social order, she changed the center of gravity of her psyche and, by extension, of her culture.

Partial explanation of the psychological reasons for Deirdre's elopement lies in her lessening need for a father image and increasing reluctance to adhere to the traditions demanded by her culture. Deirdre, who had separated herself from her symbolic father (Conchubar) and taken a youth (Naoise) as her partner, not only disclosed the awakening of her own instinctual nature but revealed a concomitant need to become an active participant in a love relationship. Unwilling to pursue an emotionally sterile and subservient existence with a *senex* figure, she chose to follow her own natural inclinations and satisfy her sexual needs by living out her destiny as an individual and as a woman (Harding 1965, 21ff.).

The next phase of Deirdre's initiation—the coming to consciousness of the antinomies of the life process—served to develop her increasingly thoughtful and spiritual attitude toward life and love. The birth of her ego, which encouraged the functioning of the rational principle, was accompanied by the emergence of an increasingly powerful inner drive. Naoise's youth, virility, and good looks had stirred some unknown power within Deirdre. Although he was an individual in his own right, he existed for Deirdre as a projection of her own quest for independence and joy in love.

As the recipient of her desire, she was irresistibly drawn to him—as if by a magical bond. After living out her exile with Naoise, however, her increasing understanding of the dangers involved and the ineluctability of conflict and choice suggests growing awareness and maturity on her part.

Yeats's play opens during the third and last phase of Deirdre's rite of passage. Against her better judgment, she has acceded to Naoise's suggestion that they return to Conchubar's kingdom. They will be in no danger, he assures her. His old friend, Fergus mac Roich, king of Ulster, has told him that Conchubar gave him his oath of peaceful intent.

Senex *Figures: Conchubar and Fergus*

In the cases of both Conchubar and Fergus, longevity is a sign of neither wisdom nor enlightenment. Because Conchubar's understanding of the female had remained undeveloped and childlike, he was convinced that he could find happiness and sexual fulfillment only with Deirdre. As the incarnation of his anima or soul image, this beautiful virginal creature was a perfect mate for the aged Celtic ruler. As previously noted, the word *virgin* for the Celts did not mean chaste. It did mean, however, "not subject to the authority of man" (Markale 1975, 133). The trauma to Conchubar caused by Deirdre's elopement with the handsome young Naoise, and his sense of humiliation vis-à-vis his countrymen—or virtual psychological castration—festered during her years in exile. Although he contained his rage, his inner chaos transformed him into the archetypal Terrible Father figure of patriarchal societies. Hiding behind the mask of a pardoning parent, the high king had become, like the god Cronus, a devouring male. Because his unleashed aggressive phallic instincts were now artfully directed, his ego could develop no further. Regression had set in (Neumann 1970, 186). Venom and hatred fed his guile. Captive of an idée fixe, Conchubar took on increasingly the characteristics of a demonic power, inviting disaster and psychological dismemberment for himself and those around him.

The question of psychological, not actual, incest is also latent in Conchubar's imprisonment of Deirdre, the child. The king's desire to live out an endogenous marriage with his adopted daughter spelled cultural devolution rather than evolution: both his own personality and, analogically, the system that had brought it into being moved in retrograde direction. Had he instead searched energetically for a mate outside the clan or tribe—exogamously—he might have broadened his own experience, thereby increasing his consciousness. Psychological incest diminishes and even abolishes the motivations to seek outside inspiration, and thus binds one to an inherited pattern of thought (Harding 1973, 143).

Despite the fact that incest was prohibited in Celtic society, kings and heroes, associating themselves with gods, transgressed, confident that the moral rule was not applicable to superior beings like themselves. Examples of incest abound in Celtic epic poetry: Mordred was the son of King Arthur and his sister Morgan le Fay; Cu Chulainn was the son of Conchubar and his sister Dechtire; Cormac Conloinges was the son of Conchubar and his mother Ness (Markale 1975, 56). Cases of psychological incest are also plentiful in literature, as witness Lady Murasaki's *Tale of Genji* and Molière's *School for Wives*.

That Fergus mac Roich, the peacemaker from Ulster, was as blind to the imminent tragedy as Conchubar is less understandable. For six years the old idealist had attempted to bring about a reconciliation of Conchubar with Deirdre and Naoise. So certain was Fergus of his persuasive powers that he had neglected to assess the situation clearly, giving free rein instead to his own hubris. Who could doubt his ability to achieve the desired reconciliation?

But, then, how could Fergus believe that the High King Conchubar would forgive Naoise, who had stolen his beautiful wife-to-be? Furthermore, had he been one to learn from past experience, he would have recalled the time when he, Fergus, had been deceived by the young Conchubar and his mother, Ness. The two in collusion had required Fergus, who was passionately in love with Ness, to abdicate his throne as the bride price for marriage with her. The possibility of another unethical action on Conchubar's part could again arise (Ellis 1991, 80).

Conchubar's bargain with Fergus not only mirrored the mythological motif of the young king plotting with his mother to overthrow the older Fergus, but it also suggested a pattern of behavior based on deception (Neumann 1970, 185). Fergus had been displaced and deserved to lose his authority or his godlike force because of his inability to *see into* Conchubar's inner workings. No longer could he play the role of venerable old man. So blurred had his inner vision become, so diminished his wisdom and sterile his understanding, that he lacked sufficient insight to lead or protect his people. He had become incarcerated in his old, stagnant, and unregenerate self-confidence. That he put himself forward as a mediator between warring factions was the naive presumption of a rambling and gullible *senex* figure. His formerly fruitful rulership had grown arid.

The First Musician warns Fergus of Conchubar's rigidity—"An old man's love / Who casts no second line is hard to cure; / His jealousy is like his love"—but Fergus fails to heed her words, and attributes her apprehension to the fact that since she and her Musician friends do not come from Ulster, they do not know the ways of its people (*Deirdre*, 49). Nor does he suspect treachery when the king's messengers do not meet him and his party.

Despite the fact that Fergus is firmly anchored to his own beliefs, he is naively convinced that others are capable of altering their behavioral patterns: "Hatred turns to love and love to hate, / And even kings forgive" (*Deirdre*, 49). So pleased is he with what he believes to be the success of his endeavors—he sees himself as the bringer of peace and harmony—that joy and love radiate in his countenance. Accordingly, he tells the wandering Musicians to sing more "sweetly," to be gentler to one whose "age is arid as a bone" (50).

At the crucial time, the powers of darkness intrude upon the stage, preluding the unleashing of Conchubar's vengeance. Ominous-looking, dark-skinned men pass by the guest house. That these men are mute adds to the mounting terror.

Nothing to fear, Fergus maintains reassuringly, they are merchants come to sell their wares. No, replies the First Musician, they are there for "murderous" purposes (50). Fergus threatens the Musicians with death or banishment for slandering the high king and for misrepresenting his intent. The king's oath of peace is his bond, he claims. Because Fergus is an aristocrat at heart, his faith in the king's lofty intentions is paramount. He thrusts aside the Musicians' "wild thought / Fed on extravagant poetry," asking them instead to sing a song welcoming the lovers back to Conchubar's kingdom. It is not without thought that they intone the tale of an ancient king and queen, "Of Lugaidh Redstripe or another. . . ." The myth, which parallels to some extent Deirdre's own drama (Rees 1971, 234), features Lugaidh and his sea mew (seagull) wife playing chess on the night that they died. Fergus must revoke his request: "no, not him, / He and his lady perished wretchedly" (*Deirdre*, 51).

Intoning their welcoming song without jubilation or any other human emotion, the Musicians, first singly and then together, vocalize their threnodies. Their otherworldly tonalities flood the stage space with a premonitory mood of sorrow. "There's so much to think about / That I cry, that I cry" (52). Both Lugaidh's and the sea mew's passions, like Deirdre's and Naoise's, mark the extremes that love may reach when "born out of immoderate thought" (52). Important symbols, such as the hunt, the "redness of the yew," the "blossoming apple-stem," and "eyes" spell aggression, blood, power, perception, sacrifice, death, and rebirth. The dirgelike lines link earthly to cosmic existence, preparing the terrain for the drama's conclusion.

Exile and Initiation

Deirdre's years of exile and adventure with Naoise, spent in youthfulness and uninhibited passion, may be viewed as part of her initiation into maturity. The acolyte is taken from one phase of existence—one basking in passionate love—to another, fraught with terror and seemingly insurmountable obstacles.

The guest house in a forested precinct, where Deirdre and Naoise are to meet Conchubar, may be viewed as a kind of shrine or sanctuary—a sacred area leading symbolically to the king's domain, or inner world. It will be the locus of the future sacrifice.

When first entering the stage space, Deirdre thanks the Musicians for their performance but then surprisingly silences their song. Is she perhaps aware that their sinister forebodings may be spinning out her own fate?

Unlike the Musicians, whose faces are painted with red ochre, giving the impression that they are "brave and confident," Deirdre wears no mask at first (52). Her pallor gives evidence that she is in the process of accepting dread as part of the life process. She grows increasingly anguished, but aided by the Musicians, who put pigment on her cheeks, she hides her feelings behind her makeup, or persona (her social face). Regal in her stance, she expresses a desire to place her jewels on her neck and coif her windblown hair prior to the king's arrival. Long and thick hair, representing aristocratic qualities, independence of character, and power, was important to the Celts. They wore it in various ways—combed back, braided, and so on—and sometimes they decolorized it. That Deirdre's hair is in disarray suggests a need to rectify and order her emotional condition, thereby dispelling the sense of dread that fills her heart. By setting "the jewels on her neck and head," she is symbolically strengthening her thinking capacity (52).

The working of precious stones and jewels by goldsmiths was a highly developed art among the Celts. Gems represented material as well as inner riches, and the rubies encrusted in Deirdre's jewelry are particularly significant in that they are associated with energy, passion, flame, enlightenment, and blood. In medieval times the ruby was believed to be a replica of the bloodred eye that dragons had in the middle of their foreheads, enabling them to cast flames upon their enemies.

Deirdre's wearing of such finely worked jewels may serve to draw attention to her glittering and dazzling presence onstage as well as to suggest psychological evolution on her part. She is no longer the spontaneous adolescent who impulsively eloped with Naoise; her manner has now become refined, ordered, reasoned—as are her polished, shaped, and mounted jewels—and *artificial*, as is the work of *art*. She evaluates the possibilities offered her at this juncture in her life, and opts for thoughtful rather than reflexive ways of confronting and solving problems. There is another ominous implication of the jewels Deirdre displays: had not Naoise stolen them from the "murderous" king of Surracha, who, when wearing them, resembled a "glittering dragon?" (53) How could one determine in this animistic society whether these pilfered rubies were "miracle workers" or "Wicked stones"? (56)

Deirdre's victory over Conchubar will depend upon mentation—that is, her ability to outwit this deceptive ruler. Because she is now conscious of her options, she also experiences the anxiety of choice. "Myself wars on myself"(53). She is no longer guided by a single thought and a unique passion; growing lucidity has given way to antinomy. What Deirdre has failed to heed as her awareness increased is the important role of instinct. Had she listened to nature as well as to her judgmental faculties, she would not have acquiesced to Naoise's bid to return to Conchubar's kingdom. Having spent her early years in the company of this high king, she knew intuitively that he would never change, that his libidinous attraction for her would not decrease, and, most importantly, that no face-saving compromises could be reached.

Because Deirdre's reasoning power fails to make logical connections, she thinks she can use feminine wiles, such as donning her jewels, to win over the king and guarantee a peaceful existence for her and Naoise in his kingdom. "It was for him, to stir him to desire, / I put on beauty; yes, for Conchubar" (58).

Unlike Deirdre, the still-naive Naoise, as credulous in his youthfulness as Fergus was in his old age, believes that Conchubar will keep his oath of peaceful intent. He reasons that as high king, he "cannot break his faith" (53). For Naoise, Conchubar was the personification of integrity, a solar force, the supreme consciousness of his tribe, a paragon of majesty, a virtual deity. The gullible Naoise fails to consider human motivations. Would not Conchubar resort to deception if pushed by rage or revenge? Hadn't Naoise— the "young bull"—run away with Deirdre, the king's bride-to-be? Why, if Conchubar was as pleased by the couple's return as Fergus claimed, had he not sent a messenger to welcome the two? Naoise is easily duped by Fergus's explanation that rather than send a subaltern, the king himself will come to greet them.

Deirdre, too, wonders why no welcoming messenger is present upon their arrival. Their entry into an "empty house upon the journey's end" suggested a breach of honor (54). Viewed as a microcosm of the macrocosm, as previously mentioned, a house represents a whole inner world. That it is devoid of any living presence may be understood as a premonitory sign of death.

The eternal optimist, Naoise tries to dispel Deirdre's fears by denigrating the weaker sex. Superior in his masculinity, contemptuous of the feminine principle, he—and Fergus—"must not speak or think as women do"— that is, they must behave like macho figures. They must not worry about slight details and eventualities, they conclude, using what they believe to be the rational principle, but what is in fact a subjective reaction: the king is certainly busy making ready for the feast of moorhen, mallard, speckled heathcock, and so on. Fergus reiterates his complete faith in the goodness of human nature: "I believe the best of every man" (55).

A dimming of stage light creates an ominous effect: one passes from the solar to the lunar world, from the masculine to the feminine sphere, from consciousness to subliminal domains. Naoise, beckoning to Fergus, looks into the distance to see if a messenger is coming. But, he realizes,

> We cannot see from this
> Because we are blinded by the leaves and twigs,
> But it may be the wood will thin again.
>
> (54)

The Forest: The Domain of the Great Mother

That "the sky [is] dimming, night closing in" as Yeats's play opens, suggests both the slow unfolding of darkness and the gradual disclosure of an archaic, primeval realm—that of the Great Mother. Appearing after the sunlight (the diurnal and conscious), the Great Mother opens up a lunar phase (the nocturnal and unconscious) where linear time no longer exists. Here one may submerge oneself in a collective unconscious—the deepest layers within the psyche, which are beyond conscious awareness. Deirdre's destiny will be thrashed out in these arcane realms through a reshuffling of feelings, notions, and sensations.

The forest, domain of the Great Mother, encircles the guest house where Deirdre and Naoise are to meet Conchubar. Although the forest symbolizes fertility and nourishment, it can also be destructive, chaotic, and devouring. Associated with the collective unconscious, the blackness of the forest, with its helpful but also dangerous and terrifying animals, encloses an individual in as yet unredeemed instinctual elements. To enter a forest or one's collective unconscious triggers both panic and revelation.

Darkening shadows cast by the thick growth of trees and shrubs may be taken as warnings not to penetrate further into the Great Mother's sacred domain—the *nemeton* of the Celts. Because of the thick overlay of greenery, humans who look upward are denied a glimpse of heaven. Indeed, wherever they turn they face only the Great Mother.

Deep in thought, Deirdre pursues her confessional inner dialogue with the Musicians. Her words are lived out on two levels—that of music, which allows her to access her fears and fantasies, and that of psychology, in a conversation between ego and elements emerging from her collective unconscious. The exteriorization of what lies deepest within her and the effort she makes to shed light on her situation occur, paradoxically, with approaching darkness.

There was a man that loved me. He was old;
I could not love him. Now I can but fear.
He has made promises, and brought me home;
But though I turn it over in my thoughts,
I cannot tell if they are sound and wholesome,
Or hackles on the hook.

(*Deirdre*, 55)

The Musicians chime in to reveal that Conchubar loves Deirdre the way "some old miser loves the dragon-stone / He hides among the cobwebs near the roof"(55). Like the spider, their message suggests, the king weaves the fateful threads of his cobweb in hiding. Outwardly indicating rectitude and honor, he hoards his love, seeking to usurp and contain ("near the roof") beauty (the feminine principle) for himself. Like the guardian dragon of the Siegfried myth, Conchubar watches over his treasure. Hadn't the possessive king, deciding to make Deirdre his wife, imprisoned her as if she were gold, to be used for his pleasure alone?

The "dragon-stone" mentioned by the First Musician is significant. For the animistic Celts, the stone as monolith (cairn, menhir), whether fallen from heaven or implanted in the earth, is a living entity that contains the spirits of dead ancestors and thus is used in religious services. For the alchemist, the "dragon" is a sulfur-spitting animal that helps the germination process but may also destroy; the imaginary stone known as the philosopher's stone represents the highest state of being: the triumph of evolution over regression. Because it is associated with both divine and earthly power, it is considered to be a regenerative androgynous force. Stones most frequently symbolize wholeness, the coming together of opposites in a primordial state. If conical in shape, they are equated with the masculine principle; if cubical, with the feminine principle.

Deirdre understands that stones are endowed with mysterious powers capable of arousing love or hatred. Like amulets, the First Musician informs her, when "sewn / In the embroideries that curtain in / The bridal bed," they move heaven and earth (56). Deirdre prays:

O Mover of the stars
That made this delicate house of ivory,
And made my soul its mistress, keep it safe

(57)

The mention of "ivory," a symbol of purity and incorruptibility but also of hardness and strength, stands as a premonition of events to come. That Deirdre's soul is "mistress" of this "delicate house," or body, reveals the infinite pulsations of her feelings and thoughts. No longer embedded in the Ouroboric domain—that preconscious stage of development which still holds Naoise and Fergus captive—she has evolved, and now understands aspects of life that go beyond the two men's experience.

Will Deirdre be able to see in time those "cobwebs"—snares, traps, death-dealing agents—hiding near the roof? Will she understand that to have commerce with dragonlike components, and to anticipate the "terrible mysterious things" of magic and spells, requires immense preparation (55)?

Like the shaman or the sibyl, Deirdre consults the voices of nature, which resound as tonalities. As prophet and poet-seer *(vates),* she reacts to the reverberations of the sonorous articulations that open her up to the invisible world of the initiate. Signs, as visual embodiments of feelings and concepts, reveal themselves everywhere to Deirdre the seer. She interprets the truth of the riddles revealed to her by the First Musician, who never speaks "at random" (56). The give-and-take between Deirdre and the First Musician serves both to intensify the mood and to enlighten her as to Conchubar's goals. As the First Musician's vocal warnings and prognostications rise from her lips and reach out inaccessible ears, they resonate throughout the cosmos with increasing impact.

Only upon reaching a peak excitement, as if in a trance or dream state, does the prophetic voice within Deirdre speak: it is the same voice that prodded Abraham to leave the land of Ur (Gen. 12:1) and Jesus to speak out his new message. Conchubar "will murder Naoise, and keep me alive," she pronounces as the bearer of revelation, of the transpersonal message transmitted to gifted individuals (56).

Naoise, still the naive *puer,* warns Deirdre not to believe the "singers of the roads" and their gossip. Turning to Fergus, he asks him to excuse Deirdre: she has the heart of "the wild birds that fear / The net of the fowler or the wicker cage" (57). But Naoise, Deirdre points out, lives on the surface of things:

> You speak from the lips out,
> And I am pleading for your life and mine.
>
> (58)

His patriarchal hubris coming to the fore, Naoise turns against Deirdre: "Born a woman . . . put evil in men's hearts." Did she not don her jewels to entice Conchubar? he cries out in a jealous frenzy. Fergus, the peacemaker, intercedes, blaming Deirdre's "crafty words" for Naoise's mounting resentment (59).

How can Deirdre change the course of events? By uglifying herself, she confides to the Musicians. They will teach her how to clip her hair, to use walnut juice to blacken her skin, and to tear her face with briars. She will mutilate a thing of beauty and thus repel the king (59).

Again, archaic figures appear on the stage, projecting a sinister mood: one by one "dark-faced men with strange, barbaric dress and arms" pass before the doors and windows of the guest house. These ghostly entities, emanations from some shadowy realm, walk about in silence, like Plato's shadows in the allegory of the cave. The presence of these supernatural beings invades the stage space, creating an atmosphere of terror. As *shadow* figures, psychologically speaking, they are manifestations of unconscious elements. They are the unregenerate, unredeemed characteristics that the individual's ego finds unacceptable and therefore frequently projects onto another person or group of people. One of these "dark-faced" individuals, no longer mute, comes to the door of the guest house to inform the protagonists that he is Conchubar's messenger: the king is awaiting them for supper (60).

Only Deirdre and Fergus, however, are summoned. Now even the *senex* and the *puer* sense treachery. The messenger has been bribed, Fergus contends, by someone who wants to arouse the king against them. Because he claims to know "Conchubar's mind" as well as he knows his own, Fergus persists in believing that the high king is himself incapable of acting deceitfully. But Deirdre asks Fergus to "ride and bring [his] friends" to help her and Naoise escape. As for the impulsive Naoise, he takes up his sword, his only means of rectifying a wrong: "For I have found no truth on any tongue / That's not of iron" (60).

The Heroic Feminist and the Ritual Sacrifice

Struggling to maintain a heroic stance in this war between patriarchal and matriarchal powers, as well as between true and only libidinous love, Deirdre, the shaman, takes her stand. Having journeyed inwardly through multiple cycles as a prelude to the great transition—from life to death—she *knows* the course she must follow. She also understands that suffering is an inner process that she must experience en route to individuation (an inner blending of opposites, a *mysterium coniunctionis*). No longer inhabiting the misty and nebulous realm of the romantic girl whose love has been full and immoderate, who braved convention to live her feelings, she is ready to pursue her voyage to that Other World—through eternity (Sharkey 1975, 21). It is she, as spiritual leader, who must make the connection between the earth and that other domain. Divine powers will endow her with the libido needed to find her way (Franz 1972, 133).

Deirdre must die. According to protocol, as a queen, she must die with dignity "In a death-chamber" (*Deirdre,* 61). Like such heroines as Isis, Andromache, and Mary Magdalene, she faces her ordeal with courage. Her virtual immobility onstage and her paring of gesture to the minimum draw attention to her harrowing plight.

Even Naoise, the *puer,* who moments before had been ready to duel with his enemy, now opts for prudence and restraint. "Calm, like a man who has passed beyond life," he, too, seemingly begins to comprehend the events in store for him:

> There is not one of the great oaks about us
> But shades a hundred men.
>
> (61)

Naoise tells his beloved in a moving love-duet that "no man and woman have loved better." Deirdre now, but for an instant only, has a change of heart: she yearns to leave with Naoise, to "break away" from the shadow world surrounding them. Impossible, he tells her, for they would be separated by the barbarous weapons wielded by the high king and his men.

The two begin their chess game, replicating those played by the mythical Lugaidh Redstripe and his sea-mew wife prior to their demise; and that of King Echoaid Airem, who, while moving his chessmen against those of Midir, did not realize his opponent was to abscond with his beautiful wife, Edain (62). Meanwhile, Naoise orders torches to be lit to cast away the shadows: "For day's grey end comes up" (63). "Solitude" and "loneliness" suggest awareness and acceptance of the enfolding tragedy.

Deirdre comports herself as an aristocrat, awaiting "a high and comely end" (62). Attempting indifference to her fate, she orders the Musicians to refrain from playing sad music. Instead she would hear music to nourish the imagination even while encouraging thinking and discrimination in the game of life. The Musicians, repeating the theme of immoderate love introduced in the early part of the play, chant the story of a passion unbound by mortal limitations—a passion heroic in dimension, immortal in intensity.

Rising from the game of chess, Deirdre kneels at Naoise's feet to confess her passion. She is unable to play the part of the cold-blooded sea-mew wife of the myth:

> I cannot go on playing like that woman
> That had but the cold blood of the sea in her veins.
>
> (63)

Fire burns within her as she recalls the six years she lived with Naoise in exile—days and nights of wandering and frantic passion. As she incants her love motif, nature seems to burst into life as does the love she now relives. The past, integrated into a present reality, serves here to expand consciousness:

> Do you remember that first night in the woods
> We lay all night on leaves, and looking up,
> When the first grey of the dawn awoke the birds,
> Saw leaves above us? You thought that I still slept,
> And bending down to kiss me on the eyes,
> Found they were open.
>
> (63)

Unforgettable was that "bewildering kiss" he had given her. Still active and alive, it catalyzes her, viscerally and spiritually. Her body speaks; it feels and sways, and remains her reality.

Conchubar enters this rapturous scene. Naoise turns to seize his spear and shield, only to see the high king depart. With the bravura and flamboyance of a born hero, he rushes out after his enemy.

"Children, beware!" the Musicians utter. Deirdre understands she must prepare for her final ordeal (64). Controlled, at least on the surface, she is determined to act decisively and responsively; she will become her lover's protector and fight for his life. She takes the knife of one of the Musicians, hides it under her robe, waits, observes, walks from door to window.

Conchubar enters with the dark-faced men, ordering them to drag Naoise into the room "entangled in a net"—Naoise, "the man she chose / Because of his beauty and the strength of his youth" (65). Turning to Deirdre, the High King tells her deceitfully that Naoise can still be saved if she yields to him voluntarily.

> If Deirdre will but walk into my house
> Before the people's eyes, that they may know,

When I have put the crown upon her head,
I have not taken her by force and guile.

(66)

Having tried in vain to win forgiveness for her beloved, Deirdre offers herself as a sacrificial victim to Conchubar. Naoise intervenes; he prefers his own death.

O eagle! If you were to do this thing,
And buy my life of Conchubar with your body,
Love's law being broken, I would stand alone
Upon the eternal summits, and call out,
And you could never come there, being banished.

(68)

That Naoise calls Deirdre "eagle," representative of royalty and power, and usually identified with the male, is an acknowledgment of her power as a masculine principle. She is logos or wisdom. The association of the eagle with Deirdre suggests that she bears all the heroic and forceful characteristics of this archetypal bird, and that she will experience death and renewal.

Kneeling before Conchubar, Deirdre confesses that she is the one to be punished, for it was she who convinced Naoise to elope with her. As she speaks, Naoise, unseen by her, is gagged and dragged behind the curtain. Moments later, the executioner returns with his blood-spattered sword. The climax of the scene is reached with the announcement of Naoise's death. The Musicians now sing their threnody.

Then the king orders Deirdre into his house. Although she refuses to obey him at first, she understands that if she is to see her dead husband once again, she must resort to duplicity. Calmly, with icy coldness, she agrees to lie in Conchubar's bed that night if he will allow her to perform the death rituals for Naoise. The king suspects that Deirdre might be carrying a knife. She goads him on to search her. Conchubar, however, ashamed of his suspicions, does not comply with her request. Her inner voice conveys her feelings of revulsion for this tottering king: "There is no sap in him; / Nothing but empty veins" (71). And he, whose life has been built on deception, fails to fully recognize Deirdre's deceit.

Shouts are heard. Fergus, returning with an army of supporters carrying scythes, sickles, and torches, demands to see Naoise. Conchubar announces that Naoise is dead; Deirdre is now his queen. The triumphant king, intent upon proving his victory, orders that the curtain be drawn back. To his horror, he sees Deirdre lying dead beside her beloved.

The twice-deceived king, now emotionally destitute, finds himself alone. While Fergus's men shout for revenge, he sorrows: "[T]he bird's gone." The Musicians sing of the "high grey cairn," the resting place for those who have gone to "their cloudy bed" (72).

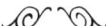

She who had been the poet's muse—the *femme inspiratrice*—born into a metaworld through song, lived on as resonance, reverberation, and word, and was renewed in *myth*.

7 I. B. Singer's "Yentl the Yeshivah Boy": Gender Deconstruction and the Fashioning of the Modern Woman

"Yentl," a short story by Isaac Bashevis Singer (1904–91), takes on mythic proportions in his dramatization of the events confronting a young girl from an orthodox Polish family as she attempts to break out of an ultrapatriarchal society. The struggle waged by the protagonist, Yentl, which takes place towards the end of the nineteenth or in the early twentieth century, is all the more acute because of her need to remain *true* to her nature. She brings sorrow upon herself and those she loves in her desire to circumvent rigid spiritual and social conditions, but the crux of the tale lies in her persever- ance in pursuing her quest.

Because of Yentl's resolve and steadfastness, she may be likened to the ancient judge Deborah. Unlike other biblical woman, Deborah was not known primarily as someone's wife, as was the case with Abraham's Sarah, or Moses' sister Miriam; Deborah's fame rested on her own merits. Although Yentl might never have made a name for herself, she nevertheless remains the prototype of the woman seeking to divest herself of intellectual constriction. That she was endowed with an indomitable will and accepted psychological pain in standing her ground brings to mind Job's assertion to God "Though He slay me, yet will I trust in Him: but I will maintain my own ways before Him" (13:15). As God allowed Satan to test Job's righteousness by visiting upon him excruciating suffering, the satanic elements erupting in Yentl's psyche, although inflicting emotional distress, had a positive effect on her, catalyzing her to complete her rite of passage.

Ectypal Analysis

Isaac Bashevis Singer, recipient of the Nobel Prize for literature in 1978, was born into a poverty-stricken family in Leoncin, Poland. Four years later, parents and children moved to Warsaw. Isaac's father, Pinchos-Mendel Singer, a rabbi and deeply mystical Hasid, was committed to the most ancient Judaic traditions. Not only was he unwilling to step into—at least intellectually—the secular world, but he remained anchored throughout his life to his closely held convictions. The very possibility of enlightening himself about such matters as socialism, Zionism, art, theater, or literature was a threat to his religious principles. Singer described his father's intellectual outlook as follows:

> My father used to say that secular writers like Peretz were leading the Jews to heresy. He said everything they wrote was against God. Even though Peretz wrote in a religious vein, my father called his writing "sweetened poison," but poison nevertheless. And from this point of view he was right. Everybody who read such books sooner or later became a worldly man and forsook the traditions. In my family, of course, my brother had gone first, and I went after him. For my parents, this was a tragedy. (Quoted in Alexander 1980, 14).

Emphasis in the home, therefore, was given to the study of the Bible, and to all the sacred writings that flowed from it: the Midrash, Talmud, Kabbalah,[1] and more.

Singer's mother, Bathsheva Zylberman, although extremely pious, was more pragmatic and less rigid in her beliefs than was her husband. Evidence of Singer's admiration for his mother as well as for her approach to worldly matters became manifest when he chose to add her name, "Bashevis," to his own.

As is frequently the case, the Singer family became a prey to conflict between old and new generations. To the horror of the parents, the oldest son, Israel Joshua, began his overt rebellion against the intellectual constriction imposed in the home by becoming not only an artist and writer, but, most incredibly for Jews at that time, a soldier in the czar's army. This said, he still maintained his commitment to Jewish enlightenment.

It was only a matter of time before Isaac would break out of the mold as well. His first step toward liberation occurred with his brother's gift to him of a Yiddish translation of Dostoevsky's *Crime and Punishment*. Although no overt rejection of his parents' traditional beliefs was in the offing, a spirit of doubt began to intrude into his world. Fearing, perhaps, further lapses, Singer's parents moved in 1917 from Warsaw and its climate of "vulgarity, boastfulness, conniving, and flattery" to the small town of Bilgoray, which they considered a safe haven—far from a world rampant with the vexatious spirit of heresy (Singer 1991, 171). Predictably, nevertheless, Isaac's parents soon realized that intransigent attitudes cannot always prevent the spread of new ideas. The excitement and tension already experienced to some extent by Singer in Warsaw could not be restrained. On the contrary, it increased in dynamism. Much to the consternation of his parents, he not only managed to ferret out some modernists in town, but worse, began writing short stories and poems, and teaching in a lay coeducational school. Despite Singer's interest in new ideas, however, the antiquated customs and traditions of Bilgoray yielded him great intellectual and creative riches. "In this world of old Jewishness I found a spiritual treasure trove. I had a chance to see our past as it really was. Time seemed to flow backwards. I lived Jewish history" (289–90).

Intent upon finding himself, by 1921 Isaac sought broader horizons and decided to move back to Warsaw. The condition imposed by his parents for his departure from Bilgoray was to enroll in the Tachkemoni Rabbinical Seminary. He acquiesced, but left a year later to return to Bilgoray.

By 1923, Isaac was committed to a literary career and returned to Warsaw. To support himself, he worked as a proofreader for the Yiddish literary magazine *Literarishe Bletter*. Emancipated to a certain degree both intellectually and sexually, he took a mistress, Runia, a devout Communist, who in 1929 bore him a son, Israel.

Although Isaac frequented emancipated circles, he was not one of those modernists who sought to imitate Western thought and comportment by fighting poverty, injustice, and persecution, and in the process failed to create an ethos for themselves. His views were more individualistic. He would retain much of his Jewish heritage and build upon it. Moreover, to idealize and then imitate the ideologies and behavioral patterns of others is tantamount to self-rejection, and thus was not congenial to his purpose or psychological makeup.

Singer's contribution to the literary field and to Judaism was to be made on another level. Although he knew that Yiddish was a dying language and that therefore his audiences would be small—and although some people, including his own brother, believed that to write in this language was degrading, since it was used by those he considered uneducated in Western ways and it diminished one's stature as an artist—Isaac stood his ground. His first novel, *Satan in Goray* (1933), takes place in seventeenth-century Poland following the large-scale killings of Polish Jews by the Ukrainian peasant revolutionary Bogdan Chmielnicki and his followers. The reception of this work was instrumental in Singer's determination to carve out a path as a creative artist based on his treasure trove of inner responses to events, traditions, people, and most importantly to an ever-effervescing imagination, rather than to yield to ephemeral modes or fads. That the novel was a success, published both in serial and book form, increased his faith in his decision. Molded from his own authentic responses and not intellectually contrived, his writings were not to be considered as status symbols or the outgrowth or imitations of the ideologies of others. With this in mind, matters dealing with psychology, philosophy, or politics would find little or no place in his short stories or novels. His groundbed was to be folklore, fantasies, dreams, and mystical spheres.

A drastic change occurred in Singer's creative potency following his move to the United States in 1935. Once he and his brother, Israel Joshua, who enjoyed quite a success as a writer, moved to the Williamsburgh section of Brooklyn, Isaac's imagination seemed to have aridified. Although he worked as a free-lance writer for the Yiddish newspaper *Forward*, he produced no creative works until 1943. Nor can one attribute his literary silence to his great poverty or his lifestyle. Seemingly, he was overwhelmed by the thought that Yiddish, although alive in Poland, had absolutely no future in his adopted country. As soon as he had accepted this intellectual truth on an emotional level, his urge to write again flowed forth. With such stories as "The Destruction of Kreshev" and "Zeidlus the First," and with a lengthy family roman-fleuve called *The Family Moskat*, published in serial form in *Forward* (and in 1950, as a book, in Yiddish and in English translation), Isaac Bashevis Singer began his steady march to fame.

Archetypal Analysis

Singer's short story "Yentl"[2] explores the extremes to which a young girl will go in order to fulfill an immense inner need. Hers revolved around a dream of revolutionary proportions: a munificent intellectual and spiritual commitment.

Yentl demonstrated a powerful will of her own early in life, following the death of first her mother, then her father. It was then that she made the momentous decision to move away from Yanev, her native town—not that she felt lonely or had not been solicited by marriage brokers, but she sought other environments that would afford her, she believed, greater intellectual (that is, religious) stimulation. Relatives and friends, however, urged her to accept a husband and begin a family. She had other plans. Very much her father's daughter, Yentl was keenly aware of her likes and dislikes. She had always found distasteful the performing of women's chores: cooking, knitting, sewing, and "chatting with silly women." Moreover, she functioned poorly in the home, burning and spoiling whatever dishes she made. Underneath it all, she rejected the entire social structure of the community. Not only were women relegated to the home; they were barred from acquiring higher religious learning.

As long as Yentl's father, Reb Todros, had been alive, life seemed to her idyllic. Daily, after seeing to it that the door of the house was locked and the windows curtained, father and daughter spent hours studying the Torah. So excellent a pupil was she that her father said to her:

> "Yentl—you have the soul of a man."
> "So why was I born a woman?"
> "Even Heaven makes mistakes."
>
> (Singer 1991, 149)

That Yentl's father had told her she had the "soul of a man," thereby equating the thinking function with the masculine gender, was an appropriate view in his time.

Yentl understood at an early age that it would be inimical to her nature to follow in her mother's or any woman's footsteps. Men's activities alone suited her. First and foremost, she was passionately interested in learning. In time, she realized that she was physically different from others of her sex— tall, thin, "with small breasts and narrow hips." Nor could the games she played as a child be categorized as women's amusements. When, for example, her father took his afternoon nap, she used to put on his clothes, including his skullcap and velvet hat, then look at herself in the mirror. With great satisfaction, she saw that "she looked like a dark, handsome young man." In fact, "there was even a slight down on her upper lip." Her braids alone revealed her gender. And these could be easily cut. "Secretly, she had even smoked her father's long pipe" (149).

When Yentl's father used to speak to her about the great yeshivas, rabbis, and men of letters in other towns and cities, she would listen in rapt silence. It was then that she decided to spend her life in study, devoting her every thought to Talmudic inquiry and disputation. She loved to reason by dialogue, to investigate abstract notions, to weigh many possibilities in an attempt to discern certain truths. Exposition, discussion, systematic reasoning, and the juxtaposition of ideas triggered by a plethora of questions and answers excited her. Such thought-provoking interaction, leading so frequently to theoretical application of mental constructs, absorbed her every minute.

Yentl was "obstinate." Despite the peer pressure applied to her following her father's death, she sold her house and furniture, willingly incurring a loss in so doing. She cut her braids, careful to keep enough hair for sidelocks at her temples, then donned her father's clothes. Placing her phylacteries, some books, and her own underclothes in a small basket that she would carry with her, Yentl left Yanev at night in the month of Av (May), with 140 rubles to her name. That her departure took place in the fifth month of the Jewish year may in part refer to God, the divine father *(av)* who comforted himself after Nebuchadnezzar's destruction of the Temple that Solomon had built in his honor in the month of Av, 587 B.C.E. Soon the Jews would be led away from Jerusalem into exile in Nebuchadnezzar's Babylonia. Yentl, too, would leave the warmth and security of a family existence as she set out on her journey into the unknown.

Yentl went to Lublin on foot. The city had once been the home of Meir Ben Gedaliah (1558–1616), the famous and much admired codifier and commentator of the Talmud, and this association may have been instrumental in dictating her choice.

Father Identification

Yentl's strong father identification implied a rejection of what she considered to be the empty life led by the women of her community, who devoted themselves exclusively to child rearing, cooking, idle conversation, and ignorance. Opting for the opposite extreme, Yentl was determined, no matter the cost, to live a life of the mind.

Although she was unaware of its ramifications, uppermost in Yentl's thinking was her repudiation of a way of life prevailing in many ultrapatriarchal societies in Eastern Europe. Not only were women imprisoned in their anatomy; even more contemptible, they were considered unworthy and unfit for advanced religious study, as previously mentioned. Although cognizant to a certain extent of the anatomical differences between the sexes, Yentl rejected taboos and regulations dictating the activities of females. To have melded cultural and religious values in an attempt to relegate women to a subordinate position, particularly in questions of education, was anathema to Yentl. Because she understood that her community would not transcend sexual differences, she would be obliged to resort to her own devices to deconstruct gender prohibitions. In time, she hoped that androcentric values would either be diminished or vanish (Reis 1991, 26). Yentl's father identification, to a great extent, worked positively for her. It gave her the necessary support and self-confidence to further her ideological struggle.

Let us examine some of the inequities involved in the social structure of Yentl's era and group. While elementary education for male children was compulsory from the ages of four to thirteen, girls were simply taught their prayers, and if they did know how to read, their learning consisted mostly of Yiddish translations of the Bible. There were, to be sure, some exceptions: women whose husbands spent their lives in study and prayer yielded the burden of earning money to their wives.

The curriculum for boys studying in community schools *(cheders)* focused, for the most part, on religious studies: the Talmud and rabbinic teachings. Poverty was so great in many communities that conditions in some schools, frequently limited to a single room in the teacher's home, were appallingly inadequate. The following is a description of a *cheder* in Vitebsk in 1894:

> Our Talmud Torahs are filthy rooms, crowded from nine in the morning until nine in the evening with pale, starved children. These remain in this contaminated atmosphere for twelve hours at a time and see only their bent, exhausted teachers. . . . Most of them are clad in rags; some of them are almost naked. . . . Their faces are pale and sickly, and their bodies are evidently not strong. In parties of twenty or thirty, and at times more, they all repeat some lesson aloud after their instructor. He who has not listened to the almost absurd commentaries of the ignorant *melamed* [teacher] can not even imagine how little the children gain from such instruction. (Baron 1964, 142)

The unsatisfactory conditions prevailing in so many schools did not deter serious adolescents from pursuing their studies. On the contrary, in many instances hardships fired their enthusiasm. From the *cheder* they went to the yeshiva (seminary). Many continued their education even after marriage. Religious study for these young men became a way of life, explaining perhaps the high rate of literacy in Jewish communities as compared to the low rate among their Christian neighbors.

The reputation of yeshivas, directed frequently by prestigious rabbis, grew in keeping with the number of advanced students attending. Since budgets were limited, the community, intent upon insuring the tradition of learning, supported and even endowed these institutions. It was the custom for poor students to be sent on specific days to take their meals at the homes of wealthier members of the community. Although the poverty of teachers and students was great, learning was so significant in their lives that they were not only devoted to their studies but also took pride in their individual houses of learning, where, they believed, they were fulfilling "Judaism's supreme commandment" (142).

Because Yentl had been nurtured in the belief that education was *sacred*, she would understandably identify with its values and with those who furthered this discipline. Moreover, hadn't the importance of education been emphasized since biblical times? In Deuteronomy we read: "[T]hou shalt teach them diligently unto the children"(6:7). Hadn't the scribe Ezra, upon his return in 458 B.C.E. to Jerusalem from his people's enforced exile in Babylonia, been empowered by the victorious Persian king Artaxerxes to institute regular public readings of the Torah? Indeed, Simeon Ben Shetah (first century B.C.E.) is known to have laid the foundations for standards of local elementary and higher-level schools that became the prototype of Jewish communal education for centuries to come.

Why were the Torah, the Talmud (teaching), and the Commentaries taught and studied so assiduously in Hebrew schools? What was it about these books that had motivated Yentl not only intellectually but emotionally as well?

The Torah (Pentateuch, or the first five books of Moses: Genesis, Exodus, Leviticus, Numbers, Deuteronomy) consists of both Written Law and Oral Law. The former, involving the teachings given by God to Moses on Mount Sinai, were recorded: "And the Lord said unto Moses, Write thou these words: for after the tenor of these words I have made a covenant with thee and with Israel" (Exod. 34: 27). To Joshua, the Divinity spoke as follows: "This book of the law shall not depart out of thy mouth, but thou shalt meditate therein day and night" (Josh. 1:8). The ancient rabbis believed this injunction to mean that one must devote one's entire life to the study of the Torah. The Oral Law was also given to Moses by divine revelation but was not originally written down; it was first transmitted by oral tradition.

The Talmud, a unique religious and literary work, includes legal and nonlegal material: legends and folklore; ethical, philosophical, theosophical, and theological speculations; parables, prayers, homilies, gnomic sayings, and historical reminiscences. Its content is a composite of studies and discussions by scholars in the rabbinic academies throughout Palestine and Babylonia from approximately 30 B.C.E. to 500 C.E. For centuries scholars had interpreted the Written Law in keeping with the specific admonitions, cases, and opinions of the various teachers and individual schools prior to the destruction of the Second Temple (70 C.E.) by Titus.

The Oral Law, the explanatory part of divine revelation, was not recorded in the Pentateuch although it was imparted to Moses on Mount Sinai, was committed to writing by Judah the Prince (second century C.E.) in the Mishnah (repetition, learning). A kind of textbook, the Mishnah was made up of interpretations and discussions of the Oral Law as understood by sages since Mosaic times. So many different and conflictual opinions of Oral Law had been handed down by scholars from one generation to the next that Judah the Prince decided to compile in book form the masses of information accepted by tradition. In that the Mishnah did not reveal all the reasons accounting for the opinions and verdicts offered by the scholars—and perhaps purposefully so—it was up to the students reading these injunctions and disputations to discover the reasons for themselves. In so doing, they would not only be refining and sharpening their own thought processes, but would be completing what was lacking in their understanding of religious doctrine. The second part of the Talmud, the Gemara (completion), not only offers discussions and analyses relating to each part of cases included in the Mishnah but also sets out to compare the similarities between them, and, unlike the Mishnah, arrives at a conclusion. The Gemara also comprises commentaries and deliberations bearing on historical figures, scriptural texts, and many aspects of daily existence (Kravitz 1972, 145).

The Mishnah, a fascinating kind of reference work, is also imbued with poetry and historicity, yielding the essence of the Oral Law transmitted by the wisest of the wise since Mosaic times. Absorbing as well as challenging in its interaction of ideas, the Mishnah involves a system of questions and answers as well as analogical and associative techniques as a basis for the discussions. Such a thinking mode is incredibly varied in subject matter and in range. In constituting or creating the Mishnah and Gemara, the mental gymnastics of such ancient sages as Rabbi Hillel, Akiva, Meir, and Johanan were not merely intended for educational, legal, or cerebral purposes. The driving force behind the disputations and ideological discussions carried on throughout the centuries, and then committed to writing, was the participants' way of discovering—at least partially—the essential truth of things. Rather than underscoring or encouraging divisiveness of opinions and principles in their nuanced disputations, and instead of separating groups and triggering schisms, the scholars tried to discern affinities between the persons involved and their ideas, thus bringing the disparate together. The subtlety and logic of the finely tuned Talmudic argumentations led scholars on many an occasion to come upon flaws in their own inquiries, which enabled them to rectify their arguments and judgments.

Like the scientist and the mathematician, the Talmudist, or pursuer of truth, had to exercise precision in measuring his ideas and weighing his views. Only in this manner could he begin to flesh out the word of God, or absolute truth. Because the Talmud was built layer upon layer, each generation becoming both receptor and imparter of knowledge, those engaging in the study and scrutiny of everything concerning the Torah and all that followed were participating in a creative endeavor as well as a religious one (Steinsaltz 1989, 2–6).

The Ten Commandments, as given by God to Moses on Mount Sinai, although comprising only ten sentences, resulted in an enormous compendium of laws—"A Torah of Life." That so much written matter had been elicited by the religious event is explained as follows in Berakhoth 2 of the Talmud: "Whatever a well-versed student of the Torah might ever expound had been given already to Moses on Mount Sinai" (Kravitz 1972, 145). Since all information is believed to exist in the Torah, it is incumbent upon the student to detect, in blessedness as well as in awe, the proper interpretation of the hidden aspects of this sacred work.

The Talmudic world for Yentl, for her father, and for the male community at large was a living expression of human joys and agonies, intellectual constructs and intuitive imagings. It comes as no surprise that everything connected with the Mishnah and the Gemara absorbed Yentl entirely. The aura and mystery surrounding the names of such great sages as Rabbi Hillel (first century B.C.E.) and Rabbi Akiva (40–135 C.E.) may have contributed to Yentl's fascination. What was of essential import to her, however, was the line of the argument undertaken and the nature of each individual's reasoning powers. Right thinking, the sages repeated always, paved the way for *right action*, the latter being the more important than the former (Goldin 1957, 14–15).

The Talmud—thanks to Yentl's father—opened up a world of abstraction to her. She seemed to thrive on the tensions the contradictory ideologies triggered in her psyche as well as the intellectual processes used to resolve them. To participate in such highly tuned dialectics harmonized with her personality. Awed by the diversity of the subjects pondered by past scholars, as well as by the movement of their minds as they flowed and sometimes jumped from theme to theme awaiting or intuiting new insights catalyzed by old ones, she was invited to experience the *numinous*. Thanks to her own talents, developed and heightened by her father's daily lessons, the logic of Yentl's contentions, the sharpness of her analyses, and the sensitivity of her interpretations of scriptural exegesis developed, tested, and strengthened her mental faculties.

The Thinking Type

Yentl's father, a dispenser of wisdom, had been a man of the Word and of the Book. Judging from his lifestyle, he believed that God, YHWH, omnipresent and invisible, revealed his presence and his creative power through the Word. In Genesis, for example, we read that "God *said*, let there be light. . . . And God *said*, Let there be a firmament in the midst of the waters" (1:3, 1:6). It was via the word/breath that the world came into being. Yentl's identification with her father had been and still was so strong that she, too, experienced intellectual and spiritual renewal through auditory mentation.

Not the image of God, whose representation was prohibited in Hebrew tradition to avoid regressing into idol worship, but rather the Word in his voice, was forever present in the Hebrews' psyche. Isaiah, for example, wrote of his numinous experience when hearing the voice of God in the temple: "A voice of noise from the city, a voice from the temple, a voice of the Lord" (66:6). Voice lived potently within Yentl's obscurity.

A hypostatized animus figure—a Master of Wisdom, protector, guide, and inspiration—not only functioned archetypally in Yentl's psyche in the form of Divinity, but throughout her young life was supplemented by the voice and presence of her *personal* father. The concept of the Wise Old Man, constellated both archetypally and personally, gave her access to the libido (psychic energy) necessary to help shape and define her future. In that the presence of this spiritual macro- and micro-Wise Old Man force emerged from the deepest sources of her unconscious, it was transformed, in keeping with her typology, into *logos*. As such, divine speech, the creative Word, and the thinking process in general became a mediating principle between God/Father and Yentl. Indeed, it became her raison d'être.

Because of this harmonious tripartite relationship, Yentl had no regrets, no guilt feelings, no psychological problem in selling her house and her belongings, and leaving the town in which she had spent all of her days. On the contrary, she understood, perhaps instinctively, that to remain in a community where she was known and where she would have to openly fight the status quo would have negative ramifications. Or, if she were to yield to marriage and a life inimical to her yearnings, she would be relegated to the deadly style of the home. Moreover, in the latter case, she would most probably have only a very superficial relationship with her husband. Had not Maimonides stated that any serious student of the Talmud should not indulge in idle chatter with women, even with his own wife?

> It is a known thing that for the most part conversation with women has to do with sexual matters. That is why Yose ben Johanan says that much talk with them is forbidden, for by such talk a man brings evil upon himself. (Quoted in Goldin 1957, 55)

Students of the Talmud were advised to acquire a male friend with whom to converse and study Scripture, "and reveal to him all his secrets, the secrets of the Torah and the secrets of worldly things" (55, 57).

Yentl was certain that even though she was not a male, she had made the right choice. There could be no other way but to devote her life to study and thoughtful discussion. It had been written in the Mishnah:

> For so long as words of the Torah enter and find the chambers of the heart unoccupied, they make their home in the person—and the evil impulse can have no dominion over him and no one can drive away these words from him. A parable is told: to what may this be likened? To a king who was on a journey; he came upon a palace whose rooms were unoccupied, and entered and occupied them. No man can expel him from there. So too, so long as the words of the Torah upon entering find the chambers of the heart unoccupied, they make their home in it; the evil impulse can have no dominion there and no one can drive these words away. (51)

Rather than experiencing a void after her father's death, Yentl felt strong enough to make the transition from passive to active learning. She was certain she would not only enrich her understanding of the written text but would also deepen her knowledge of spiritual matters by questioning, supposing, and receiving clarification of elements beyond her ken. She was also aware of the fact that now that her father was gone, she would have to search for a master or teacher capable of enlightening her with regard to new concepts, precise argumentation, and consistency in her disputations, while also inviting her to fathom the moral and theological implications of the suppositions under scrutiny.

Study, for a thinking type such as Yentl, was the main source of her nourishment. Because mentation had been awakened under her father's tutelage, she considered herself certainly equal, if not superior to, others of her age, at least in analytical matters. Because she knew so little about the outside world, however, she was oblivious to the obstacles that might beset her once she left the security of her home environment. She did understand that in moving from a cloistered existence into the external world, she would be unable to adhere to the strict religious laws and prohibitions regarding her sex. Henceforth, her behavior would adhere to a pattern of gender deception.

Because her father had both loved and respected Yentl for her mental capabilities, he had inculcated in her feelings of self-worth. The archetypal pattern that had been set since her earliest days had served not only to activate her libido but to fix such concepts as learning—a godly undertaking—as primordial. She minimized the difficulties, gender-related or not, that might present themselves in the pursuit of her goal. Such a positive and energetic approach to life had also been instrumental in Yentl's acceptance of her father's death as a fact of life. Rather than spending her days lamenting his demise and the void it left in her world, she looked forward to fulfilling herself as a scholar, thus following in his footsteps or recreating his image in herself. In so doing, she was in fact obeying, rather than defying, her father's way.

The "soul of a man" that her father had discerned in Yentl helped her to deal with and adapt to each new problem as it arose (Harding 1973, 57). The direction taken by her thoughts, emerging as they did from unconscious roots, divested her of any conflict between her judgmental faculties and her conscious objective. Perhaps such mental mechanisms posed a problem of which she was unaware: she was not sufficiently cognizant of the possible ramifications of her acts or statements. Because Yentl's rational function was forever arranging possibilities and formulating suppositions in accordance with her subjective needs, she overlooked and therefore remained untroubled by a fundamental *untruth*: her comportment. The fact that she would be posing as a man, thereby resorting to distortion, thus disobeying the Talmud's interdict, seemed not to bother her in the slightest. If any problem concerning her gender were to occur, she felt, her reasoning powers would always be on the alert to quell any stressful thought that might arise.

Because Yentl's forte was abstraction, her perception and cognition, when focused on Talmudic matters, were objective and wonderfully sharp, as evidenced by the admiration of her father. As defined by Jung: "Abstraction . . . is a form of mental activity that frees this content from its association with the irrelevant elements by distinguishing it from them, or, in other words, *differentiating* it" (Jung 1990, par. 677).

Yentl's propensity for abstraction had developed her rational function to the extreme. Through conceptualization she had learned how to separate, differentiate, and distinguish one theme or idea from the whole. A world revolving around such mental feats required isolation on her part: the divestiture of everything that was not connected with her projected goal. Thus, she was cut her off from her feeling function and further removed from the world of reality. Because she identified exclusively with books, thinking, and disputation, the question arises as to whether she risked being swallowed up by her excessive needs.

Until her departure from her hometown, her thinking was so well regulated that it held her inferior feeling function in check. Under stressful conditions, however, would her conscious attitude always be capable of weighing the full value or impact of the objective conditions at hand? Would her actions always be based on an impartial and impersonal examination of the entire scheme of things? Or, on the contrary, might she condition them subjectively? (paras. 830–33)? The fact that she did not fully consider, prior to acting, those things which remained outside her realm of experience might, at least in part, account for the painful events to follow.

Persona

Yentl considered it crucial to wear her father's clothes. Only under such a disguise could she cope with—in her way, challenge—the conventional society in which she lived. By so doing, however, she was putting on a male persona (social face). Unlike the ruler in Andersen's fairy tale "The Emperor's New Clothes," Yentl was very much aware of hiding the naked truth. Only with a disguise would she be able to function as she wished, without earning castigation. At least, this is what she believed.

Yentl's clothes represented a secret attitude, enclosing her in the dark, or the unconscious. Let us recall that her father had always drawn the curtains before they began studying the Talmud. Yentl was resorting to a similar device—extreme privacy (or could one refer to it, possibly, as deception?)—in order to protect her treasure: *logos*. Indeed, wasn't she merely following her father's example (Franz 1972, 21–22)?

When adherence to ethics, morality, and traditional rules of behavior—a prerequisite to Talmudic study—is transgressed, a serious breech has been committed. Perhaps her father's example taught her ingenuity rather than a set truth. Her own well-developed cognitive sense simply took it a step further. Were she to have probed spiritual paths as she had legal questions, she would have realized that by circumventing the very fabric of Judaic rules of behavior, she was blaspheming. Grave dangers lay ahead for those taking such a route. To step beyond what is considered a respectful attitude toward one's coreligionists required enormous inner drive on her part, as well as a finely tuned and well-equipped mind able to see clearly amid the complex twistings and turnings of casuistry. Yentl was endowed with both.

Unlike Job, who laid bare his heart, Yentl resorted to an interplay of right and wrong to gain her ends. By drawing a veil over her physical being she would be allowed the freedom to develop her mental pursuits in the name of God. The lowering of her ethical values had not even come into question. Living in the world of the mind as she did, she was convinced that she was serving God in her own special way. And perhaps she was! That her personal moral code did not coincide with what she considered to be intransigent collective obligations in no way discouraged her zest to reach her goal nor diminished her self-confidence. Because she believed God to be with her, she felt capable of fulfilling her innermost ideal. The numinousness of her religious experience imbued her with a strange sensation of certainty.

A Collision Course

Conceptual approaches via the word-and-thought complex as adumbrated in the Talmud had always been Yentl's daily fare as well as her daily challenge. Such mental meanderings invited her to draw upon conventional and nontraditional interpretations when arguing the multiple meanings of scriptural content. The stimulation provided by the Talmud, with its analyses, interpretations, explications, and hermeneutical approaches to every phase of existence, enveloped her very being. Her world was *aflame*. In Exodus, however, we are warned: "If fire break out, and catch in thorns, so that the stack of corn, or the standing corn, or the field, be consumed therewith; he that kindled the fire shall surely make restitution" (22:6). A price must paid whenever an inner flame breaks out of its protective sheath, and Yentl would pay the price for her desire to become a "Man of the Book."

Let us recall that Yentl left her hometown at night, when everyone was asleep. A strong ego (center of consciousness) had motivated her to leave the safety of a community, to go against the collective code, and to indulge in deception. Yentl, in this area, was no different from young heroes like Siegfried or Parzival starting out on their great quests. Lacking in judgment and experience and devoid of sophistication, these figures were not cognizant of fear as they forged ahead in their search for a new spiritual life.

Yentl, unlike Siegfried and Parzival, had been well grounded. Her study of the Talmud was not only a record of a mental, spiritual, and psychological process but was a living monument of her ability to partake in the intellectual food it offered. It was a measure, to some extent, of her own spiritual and intellectual evolution. After feasting with the greats of all time, how could anything in the mundane world generate in Yentl anything but boredom? But because she was so cut off from the world of reality, obstacles and trials would beset her, as they had so many heroes of the past, in order to rectify a blatant imbalance in the psyche. The problems and stressful circumstances she would have to face may be viewed as tests intended to develop her discretionary faculties and deepen her ethical understanding.

The agonizing choices of the biblical Deborah, let us recall, also led her on a collision course. Although she was a prophetess who had "dwelt under the palm tree" waiting "for the children of Israel to come up to her for judgment," she took an extraordinarily hazardous stand when, in God's name, she requested that the warrior Barak liberate the Hebrews from domination by King Jabin of Hazor (Judg. 4:5).[3] Because of her evidently well-developed and harmonious thinking and feeling functions, she was prepared to compromise with Barak when he demanded that she accompany him in his military campaign: "If thou wilt go with me, then I will go: but if thou wilt not go with me, then I will not go" (4:8). After acquiescing to his terms, she replied by posing her own. She let Barak know that he was to expect no sexual favors from her: "[N]otwithstanding the journey that thou takest shall not be for thine honour"(4:9). In so doing, she fought the sexism prevalent in the society of her day. She was her own person, openly and vehemently.

Like Deborah, Yentl would have to fight her own war, not only with regard to the outside world, but, even more seriously, in terms of her own inner attitude based on ethical values and a whole repressed-feeling domain. She would likewise have to learn the meaning of conciliation and malleability along the way.

The Main Road

Once Yentl reached the main road after leaving her hometown, she was offered a ride to Zamosc, after which she walked on alone until she reached an inn. There she met other students en route to study with famous rabbis. She listened attentively to their discussions, centering for the most part on how some yeshivas in Lithuania and Poland were greater than others. Since she had never been in the company of young men before, although she was impressed by the tenor of their conversations Yentl did not join in, fearing perhaps that she might say the wrong thing. No sooner had the conversations taken a less serious turn than one of the young men poked her on the shoulder and asked: "Why so quiet? Don't you have a tongue?" After she replied by telling him she had nothing to say, he tweaked her nose. Although angered by his words and gesture, she restrained herself. Meanwhile, Avigdor, a slightly older student, "tall and pale, with burning eyes and a black beard, came to her rescue" (Singer 1991, 150).

Yentl, now calling herself Anshel, after a dead uncle, warmed to Avigdor's thoughtful and understanding ways. When she told him she was looking for a quiet yeshiva, he suggested she come with him to Bechev. There she could study with the head of his religious academy, who was, in his words, a "genius." So brilliant was he that "he could pose ten questions and answer all ten with one proof." Added incentives: the yeshiva was small, with only thirty students attending; the families in the town provided the students with food and took care of their laundry and sewing; lastly, most of them found wives in the community.

Avigdor explained to Yentl that because his mother had died in the middle of the last term, he had left the yeshiva and was now returning to complete his studies. When Yentl asked him why he was not married, he told her he had been in love with and engaged to Hadass, the only daughter of Alter Vishkower, the wealthiest man in town. For no apparent reason their engagement had been broken off. Since that incident, he had turned down other suggestions offered him by marriage brokers. (Later he learned that his engagement had been called off because his brother had committed suicide.) Tense, shy, perhaps embarrassed at his ill luck, "with a high furrowed brow" behind which "his thoughts seemed to race," and perhaps annoyed for having disclosed such intimate details to a stranger, he spoke defensively: "Well, what of it. I'll become a recluse, that's all" (151).

Was it an example of synchronicity that Yentl should have been the one to be sent to Hadass's home for her weekly meals? When an outer happening seems to coincide in a *meaningful* way with an inner psychological condition, it may be said that an unconscious identification has occurred between the individual and the external world. Such a phenomenon, Jung suggested, brings a "border zone" into being, in which contents from conscious and subliminal spheres contiguous to each other flow into one another, thereby triggering an *abaissement du niveau mental*. In that the unconscious exists in a space/time continuum, it functions in a fourth dimension, thereby eliminating such three-dimensional notions as past, present, future, causality, and space differentiation (Jacobi 1959, 62–63).

The coincidental happening of seemingly unrelated events experienced by Yentl/Anshel not only had meaning for her but may have been viewed by her as an apriori fact, that is, one derived by reasoning from self-evident propositions. Such a deductive premise was perfectly logical for a thinking type. The synchronistic event did not appear incompatible with Yentl's strong ego, which seemed, at this juncture, to be in harmony with the Self (total psyche). Jung defines the Self as

> an inclusive term that embraces our whole living organism, not only contains the deposit and totality of all past life, but is also a point of departure, the fertile soil from which all future life will spring. This premonition of futurity is as clearly impressed upon our innermost feelings as is the historical aspect. The idea of immortality follows legitimately from these psychological premises. (Quoted in Jacobi 1959, 65)

Yentl's access to archetypal levels, and the unfortunate contamination that could emerge between subliminal and rational spheres, might not necessarily work in her favor in human relationships or in life situations. For the time being, however, things seemed to be going well. Since the students at the yeshiva studied in pairs, she and Avigdor, soon on friendly terms, chose each other. Not only did he help her with her studies, but he invited her to share his lodgings. (For obvious reasons, Yentl/Anshel chose instead to live with an aged and nearly blind widow.) Despite the strength of the new friendship, during their study periods together Avigdor always questioned Yentl about Hadass. How did she look? Was a marriage being planned for her? Yentl's answers were so perfunctory that he concluded that Hadass did not appeal to his study partner.

So fond did Yentl become of Avigdor that to show her feeling for him she began buying him presents: a silk handkerchief, a scarf, and other items. He in turn felt so much affection for Yentl/Anshel that he even suggested that his friend marry Hadass. "Never," she replied. Some time later, Avigdor informed Yentl that he had accepted the matchmaker's offer to marry the wealthy widow Peshe. Although Peshe was the owner of a herring, tar, pot, and pan shop, Yentl advised him against such a plan, declaring that Peshe was neither clever nor pretty, and because her husband had died during the first year of their marriage she was to be typed as a husband-killer. He agreed, but much embarrassed, he confessed, "I need a woman. I can't sleep at night." Startled by such an admission, Yentl asked him why he could not wait for the right girl to come along. Because "Hadass was my destined one," he responded. Avigdor became engaged to Peshe, and predictably, his problems began, as did Yentl's.

Because the weeks prior to Avigdor's marriage were taken up with material concerns, such as outfitting the groom, the head of the yeshiva asked Yentl/Anshel to choose another study partner. No one, she told herself, could begin to take Avigdor's place, spiritually or intellectually. Indeed, "without Avigdor the study house seemed empty." At night, alone in her room, after having removed her men's clothes, she was once again a woman— and a woman in love. "Perhaps I should have told him the truth?" she thought. On the other hand, now that she had been indoctrinated into the world of books and study, she realized she could not possibly turn back the clock and live like a girl. Disturbed by her great—and really first—conflictual episode, Yentl/Anshel believed herself close to madness (Singer 1991, 155).

Although warm and authentic, Yentl was so introverted and her feeling function so primitive, that when it was a question of human relationships she seemed to lose all ability to judge or calculate. Had she been capable of assessing her feelings objectively, she might have better understood the risks at stake: including losing sight of life.

The Dream

So intense was Yentl's dilemma that she awakened from a dream one night with a start. "In her dream she had been at the same time a man and a woman, wearing both a woman's bodice and a man's fringed garment." Even more emotionally assaulting than her dream was the real-life fact: the lateness of her menstrual cycle. She feared the worst, and perhaps understandably. Had the Medrash Talpioth of the Talmud not told of the plight of a woman who had conceived simply by desiring a man? For the first time, she understood why the Torah prohibits wearing the clothing of a person of the other sex. Such deception served to confuse not only society but the individual as well. "Even the soul was perplexed," she thought, upon "finding itself incarnate in a strange body."

Clearly, Yentl/Anshel's rational domain was no longer in command. She found herself unable to eat or even talk. No longer could study, once her main nourishment and that healthy sustaining factor in her psyche, come to her rescue. Her archetypal dream had pointed to the schism between the persona that she had so cavalierly donned and what lay hidden beneath the mask: the woman. The two not only did not fit together any longer but had become incompatible with one another. Even more significant was the possibility of a takeover by her inferior *feeling* function. No longer would she be reasoning her way out of unpleasant or difficult situations as before. Instead, the woman in love would be directing the way. Slowly, but incisively, her manly mask was corroding, obliterating that self-confidence, that joy, she had formerly experienced during her many intellectual disputations with Avigdor. How could anything but psychological dismemberment follow? So dissociated and intertwined had her two personalities become that one overflowed into the other.

Where would her next step take her? The environment Yentl had chosen to inhabit required her to maintain her persona at all times. If outer factors had not intervened to upset the delicate balance, such a disjunctive situation could perhaps have prevailed. But, on the other hand, when an individual is deeply stressed, as Yentl was, unsettling results cannot help but intrude. Because her persona, identified with a conscious intent, was being perpetually bombarded by upsurges of feeling tones emanating from her subliminal sphere, the dichotomy between the increasingly disjointed facets of her inner and outer personalities invited chaos. Alone, with no one to share her secret, she failed to understand how to deal with the inner stirrings leaping about within her. Each claimed authority over the other; each took possession of her at different moments. Unrelated to herself as well as to her milieu, she felt tyrannized by the emotions that her thinking function failed to understand. She longed for truth, relatedness, and love, but her feeling world was at odds with the rational construct she had created for herself in order to carry out her life's goal. The friction between both extremes intensified, bringing into being what Jung called a condition of *enantiodromia* and serving to activate unconscious contents that became manifest in her archetypal dream.

The gender confusion projected in her dream colored Yentl/Anshel's whole existence. Life, so exciting and fruitful a force prior to the broadening of her inner schism, had taken on a negative cast. Gloom, fear, and an abrasive view of her existential sphere haunted her every thought. No longer independent, she had become increasingly impressionable, her former strength becoming a weakness. The once intellectual persona was yielding to the emotional, sentimental, and tender woman beneath.

That Yentl/Anshel found herself unable to eat or even function in the real world indicated the immediacy of her stressful situation. Her libido, channeled so successfully prior to Avigdor's engagement, could no longer be dammed up. It exploded with such power that her thinking process shriveled. Incredibly, therefore, when Yentl/Anshel next visited Hadass, she asked the young lady to become her wife. Only after uttering her marriage proposal did she begin to understand the depth of her entanglement "in evil." Why had she spoken as she had? she wondered, concluding that it was some power within her that "kept urging her on."

The Autonomous Complex

Yentl's emotional development had not kept pace with her mental growth. Because ancient or traditional attitudes simply do not fade away even if new needs emerge, the powers within her could no longer contain the increasingly demanding polarities inhabiting her psyche. The energy centers, or nuclei of fiery essences, making up these warring extremes had displaced and fragmented what had once been her formerly smooth-running thinking function.

Yentl's error was in part brought on by her undervaluation of her feeling world. Overly hungry for knowledge, as Faust had been prior to the onset of his initiatory journey, she had been unaware of how much she yearned for relatedness and, more importantly, for love. She had advanced her thinking function at the expense of a whole underdeveloped feeling domain that she associated, unfortunately, only with the feminine. In so doing, she became inflated, considering herself superior to women in general: "With girls I can play as I please!" Wasn't Yentl, then, unconsciously attempting to destroy what she considered inferior, that is, her own feminine, feeling side? Hadn't she, moments after proposing to Hadass, gasped and said: "What have I done? I must be going mad." Only later did she realize that Avigdor, not she, had been the one who wanted to marry Hadass. So disconnected had Yentl/ Anshel become that she had identified with Avigdor. Not only had she lost sight of her own identity but she had unconsciously proclaimed herself Avigdor's self-appointed guardian, capable of fulfilling his desires.

Suffering most frequently lies ahead a person when the ego, arrogating unto itself what is not properly within its dominion, becomes so inflated as to lead the individual out of the world of reality. As psychopomp, Yentl's ego had so altered her mode of behavior as to direct her actions and thoughts into borderline channels. Such steps led to her rebellion against the social and ethical conventions of her religious upbringing.

In a well-adjusted person, the ego is made up of many complexes—that is, connected groups of ideas pertaining to the ego. This ego-complex, as it is termed, is able to cope with most problems relating to the individual and is considered "the highest psychic unity of authority" (Jung 1960, par. 82). When it is disturbed, however, the psychic totality may become fragmented and split up into various complexes. When such a splitting-off occurs, each complex may be looked upon as a kind of "miniature self-contained psyche which . . . develops a peculiar fantasy-life of its own" (paras. 59, 60). Under such circumstances, a complex may become virtually autonomous, as occurred in Yentl/Anshel's case, the resulting fantasies assuming abnormal proportions.

Autonomous complexes may be looked upon as toxins, because they do not fit into the conscious mind harmoniously and may resist all attempts on the part of the will to cope with them. Complexes are endowed with a type of electric current; they possess affective charges and feeling tones. The affects given off by a complex are sometimes so great as to be capable of acting physically upon the person experiencing the complex. Respiration, blood pressure, and the circulatory system may all be altered, depending upon the power of the complex over the individual. Let us recall in this regard that Yentl could neither eat, sleep, nor talk. When certain exceptionally deep-rooted complexes break through into consciousness, they can erupt with such extreme violence that they invade the entire personality. Such an explosive condition had led Yentl/Anshel to propose marriage to Hadass.

Although Yentl/Anshel had no evil intent in asking for Hadass's hand, by doing so she showed herself to be completely cut off from reality. Rather than integrating what was split off, the autonomous psychic complex had gone its own way, inviting her to transgress *all* ethical and moral rules of behavior. Disrespectful of all decorum, these unredeemed packets of energy had encouraged her to step over the borderline of acceptable and accountable modes of behavior: her *shadow* prevailed.

Whether identified with the *shadow, evil,* or *Satan,* that power within Yentl/Anshel which, she claimed, "kept urging her on" now dominated her rational sphere. A whole secret, negative, and devilish world living inchoate within this formerly noble girl, who had once set out to rectify a weak link in collective thinking, was now fermenting. Because she had hitherto known only paternal and godly affection, and never those catalytic emotions inspired by love between man and woman, she was unable to shackle these unbridled powers. Although seeking to go her way, as Job had, unlike the biblical figure she had not laid her heart bare. She had merely drawn a curtain over the living and earthly part of her personality. Mistakenly, she thought that by wearing man's clothing and applying her mind to manly studies, she would succeed in blocking out and even destroying the woman beneath. The opposite occurred: the passionate feeling force repressed for so long had now been transformed into a deeply demanding power.

Irrationally, Yentl/Anshel forged ahead. So inflated and distended had her ego become, so blind to its own limitations, that it felt ready to take on the whole world. "The public are fools," she mused. Her projected marriage to Hadass encouraged her to say to herself: "Now I'll really start something." Because her entire psyche had fallen under the dominion of her complex, everything she did, thought, and felt centered around her distorted views. Balance had been lost.

As the complex gained in strength and vigor, the rest of the psyche starved and atrophied. Events and statements in her daily life not pertaining in some way to her complex were sloughed off, while relatively insignificant statements or acts that she felt were related to her complex became all-important. As the day of Avigdor's impending marriage approached, Yentl began suffering other physical symptoms besides inability to eat or speak: she could not sleep, her throat was parched, her forehead was feverish, her knees were weak, and her stomach began playing tricks on her. "A quarrel seemed to be going on inside her. It was as if she had sealed a pact with Satan, the Evil One who plays tricks on human beings, who sets stumbling blocks and traps in their path" (Singer 1991, 160). So distraught had she become that she spent her days in the study house, hoping to find some help in the patriarchal sphere of law, dogma, order, and knowledge.

Satan: Spiritus Agens *of Change*

Had Satan really entered her being? Had Satan been the one to involve her more deeply and virtually inextricably in a blasphemous situation? Before exploring these questions, let us first examine Satan's place in Hebrew religious thought.

Because the Hebrew God is suprapersonal, infinite, and immanent, he incorporates All, including the empirical concepts of good and evil. Exodus acquaints us with Divinity's thirteen attributes, which include love and hate, kindness and punishment (34:5–7). God for the Hebrew, then, is a composite of opposites. In Deuteronomy, he states: "See, I have set before thee this day life and good, and death and evil" (30:15). In Isaiah we read: "I form the light, and create darkness: I make peace, and create evil: I the Lord do all these things" (45: 7). Unlike the Hebrews, the Christians conceive of Christ as all good (all light, all spirit), thereby rejecting the notion of evil as implicit in him; and relegating it to the Antichrist.

In Judaism, evil (or anything connected with this cosmic power, such as demonic spirits, which were creatures of the Lord and thus part of him) was and is part of Divinity. In Deuteronomy it is stated: "[T]hou mightest know that the Lord he is God; there is none else beside him" (4:35). Under the influence of Persian and Hellenistic schools of thought, the concept of evil became concretized in Satan, Belial, and Beelzebub. Satan, a son of God, was the "adversary," the "accuser," the one to inject feelings of suspicion into Job, among others, thus becoming instrumental in his suffering. In this regard, Satan was both finite and infinite: finite in his malevolent attitude toward Job and infinite as a negative principle in God himself. The confrontation that took place among the three forces involved—Job, Satan, and God—may be conceived as a concretization of antagonistic principles within the Godhead (Kluger 1967, 52).

That Yentl blamed her malaise on Satan, the adversary within her, was her way of explaining away the inner antagonism invading her world. Satan was, indeed, that power that incited her to go ahead with her plan and to marry Hadass. It was he who disturbed her peace of mind, thereby upsetting the smooth-running rational plan she had mapped out for herself upon leaving her hometown. As an aspect of God (psychologically, the Self), he had been sent to hinder and obstruct, thereby to activate contents in Yentl/Anshel's unconscious. Only after experiencing such spiritual and physical malaise would she begin to clarify and then rectify the deception she was perpetrating with regard to others and to herself. Satan, in Yentl/Anshel's case, may be considered to be a hypostatized or personified divine function of "opposition," a demon ready to confront her dialectically on her own turf and force her to examine at greater length her deeply manipulative stand (40).

One might question Satan's timing. Why had he chosen to manifest himself at this point in Yentl's development? Evidently his appearance corresponded to a need to make conscious what had not thus far been expressed. By allowing that satanic or colliding force—that which was split off within her psyche—to brush against the will of God or the Self, he was involving himself in the struggle. The ensuing dramatic opposition between Satan and God could, as in Job's case, be instrumental in bringing shadowy and vitiated subliminal matters into consciousness, thereby paving the way for redemption. Under such circumstances, Satan, as activator, would no longer be considered evil, but rather a positive and deeply spiritual agent—

a "divine being" (76). Hence, Yentl/Anshel's drama takes on numinous proportions, becoming an expression of an inner process leading to the birth of a new consciousness.

Luminosity in Darkness

After Avigdor married the domineering Peshe, a woman whose life was focused on material things rather than on human relationships, all went from bad to worse. When he complained of Peshe's loathsome character (shrew, miser, nagger, materialist) to Yentl/Anshel, the latter would simply list Avigdor's virtues (height, manliness, wit, erudition) and respond: "If I were a woman and married to you, I'd know how to appreciate you." Avigdor's sorrow reached such proportions at times that his "speech was incoherent, like that of a man possessed."

Yentl/Anshel also felt agony at her projected marriage to Hadass.

> Many times each day Anshel warned herself that what she was about to do was sinful, mad, an act of utter depravity. She was entangling both Hadass and herself in a chain of deception and committing so many transgressions that she would never be able to do penance. One lie followed another . . . she was in the grip of a power she could not resist. (Singer 1991, 160)

Despite her distress, her ethics had become so distorted that she decided to go through with the marriage because she "could not bring herself to destroy Hadass's illusory happiness" by canceling the wedding. Only when Avigdor and Yentl/Anshel met twice a day to study the Talmud did they find momentary release from their misery.

The wedding date was set: about the time of Hanukkah. Yentl allowed herself to be outfitted for the event, resorting to all kinds of subterfuges. So adept had she become in this domain that she felt herself capable of doing the impossible. "Fooling the community had become a game" (160) for her. Would the truth ever surface? Although admittedly a transgressor, she justified her conduct by arguing that "her soul thirsted to study Torah" (160); thus she had to commit such an infraction.

Why were the nuptials set at the time of Hanukkah? The Hanukkah festival commemorates the rededication of the Second Temple by Judah the Maccabee in 165 B.C.E.), on the third anniversary of its desecration by Antiochus Epiphanes (1 Macc. 4:59). The festival lasted eight days, the Talmudic legend (Shab 21b) tells us, because the pure oil found burning in the temple, although sufficient for but a single day, miraculously burned for eight days.

One of the most important features of the Hanukkah celebration is the kindling of the eight-branched menorah (candelabrum) from a light placed in a ninth socket *(shammash)*. The menorah represents the "lights of holiness"; it is a manifestation of the spiritual light given by God to Moses on Mount Sinai, and thus the "lights of the commandments" as well as the Primordial Light. In Exodus we read:

> And thou shalt make a candlestick of pure gold: of beaten work shall the candlestick be made: his shaft, and his branches, his bowls, his knops, and his flowers, shall be of the same. (25:31)
>
> And thou shalt make the seven lamps thereof: and they shall light the lamps thereof, that they may give light over against it. (25:36)

That Yentl/Anshel's marriage took place before the holiday commemorating the miracle of the lights, thereby diminishing the role of darkness, suggested the symbolic birth of her increased understanding. The interplay of light and darkness—the dazzling luminosities cast throughout the synagogue, representing enlightenment of the soul—was particularly significant in Eastern Europe at this time, when only the wealthiest groups could afford electricity.

Following the marriage of Yentl/Anshel and Hadass and the performance of the "virtue dance," bride and groom were "led separately to the marriage chamber. The wedding attendants instructed the couple in the proper conduct and enjoined them to 'be fruitful and multiply.'" Early the following morning, the bride's mother and her group of ladies entered the marriage chamber, found traces of blood on the sheets, and "the company grew merry and began kissing and congratulating the bride" (Singer 1991, 161).

Singer omits all details concerning the sexual activities in the bridal chamber. With tongue in cheek, however, he writes: "Anshel had found a way to deflower the bride. Hadass in her innocence was unaware that things weren't quite as they should have been. She was already deeply in love with Anshel."

Months passed. The marriage seemingly was a happy one. The only dark cloud on the horizon was the fact that Hadass had not become pregnant. Avigdor's relationship with his wife, Peshe, however, had grown impossible. Because she had refused to give Avigdor enough to eat, Yentl/Anshel not only brought him a buckwheat cake daily, but invited him to eat with her and Hadass.

Avigdor, refusing categorically to have a child with Peshe, preferred, he said, to "act like Onan, or, as the Gemara translates it: he threshed on the inside and cast his seed without." Of the biblical Onan, who refused to honor his father's command to inseminate his brother's widow, Tamar, it is written: "and when he went into his brother's wife . . . he spilled it on the ground, lest that he should give seed to his brother" (Gen. 38:9).

Avigdor's autoerotic activities, which brought him to a climax, were a means toward an end and not intended to provoke fantasies which would then result in orgasm (or, psychologically, the discharge of instinctual tension). Had he not been deprived of love, had he been able to marry Hadass, his sexual practices would have been both normal and harmonious. "Oh, Anshel, how I envy you," Avigdor confessed. "There's no reason for envying me," was the reply. "Everyone has troubles of his own" (Singer 1991, 162).

As the weeks and months passed, Yentl/Anshel was experiencing increasing torment. "Lying with Hadass and deceiving her had become more and more painful. Hadass's love and tenderness shamed her." Life's complexities were also growing intolerable. When, for example, on Friday afternoons the townspeople went to the baths to welcome the Sabbath in purity and cleanliness, Yentl had to keep finding excuses for not going along. The townspeople grew suspicious. Did he have a hidden unsightly birthmark? Had he been improperly circumcised? And why wasn't Hadass pregnant?

The more aware Yentl became of her deception, the greater was her torment. "The lie was swelling like an abscess and one of these days it must surely burst." She understood that she could not long continue such dissimulation.

Passover

During Passover week it was the custom for young men to take a trip to nearby cities to buy things they wanted or needed, such as books, or to find new business opportunities. When Yentl invited the impoverished Avigdor to spend a few days at a nearby town, Bechev, he accepted with delight.

The Passover holiday, called "the festival of freedom" because it commemorates the exodus of the children of Israel from Egypt, would also be auspicious for Avigdor and Yentl/ Anshel. It would mark the beginning of their liberation or rebirth—as well as of nature's. "The fields were turning green; storks, back from the warm countries, swooped across the sky in great arcs. Streams rushed toward the valleys. The birds chirped. The windmills turned. Spring flowers were beginning to bloom in the fields."

During their merry carriage ride, Yentl/Anshel told Avigdor that she had a secret she would reveal to him when they reached their destination. Understandably, he thought it concerned an essay that his friend had written or some hidden treasure he had discovered. That night, after Yentl/Anshel had made certain the door of the room they shared was locked, she said to him: "Prepare yourself for the most incredible thing that ever was." Whereupon she confessed to being a woman and not a man. Because Avigdor burst out laughing, Yentl said: "Then I'll get undressed." Avigdor suddenly became nervous: "Anshel might want to practice pederasty," he feared. When Yentl started disrobing, Avigdor turned "white, then fiery red." So stunned was he that he began to tremble. Moments later, he murmured: "How is it possible? I don't believe it!" Yentl answered defiantly: "Should I get undressed again?" (163).

Even after she related her entire story to Avigdor, he still thought he was living a nightmare and that nothing she said was true. Why hadn't she told him before? "We could have. . . ." No, Yentl said, attempting once again to dissimulate her real feelings for him: "I'm neither one nor the other." She revealed her secret, she told him, so that he would be able to testify at the courthouse as to her gender, after which Hadass would be granted a divorce. Avigdor would also be granted one, and finally he and Hadass would marry.

Still Avigdor could not believe the story. Were all of their intimate conversations and their friendship delusions? Were their disputations spurious? Was Anshel a demon? "He shook himself as if to cast off a nightmare; yet that power which knows the difference between dream and reality told him it was all true" (164).

When the two began discussing the commentaries concerning the legality of a divorce under certain conditions, their conversation became so involved that they were soon lost in Talmudic speculation: "[T]he Torah had reunited them. Though their bodies were different, their souls were of one kind." And as they talked "a great love for Anshel took hold of Avigdor, mixed with shame, remorse, anxiety. If I had only known this before, he said to himself." Only then did Avigdor realize that he had always longed for a wife "whose mind was not taken up with material things. . . . His desire for Hadass was gone now, and he knew he would long for Yentl, but he dared not say so" (165).

The two counted their sins in the darkness of the room, Avigdor's by association, Yentl's by design. She told him that the only reason she had married Hadass was to be near him. "You could have married me," he replied. "I wanted to study the Gemara and Commentaries with you, not darn

your socks!" she answered. Again Avigdor asked: "If you're willing. . . ."
And she replied: "No, Avigdor. It wasn't destined to be. . . . I'll live out my
time as I am" (166).

To spare Hadass greater heartache it was decided that Yentl would not
return to Lublin. Instead, she would send her a divorce by mail. This she did.
So heartbroken was Hadass that she began wasting away. Why had her husband left her? She, who loved him so tenderly. The townspeople as well
tried to understand the reasons for his departure. Had he been seduced or
converted? Was he a demon? Had he so transgressed that he went into exile
to do penance?

In time, Peshe granted Avigdor a divorce, after which he married Hadass.
Everything about the wedding feast was perfect, but neither Avigdor nor
Hadass knew joy. That the couple named their first child Anshel stunned the
townspeople. Guesses are still forthcoming as to what really occurred. And
Singer writes with his inimitable humor:

> It is a general rule that when the grain of truth cannot be found, men will
> swallow great helpings of falsehood. Truth itself is often concealed in such
> a way that the harder you look for it, the harder it is to find. (169)

⋰⊙⌒⊙⋱

No mention is made of Yentl's fate. Now that she had confessed her
"sin" to the one person she loved and had sacrificed that love for the dazzling luminosities of the mind, her newfound purity of spirit enabled her to
come to terms with what the community might look upon as her shadowy
and deceptive side. But might not Yentl, as a struggling, sacrificing, and
sorrowful individual who longed to develop her mind and to live as an equal
among her male brethren, be looked upon as the prototype of today's woman
in the world at large? Now that she had completed her rite of passage, and
had made her choice in full awareness of the difficulties and deceptions involved, could she not be considered one of many Yentls rising up throughout history, all somehow paving the way for the breakup of the old order?
Isn't it her voice that looms strong—like Deborah's—after centuries of silence?

CONCLUSION

Women, Myth, and the Feminine Principle has introduced its readers to the roles played by females in seven myths covering different centuries and a variety of cultures. The trajectory has also included an exploration of the social structures and the religious, philosophical, and psychological ideations contained within each of the texts scrutinized. Knowledge of the manner in which women were frequently (but not always) neglected, devalued, and repressed in the past—and they still are in some societies—may better equip readers to assess their own lifestyles and examine their own behavioral patterns. From this vantage point they may perhaps be inspired to peer into future possibilities for themselves and for humanity at large.

Because *Women, Myth, and the Feminine Principle*, like *Women in Myth*, may be used as a text for teaching, it seems necessary to refer briefly to the history and times in which these living documents of the soul were—and are still—experienced. Students may thereby familiarize themselves with the conditions and needs that ushered certain heroines or deities into the world. What societal factors encouraged or drove some protagonists to take certain actions and to subsume them under larger purposes? Students may be prompted to draw parallels between former and contemporary worlds, put their existential situations into perspective, and, hopefully, learn from past happenings. The truism "History repeats itself" is, after all, self-evident.

Myths being both ectypal (inasmuch as they deal with the existential world) and archetypal (inasmuch as they deal with eternal experiences), they reveal the "the structure of reality." Mircea Eliade explains: "That is why they are the exemplary models for human behaviour; they disclose the *true* stories, concern themselves with the *realities* (Eliade 1967, 15).

The myth, then, may become the model or prototype of the period or

239

periods in which it originated. Since myths are embedded in linear as well as nonlinear schemes, they are at once time-ridden and time-transcending. Time becomes reversible, and the myth speaks to today's as well as to earlier audiences. In view of the many transformations and recountings that myths undergo during the course of centuries, they may be said to reflect various aspects of the needs, obsessions, phantasms, terrors, joys, and longings of individuals as well as of the collective.

Enigmas have always haunted our mind/feeling axis and have prodded us into ferreting out untold secrets. Each person or culture has attempted in a particular way to fathom the unknown—that is, to transcend humankind's finite parameters. A plethora of solutions have been formulated and a profusion of conclusions offered. Framed, voiced, or written, they seem to justify and solve the needs of both the individual and the society that generated these beliefs. Because myths are spawned in and nourished by both the *finite* and the *infinite,* the many judgments forwarded are, at best, uncertain and ephemeral. The presumption that they are equipped to solve cosmic mysteries or the ways of immortals may promote what Jung calls a condition of "inflation"—what the Greeks termed *hubris.* At this time, Nemesis—the goddess of due proportion—was called into action to restore moderation and to balance the individual and the collective.

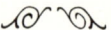

The seven myths—Tibetan, Hindu, Middle High German, Quiché Mayan, French, Irish, and Polish—contained in *Women, Myth, and the Feminine Principle* have been explored, as we know, from a hermeneutic, historical, and archetypal point of view. Such an approach permits an appraisal of the labyrinthian problems facing the protagonists of the myths—and people in general. The actions observed and the voices heard within the narrative structure of the epic poem or of the religious texts figuring in *Women, Myth, and the Feminine Principle* may impact powerfully and pertinently on today's individual or groups. Because ancient as well as contemporary societies have experienced myths according to their cultural canons, they answer a need, a yearning, and an inner pulsation, on both a personal and collective level. In the words of the renowned French philologist Georges Dumézil:

> The function of that particular class of legends known as myths is to express dramatically the ideology under which a society lives; not only to hold out to its conscience the values it recognizes and the ideals it pursues

from generation to generation, but above all to express its very being and structure, the elements, the connections, the balances, the tensions that constitute it; to justify the rules and traditional practices without which everything within a society would disintegrate. (Dumézil 1970, 3)

The empirical, spiritual, and psychological interpretations in this book may elicit speculations and contentious ripostes from our readers. To some extent, our intent is to parallel the path of the devil's advocate, and hopefully to encourage individuals to wrestle with the problematics of an increasingly complex society. May they thus be dissuaded from naively "hopping on the bandwagon" and joining forces in the marketplace with the flaunters of ready-made placebos.

To believe, as many do, that one religious persuasion, one political or psychological agenda, one creed or school of thought —be it feminist or other—contains all the answers is the path of the credulous. Or, better still, of the simpleminded. The bypassing of cogitation and judgment may encourage extreme action and volatile behavior deleterious to both the actor and the one who is adversely affected.

It is incumbent upon readers to *make the connections* between the joys and sorrows experienced by the protagonists in the texts and their own reality. The reader alone—not the author—knows what arouses irksomeness or excitement in her or his mind, heart, and psyche. An event or a personality in a myth may trigger within the reader an image—archetypal or not—that will energize something resting *in potentia* in that inner ocean referred to as the collective unconscious.

The protagonists in the texts analyzed open up their minds to nature in many of its vestments and forms. The experience has unfortunately been seen by some modernists as indicative of a "primitive mentality," but the Jungian analyst, Sibylle Birkhauser-Oeri, could not have presented more forcefully the necessity of reading into nature's multitude of colors, shapes, and densities, of listening to its soundings and inhaling its aromas. Therein lie new radiant displays of knowledge and even glimmerings of new languages.

Trees and animals had voices and expressed humanity's own unconscious thoughts and feelings. We can still observe this state of mind very well by studying primitive religions. But the primitive is still alive in each of us, a part of our psyche with which most of us have lost contact. If it were merely an inferior part, we would not suffer by the loss. But such is not the case. A single night's dream can be enough to make us understand how helpful the advice of this voice from the unconscious can be. (Birkhauser-Oeri 1988, 11)

Through a broadening understanding of nature evidenced in myths, readers are given the opportunity expand their sense perceptions, to heighten their intuitions, and to draw upon their scientific, literary, and artistic knowledge. Yet here, too, obstacles and frustrations are in store. Nature so frequently is unwilling to reveal her mysteries and holds us at bay! "Nature has a master agenda," writes Camille Paglia, that "we can only dimly know" (Paglia 1991, 1).

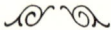

Although women's movements have made immense strides in bettering the lot of females in certain cultures, they have not yet impacted on certain still restrictive and destructive societies on this globe. Yet even in cultures that we label highly advanced—where *awareness* is encouraged, and harmony, balance, and interconnectedness are sought—behavioral extremes sometimes prevail. The Jungian analyst Marion Woodman, for example, has words of warning for the power-driven woman unable to accept the slightest failure. She is the prototype "of the woman robbed of her femininity through her pursuit of masculine goals that are in themselves a parody of what masculinity really is" (Woodman 1982, 7). This one-sided woman, or rather this woman who is unable to blend the polarities within her psyche—alluded to frequently as its feminine and masculine aspects—divests herself of the richness of a cohesive personality. She is impeded in the course toward *psychic wholeness*; nor can she *know* real accomplishment.

Women, Myth, and the Feminine Principle has sounded the divergent voices and pulsations of goddesses and mortal women in various centuries and cultures. The notion of the "divine feminine" in Tibet's *Gesar of Ling* is experienced as an emanation of the Great Mother. She is invoked at times as a personal divinity whose character traits correspond to the psychology of the adept calling her into being. Depending upon her manifestation, she can be beautiful or horrific, peaceful or belligerent. Each of the many feminine apparitions (projections of subliminal contents) or viable flesh-and-blood women play a significant role in the world of Gesar, the protagonist. Not merely messengers but independent spirits as well, they display profound insights and intelligence, particularly at crucial periods during Gesar's earthly trajectory.

Kalidasa's *Sakuntala* is an ascesis. Each dramatic sequence in this Sanskrit drama indicates a step forward in the principal's growth. Hers is a progressive extraction from the *prima materia* —or what is considered bondage to the phenomenological world. It comes as no surprise, then, that throughout the happenings Sakuntala is the one to be accused of having committed an irreparable fault; it is she who stands guilty of having offended society and kingship. Yet it is she as well who is the catalyst for the king's—and her own—spiritual and psychological growth. The special disciplines she practices teach her to free herself from her physical dependency on others and to develop multidimensional consciousness and immutable wisdom.

Mood swings—barometers of happiness and stress—are implicit in the *Nibelungenlied*. Particularly impressive are the personalities of the two protagonists—Kriemhild and Brunhild. Although the ego of the former seems cohesive and relatively well integrated at first, emotional hurt affects her so deeply that in time her rational sphere is submerged and her entire personality seems to break apart. Synergy yields to chaos: from tender gentleness she veers to the extremes of cruelty. In the case of Brunhild—a "warrior-maiden"—we are exposed to a woman who has found her groundbed, and who lives out her joyous and fulfilling existence productively according to her needs and wants. Hers is a connected and cohesive personality. But the imposition of society's marital regulations and its insistence on conformity injures her sense of identity and spirit of independence. Once deprived of her self-image and self-esteem, she is reduced to the status of a nonperson.

The Quiché Mayan *Popol Vuh*, although it reflects a mainly patrilineal, patriarchal, and patrilocal society, invites the feminine principle, or primordial Mother, to participate in the creation of humankind. The very existence of an archetypal couple —the "mother-father of life, of humankind"—in the myth's creation motif is all the more striking in that the female (Xmucane) is named first, and then the male (Xpiyacoc). The archetypal Maiden in the *Popol Vuh*, determined to enter what may be called the life experience, reveals her courage and spirit of independence by breaking away from the patriarchal fold. Alone and friendless at first, it is she who, gives birth—immaculately—to Hunapu and Xbalanque, the Quiché Maya's culture heroes.

Racine's mythic heroine, Phaedra, suffers from debilitating guilt, provoked in her by the extremes of her highly moral standards. Though she declares herself guilty of harboring an incestuous passion for her stepson, Hippolytus, her feelings of entrapment at first do not crush her spirit. By clinging to the notion that as long as her crime lies buried within her—nonverbalized—it will exist only as an abstract notion of the mind, she feels she will be spared society's martyrizing castigations. Her tragedy erupts following the revelation of her corrosive secret.

The guiding value and single passion of Yeats's mythic heroine, Deirdre, whose life is shared with the young warrior Naoise, is her will for independence. The strength of the fire burning in the deepest folds of her psyche, viewed from either a feminine or masculine point of view, produces the power for her to seriously threaten the reigning patriarchal standards of her society. Her willingness to die for her passion and for her principles made a powerful impact in her time, as it does in ours, as attested to by the popularity of legends and fairy tales paralleling the Deirdre motif.

A product of the Polish/Russian shtetls, Singer's short story explores the extremes to which a young girl will go to fill an immense inner need. Endowed with resolve and steadfastness, Yentl's is transformed by her struggle and endurance into the archetypal woman seeking to divest herself of intellectual constriction. That she is endowed with an indomitable will and accepts psychological pain brings to mind Job's assertion to God: "Though He slay me, yet will I trust in Him: but I will maintain my own ways before Him" (13:15). Yentl's drama revolves around a dream of revolutionary proportions: a woman's unprecedented intellectual and spiritual commitment to learning. She is the prototype of the struggling, sacrificing, sorrowful female who longs to develop her mind and to live as an equal among her male brethren. Are not the many Yentls rising up through time somehow instrumental in paving the way for the breakup of the old order?

Myth is *mystery!* So reads the inscription on the Temple to Isis at Saïs in ancient Egypt.

I am that which was, is or will be and no mortal yet has raised my veil.

As we delve into the myths of past times narrated in *Women, Myth, and the Feminine Principle*, let us heed Robert Graves's suggestion:

[T]hink mythically as well as rationally, and never be surprised at the weirdly azoölogical beasts which walk into the circle; they come to be questioned, not to alarm. (Graves 1966, 409)

Let us, therefore, be unafraid to ask the questions, as we encounter and reencounter a wealth of images, ideas, and beings—unfamiliar and even exotic, but, when all is said and done, so intimately ours.

NOTES

Chapter 1. *The Divine Feminine in Tibet's* Gesar of Ling

1. The appellation "Bön Po" designates priests whose functions included divination, invocation of good powers, and the performing of funerary rites.

2. Heaven was said to be made up of nine strata or degrees; three in particular—heavenly, cloud, and rain degrees—were of utmost importance.

3. *Prajna* is not to be compared with the Hindu *Sakti*, an active manifestation of the passive and immobile god.

4. The edition used is David-Neel and Yongden 1981. In the text and the notes this will be referred to as *Gesar*, followed by the page number.

5. Associations are made between a variety of Mother types and animals, gardens, rocks, caves, trees, wells, vessels, fertility, etc. Identification of Mother figures also includes more abstract images, such as the mandala, the magic circle, because, like the mother, these forms symbolize her protective nature (Jung 1968, par. 81).

6. "Turn the Wheel of the Law" means "preach the Doctrine" (*Gesar*, 49).

7. These included, among other things, three giant figures of gold, personifications of Spirit, Word, and Form; twelve volumes of the Bum (the *Prajnaparamita* in a hundred thousand verses); a gold drum as large as a sun; two Tibetan trumpets, gold and copper vases, turquoise plates, etc. (*Gesar*, 91).

8. Tibetans practice *tumo* in order to arrive at illumination, but also to protect themselves from the intense cold of their climate.

9. Vulnerability of a part of the body evokes Achilles' heel and a spot on Siegfried's back.

10. "Spirit" is *not* the equivalent of the Westerner's soul, but rather "one of the multiple 'consciousnesses' cataloged by the lamaists" (*Gesar*, 129).

11. Machig labdrön ("the one mother, the lamp of practice"), a *dakini* in Tantric texts, is unlike other iconographically gruesome, yet positive, figures. She is deeply revered for herself as well as for having been the consort of the ascetic Father Dampa

Sangje, the founder of the contemplative ritual of *chöd*, a branch of Tibetan Buddhism. A historical figure, Machig (1055–1145) was said to have transmitted the teachings of her master to future generations.

12. *Chöd* ("cutting off") is based on the belief that anguish, illusions, and/or ideas are connected with a person's ability to control his or her thoughts, thus states of mind. A practitioner of *chöd* must arrive at a state of such mind control as to succeed, metaphorically speaking, in severing or detaching mind from body. In some cases, "the practitioner offers up his body to be eaten by demons, as an exercise both in compassion toward all hungry beings and in the realization of the Emptiness of his corporeal structure" (Beyer 1973, 47, 282).

13. The *Hik!*, an abnormally shrill tone, "is the ritualistic cry that the officiating lama shouts beside a man who has just died, in order to free the spirit and cause it to leave the body through a hole that this magic syllable opens in the summit of the skull" (David-Neel 1971, 14).

Chapter 2. Kalidasa's Sakuntala: *From Passivity to Adamantine Essence*

1. In act 1, line 35 of his lyrical work *Meghaduta* (The Cloud Messenger), Kalidasa alludes to dancing girls in the Mahakala temple of Ujjayini at the time of evening worship (Altekar 1983, 182).

2. Translations of passages from *Sakuntala* quoted in the text are from Lal 1959. The work will be abbreviated in the text as *S*, followed by the page number in Lal's edition.

Chapter 3. The Nibelungenlied: *Kriemhild and Brunhild— The Obsessive/Compulsive Stress Syndrome*

1. The shadow has been defined as "a composite of personal characteristics and potentialities concerning which the individual is unaware. Usually the shadow, as indicated by the word, contains inferior characteristics and weaknesses which the ego's self-esteem will not permit it to recognize" (Edinger n.d., 8).

2. Translations of the *Nibelungenlied* are taken from Hatto 1969. In the text and notes this work will be referred to as *N*, followed by the page number.

3. Other legends tell us that Siegfried had been affianced to Brunhild and that she was still in love with him.

4. In Skaldic verses women in general are depicted in such passive roles as observers, judges in contests, unwitting instigators of wars, and victims. Exceptions to the rule are made in mythical portrayals in such epics as the *Nibelungenlied*.

5. In Walter of Aquitaine's epic, Hagen was said to have once been a hostage at Etzel's court (*N*, 180).

Chapter 4. The Quiché Mayan Popol Vuh:
Mother Participates in the Creation

1. The translation is that provided in Tedlock 1985. In the text and notes this edition will be referred to as *PV,* followed by the page number.

2. So important were the *chilans* that men carried them on their shoulders whenever they were away from their land.(The *nacom* and *chacs,* other classes of priests, assisted in ritual and sacrificial ceremonies.) The *chilan* in the Mani manuscript followed a certain pattern: he went into a room in his home, lay on the ground, virtually "prostrate," in a trance, while the god or spirit on the ridgepole of the house spoke to him. The priests standing in the reception hall of the house heard the revelation. He predicted in a trance that "bearded men would come from the east and introduce a new religion." However, what he "had in mind was the return of Quetzalcoatl and his white-robed priest" (Roys n.d., 187). Some of the contents of the *Chilam Balam* were chanted to the accompaniment of a drum, or sung, and even dramatized.

3. Kings, such as Bird-Jaguar of Yaxchilan, also performed bloodletting rituals, one of which is described by Schele, Freidel, and Parker as follows: "Face impassive, Bird-Jaguar squatted on his heels, spreading his muscular thighs above the basket. He pulled his loin cloth aside, took the huge stingray spine, and pushed it through the loose skin along the top of his penis. He pierced himself three times before reaching down into the bowl for the thick bark paper strips it contained. Threading a paper strip through each of his wounds, he slowly pulled it through until the three strips hung from his member. His blood gradually soaked into the light tan paper, turning it to deepest red. From the saturated paper, his blood dripped into the bowl between his legs. When he was done, his wife (Great-Skull-Zero) reached down for the bowl and placed the blood-stained paper of his sacrifice in the nearby censer along with offerings of maize kernels, rubber, and the tree resin called *pom*" (1990, 281).

4. Shield-Jaguar and his son, Bird-Jaguar, ruled collectively from 681 to 771.

5. "A tree known in Spanish as *palo pito (Erythrina coralloden-dron),* [f]or its hard, red, beanlike seeds. The seeds are used by Xpiyacoc and Xmucane in performing calendrical divination for the gods, who seek the proper materials for the human body; the wood of the tree is then used in making an experimental male figure" (*PV,* 332).

6. Jung points out that just as Cybele's son, Attis, castrated himself "for the sake of his mother, and his effigy was hung on the pinetree in memory of this deed, so Christ hangs on the tree of life, on the wood of martyrdom . . . and ransoms creation from death. By entering again into the womb of the mother, he pays in death for the sin which the Protanthropos Adam committed in life, and by that deed he regenerates on a spiritual level the life which was corrupted by original sin" (Jung 1956, par. 671).

7. The aromatic smoke issuing from the concoction introduced by Blood Woman was incense: copal, henceforth used in religious ceremonies.

8. Although the concept of staples such as corn was understood by the ancient Mayas, the reality of these discoveries remained beyond their ken and thus was legendified. A story is told about a fox, a coyote, a parrot, and a crow who revealed the existence of yellow and white corn, cacao, sapotes, ananas, jocotes, nances, and matasanos in a cleft in a mountain ("Split [or Cleft] Mountain Place") to the primordial couple (Freidel, Schele, and Parker 1993, 111).

9. Corn, out of which man was formed, and blood, which was sacrificed to the gods, were considered by the Mayas to be the most powerful of substances. In Early Classical Mayan art, the corn god is featured as a handsome youth with stylized corn on his head; in Late Classic times, he represents One Hunahpu, appearing with an elongated, tonsured head.

10. In Mayan sculpture the courtesan, although sometimes depicted as wearing a cape, is most frequently seen with exposed breasts. In paintings and sculptures she is seen embracing lustful, doddering men who in some cases lift her skirts or touch her breasts. Like the Moon Goddess, Ixchel, who appears in various poses, the hierodule may give the impression of being prudish and shy; at other moments, vamplike, as she sits and spins (Schele and Miller 1986, 143).

Chapter 5. Racine's Phaedra: *"The Horror of Remorse"*

1. Racine mentions Seneca's *Phaedra* also, but observes that it differed from his own. He does not, however, refer to Garnier's *Hippolytus* (1573) or to La Pinelière's play (1635) of the same name, both of which were inspired by Seneca's work. Racine's attention may have been attracted to the Phaedra legend by Quinault's *Bellérophon* (1671) and Thomas Corneille's *Ariane* (1672), plays in which love becomes the instrument of fate. This, however, is merely supposition. There is no question that ancient literature worked most forcefully on Racine's imagination and temperament—Ovid's *Heroides*, for example, a series of dramatic monologues in the form of love letters written between mythological lovers that included Paris and Helen, and Phaedra and Hippolytus. The subtlety of Ovid's thought and his extreme insight might have captivated Racine's own fervent feelings. Analogies can also be drawn between Phaedra's love and Virgil's description of Dido's passion for Aeneas. Whatever the inspiration, Racine's tragedy bore his own personal stamp.

2. In Euripides' tragedy, Aphrodite, angered by Hippolytus's devotion to Artemis and his lack of interest in women, seeks revenge. Phaedra is her victim. Aphrodite causes her to fall in love with Hippolytus. Although Phaedra is dying from unrequited love, she refuses to reveal the truth of her passion. Her nurse, in Theseus's absence, attempts to heal the queen's illness by revealing Phaedra's love to

Hippolytus. Although shocked by the nurse's confession, Hippolytus never reveals this truth to anyone. Prior to her suicide, Phaedra accuses Hippolytus in writing of the crime. Theseus, upon his return, refuses to listen to Hippolytus's denials. He sends on his son one of three unfailing curses that his father, Neptune, had awarded him. Hippolytus is killed as a bull rising from the sea frightens his horses. Diana, protective of her beloved servant Hippolytus, discloses Phaedra's culpability to the now grief-ridden Theseus. Hippolytus's last words pardon his father.

3. The failure of Racine's and the success of Pradon's *Phaedra* was prearranged. The duchesse de Bouillon, La Fontaine's protectress, leading the frontal attack, divided public opinion. According to Louis Racine, she "reserved the first boxes for the first six performances of both plays, and consequently the boxes were either filled or empty, as [she] wished" (Racine 1950, 1:790; translation mine).

4. So great was Racine's passion for the ancients that he allegedly committed many classical dramas to memory. Still a boy in many ways, he loved what was forbidden. An incident has been reported in which Racine was taken by surprise savoring an unsavory work: *The Loves of Theagenes and Chariclee*, a novel considered undesirable by his master at Port-Royal. Claude Lancelot demanded the book, which he burned. The irate youngster availed himself of another copy. The second met a similar fate. A third copy was bought by Racine who, after memorizing the entire volume, handed it to M. Lancelot saying, "You can burn this one as you burned the others" (Racine 1950, 1:12; translation mine). Such an incident is an indication of Racine's strong will and his utter disregard for regulations that hampered the pursuit of his own desires.

5. Translations in the text from Racine 1950 are my own.

6. Translations of Racine's plays in the text are by S. Solomon and are taken from Racine 1967. This translation is abbreviated in the text as *CP*, followed by the page number.

Chapter 6. Yeats's Deirdre: *An Irish/Celtic Feminist and Heroine*

1. All quotations of *Deirdre* are taken from Yeats 1964. Numbers following the play title are page numbers in this edition.

Chapter 7. I. B. Singer's *"Yentl the Yeshivah Boy"*: *Gender Deconstruction and the Fashioning of the Modern Woman*

1. *Midrash* means "inquire" or "investigate," and the Midrash is a codification of Oral Jewish Law, upon which the Talmud is based. The Talmud is a body of eight centuries of work based on discussions and study by Jewish scholars. *Kabbalah* means

"that which is received," thus "tradition." These writings are mystical in nature. Further explanations of these and other sacred texts will be given at appropriate times within the body of the chapter.

2. All quotations of "Yentl" are taken from Singer 1991.

3. Although victory over Barak's enemy followed, its fruits were far sweeter, as related in the Talmud, centuries later when Rabbi Akiva, a descendent of Sisera, Barak's foe, not only laid the foundations for the Oral Law but also codified the Mishnah. Thus did former adversaries work together in the name of God (Telushkin 1991, 71).

BIBLIOGRAPHY

Alexander, Edward. 1980. *Isaac Bashevis Singer.* Boston: Twayne Publishers.
Allentuck, Marcia, ed. 1969. *The Achievement of Isaac Bashevis Singer.* Carbondale: Southern Illinois University Press.
Altekar, A. S. 1983. *The Position of Women in Hindu Civilization.* Delhi: Motilal Banarsidass.
Andersson, Theodore M. 1980. *The Legend of Brynhild.* Ithaca: Cornell University Press.
———. 1987. *A Preface to the Nibelungenlied.* Stanford, Calif.: Stanford University Press.
Bacot, Jacques. 1962. *Introduction à l'histoire du Tibet.* Paris: Société asiatique.
Bamberger, J. 1974. "The Myth of Matriarchy." In *Women, Culture and Society,* edited by M. Z. Rosaldo and L. Lamphere, pp.263–80. Stanford, Calif.: Stanford University Press.
Baring, Ann, and Julius Ashford. 1993. *The Myth of the Goddess.* London: Penguin Books.
Baron, Salo W. 1964. *Russian Jew Under Tsars and Soviets.* New York: Macmillan.
Barthes, Roland. 1964. *On Racine.* Translated by Richard Howard. New York: Hill and Wang.
Bekker, Hugo. 1971. *The Nibelungenlied: A Literary Analysis.* Toronto: University of Toronto Press.
Bell, Sir Charles. 1968. *The Religion of Tibet.* Oxford: The Clarendon Press.
Bénichou, Paul. 1948. *Morales du grand siècle.* Paris: Gallimard.
Bentley, Eric. 1954. *In Search of Theatre.* New York: Vintage Books.
Berriedale, Keith A. 1964. *The Sanskrit Drama.* London: Oxford University Press.
Berryman, Charles. 1967. *W. B. Yeats.* New York: Exposition Press.
Berthelot, Marcelin. 1885. *Les Origines de l'alchimie.* Paris: Georges Steinheil.
Beyer, Stephan. 1973. *The Cult of Tara.* Berkeley: University of California Press.
Bierhorst, John. 1986. *The Monkey's Haircut and Other Stories Told by the Maya.* New York: William Morrow.

———. 1990. *The Mythology of Mexico and Central America*. New York: William Morrow.

Birkhauser-Oeri, Sibylle. 1988. *The Mother: Archetypal Image in Fairy Tales*. Translated by Michael Mitchell. Toronto: Inner City Books.

Brahenda, Nath Seal. 1958. *The Positive Sciences of the Ancient Hindus*. Delhi: Motilal Barnasidass.

Brasseur de Bourbourg, Charles Etienne. 1857. *Popol Vuh. Le Livre Sacré et les mythes de l'antiquite américaine, avec les livres héroiques et historiques des Quichés*. Paris.

Brinton, Daniel G. 1881. "The Names of the Gods in the Kiché Myths of Central America." In *Proceedings of the American Philosophical Society*. Philadelphia.

———. 1982. *The Maya Chronicles*. Reprint, New York: AMS Press.

Burns, Allan F. 1983. *An Epoch of Miracles: Oral Literature of the Yucatec Maya*. Austin: University of Texas Press.

Brun, Jean. 1969. *Héraclite*. Paris: Seghers.

Byrne, Francis John. 1973. *Irish Kings and High-Kings*. New York: St. Martin's Press.

———. 1976. "Early Irish Society." In *Irish History and Culture,* by H. Orel. Lawrence: University Press of Kansas.

Campbell, Joseph. 1974. *The Masks of God: Oriental Mythology*. New York: Viking Press.

Carlson, Kathie. 1990. *In Her Image: The Unheaped Daughter's Search for Her Mother*. Boston: Shambhala.

Carmack, Robert M. 1981. *The Quiché Maya of Utalan*. Norman: University of Oklahoma Press.

Castedo, Leopoldo. 1969. *A History of Latin American Art and Architecture*. New York: Praeger.

Chadwick, Nora. 1976. *The Celts*. Harmondsworth, U.K.: Penguin Books.

Chodag, Tiley. 1988. *Tibet The Land and the People*. Translated by W. Tailing. Beijing: New World Press.

Clark, A. F. S. 1939. *Jean Racine*. Cambridge: Harvard University Press.

Clark, David R. 1978. "Deirdre: The Rigour of Logic." In *Critical Essays of W. B. Yeats,* edited by Richard J. Finneran. Boston: G. K. Hall.

Coe, Michael D. 1984. *The Maya*. London: Thames and Hudson.

Coe, William R. 1985. *Tikal: A Handbook of the Ancient Maya Ruins*. Philadelphia: University of Pennsylvania Press.

Coulson, Michael. 1981. *Three Sanskrit Plays*. London: Penguin Books.

Craine, Eugene R., and Reginald C. Reindorp, eds. 1979. *The Codex Perez and The Book of Chilam Balam of Mani*. Translated by Eugene R. Craine and Reginald C. Reindorp. Norman: University of Oklahoma Press.

Craven, Roy, C. 1976. *Indian Art*. New York: Praeger.

Crouzet, Paul. 1940. *Tout Racine ici, à Port-Royal*. Paris: Didier.

Dalai Lama, The. 1992. Foreword to *Tibetan Book of Living and Dying*, by Sogyal Rinpoche, edited by Patrick Gaffney and Andrew Harvey. San Francisco: HarperCollins.

Daumal, René. 1970. *Bharata*. Paris: Gallimard.

David-Neel, Alexandra. 1931. *With Mystics and Magicians in Tibet*. London: John Lane, The Bodley Head.

———. 1971. *Magic and Mystery in Tibet*. New York: Dover.

David-Neel, Alexandra, and the Lama Yongden. 1981. *The Superhuman Life of Gesar of Ling. La vie surhumaine de Gésar de Ling*. Translated by Violet Sydney. Boulder, Colo.: Prajna Press.

———. 1982. *The Power of Nothingness*. Translated by J.van de Wetering. New York: Houghton Mifflin.

———. 1983. *My Journey to Lhasa*. London: Virago Press.

Davidson, H. R. Ellis. 1969. *Scandinavian Mythology*. London: Paul Hamlyn.

Davy, Marie-Madeleine. 1972. *Encyclopédie des mystiques*. 4. Conception et réalisation de Marian Berlewi. Paris: Seghers.

de Bary, Wm. Theodore, ed. 1958a. *Sources of Indian Tradition*. Vol. 1. Compiled by A. L. Basham, R. N. Dandekar, Peter Hardy, V. Raghavan, and R. Weiler. New York: Columbia University Press.

———. 1958b. *Sources of Indian Tradition*. Vol. 2. Compiled by Stephen Hay and I. Hl. Qureshi. New York: Columbia University Press.

Deltour, Félix. 1959. *Les Ennemis de Racine au XVIIe siècle*. Paris: Didier.

Donnington, Robert. 1963. *Wagner's "Ring" and Its Symbols*. London: Faber and Faber.

Donovan, Josephine. 1991. *Feminist Theory*. New York: Continuum.

Duby, Georges. 1977. *The Chivalrous Society*. Translated by Cynthia Postan. Berkeley: University of California Press.

Dumézil, Georges. 1970. *The Destiny of the Warrior*. Translated by Alf Hiltebeitel. Chicago: University of Chicago Press.

Easwaran, Eknath, trans. 1992. *The Upanishads*. Berkeley, Calif.: Nilgiri Press.

Edinger, Edward. N.d. "An Outline of Analytical Psychology." Unpublished.

———. 1962. "Symbols: The Meaning of Life." *Spring*.

———. 1966. "Christ as a Paradigm of the Individuating Ego." *Spring*.

———. 1969. "Metaphysics and the Unconscious." *Spring*.

———. 1978. *Melville's Moby-Dick*. New York: New Directions.

Edmonson, Munro S., trans. 1971. *The Book of Counsel: The Popl Vuh of the Quiché Maya of Guatemala*. New Orleans: Middle American Research Institute, Tulane University.

Ekvall, Robert B. 1964. *Religious Observances in Tibet: Patterns and Functions*. Chicago: University of Chicago Press.

Eliade, Mircea. 1962. *Méphistophélès et l'androgyne*. Paris: Gallimard.

———. 1965. *Rites and Symbols of Initiation*. New York: Harper Torchbooks.

————. 1967. *Myths, Dreams, and Mysteries*. New York: Harper Torchbooks.

————. 1971. *The Forge and the Crucible*. New York: Harper Torchbooks.

————. 1972. *Shamanism*. Princeton: Princeton University Press.

————. 1973. *Yoga*. Princeton: Princeton University Press.

————. 1974. *Patterns in Comparative Religion*. New York: New American Library.

Ellmann, Richard. 1978. *Yeats: The Man and the Masks*. New York: Norton.

Ellis, Peter Berresford. 1991. *A Dictionary of Irish Mythology*. Oxford: Oxford University Press.

Euripides. 1977. *Ten Plays*. Translated by Moses Madas and John McClean. New York: Bantam Books.

Evans-Wentz, W. Y. 1960. *The Tibetan Book of the Dead*. Translated by Lama Kazi Dawa-Samdup. New York: Oxford University Press.

Fackler, Herbert V. 1978. *That Tragic Queen: The Deirdre Legend in Anglo-Irish Literature*. Salzburg: Institut für Englische Sprache und Literatur, Universität Salzburg.

Finneran, Richard J. 1986. *Critical Essays on W. B. Yeats*. Boston: G. K. Hall.

Franz, Marie-Louise von. 1972. *The Feminine in Fairytales*. New York: Spring Publications.

————. 1974. *Shadow and Evil in Fairy Tales*. Zurich: Spring Publications.

————. 1980a. *On Divination and Synchronicity*. Toronto: Inner City Books.

————. 1980b. *Projection and Re-Collection in Jungian Psychology*. Translated by William H. Kennedy. London: Open Court.

————. 1986. *On Dreams and Death*. Translated by E. X. Kennedy and Vernon Brooks. Boston: Shambhala.

Freidel, David, Linda Schele, and Joy Parker. 1993. *Maya Cosmos*. New York: William Morrow.

Gallenkamp, Charles. 1959. *Maya: The Riddle and Rediscovery of a Lost Civilization,*. New York: David McKay.

————. 1979. Introduction to *The Codex Perez and The Book of Chilam Balam of Mani,* edited and translated by Eugene R. Craine and Reginald C. Reindorp. Norman: University Of Oklahoma Press.

Genêt, Jean, and Chelbatz Genêt. 1927. *Histoire des peuples maya-quichés*. Paris.

Gilard, Madeleine. 1977. *Sortilège Maya*. Paris: Editions La Farandole.

Girard, Rafael. 1977. *Le Popol Vuh. Histoire culturelle des Mayas-Quiché*. Paris: Payot.

Goetz, Delia, and Sylvanus G. Morley, trans. 1983. *Popol Vuh*. Norman: University of Oklahoma Press.

Goldin, Juda. 1957. *The Living Talmud*. New York: New American Library.

Goldmann, Lucien. 1955. *Le Dieu caché*. Paris: Gallimard

————. 1956. *Racine*. Paris: L'Arche.

Gordon, G. B. 1915. "Guatemala Myths." *Museum Journal* 6:103–44.

Gottlieb, Freeman. 1989. *The Lamp of God*. London: Jason Aronson.

Graves, Robert. 1966. *The White Goddess*. New York: Farrar, Straus & Giroux.

Greely, Andrew M. 1977. *The Mary Myth*. New York: Seabury Press.

Gregory, Lady. 1987. *Gods and Fighting Men*. Vale, Guernsey, U.K.: Guernsey Press.

Hammond, Norman. 1982. *Ancient Maya Civilization*. New Brunswick, N.J.: Rutgers University Press.

Harding, Esther. 1965. *The Way of All Woman*. New York: Harper Colophon Books.

———. 1973. *Psychic Energy*. Princeton: Princeton University Press.

Harris, Mary B. 1936. *Kalidasa: Poet of Nature*. Boston: Meador Press.

Hatto, A. T., trans. 1969. *The Nibelungenlied*. London: Penguin Books.

Haymes, Edward R. 1986. *The Nibelungenlied: History and Interpretation*. Urbana and Chicago: University of Illinois Press.

Hillman, James. 1975. *Re-Visioning Psychology*. New York: Harper and Row.

Hoffmann, Helmut. 1961. *The Religions of Tibet*. Translated by Edward Fitzgerald. Westport, Conn.: Greenwood Press.

Hopkins, Thomas, J. 1971. *The Hindu Religious Tradition*. Encino, Calif.: Dickenson.

Jacobi, Mario. 1985. *Longing For Paradise*. Translated from German by Myron B.Gubitz. Boston: Sigo Press.

Jacobi, Yolande. 1959. *Complex Archetype Symbol in the Psychology of C. G.Jung*. Translated by Ralph Manheim. Princeton: Princeton University Press.

Jasinski, René. 1958. *Vers le vrai Racine*. Paris: Armand Collin.

Jesch, Judith. 1991. *Women in the Viking Age*. Woodbridge, U.K.: Boydell Press.

Jung, C. G. 1953. *Collected Works*. Vol. 1. Translated by R. F. C. Hull. New York: Pantheon Books.

———. 1956. *Collected Works*. Vol. 5. Translated by R. F. C. Hull. New York: Pantheon Books.

———. 1959. *Collected Works*. Vol. 9_1. Translated by R. F. C. Hull. New York: Pantheon Books.

———. 1960. *Collected Works*. Vol. 3. Translated by R. F. C. Hull. New York: Pantheon Books.

———. 1963. *Collected Works*. Vol. 11. Translated by R. F. C. Hull. New York: Pantheon Books.

———. 1964. *Collected Works*. Vol. 10. Translated by R. F. C. Hull. New York: Pantheon Books.

———. 1968. *Collected Works*. Vol. 9_2. Translated by R. F. C. Hull. Princeton: Princeton University Press.

———. 1969. *Collected Works*. Vol. 8. Translated by R. F. C. Hull. Princeton: Princeton University Press.

———. 1976. *The Visions Seminar*. 2 vols. Zurich: Spring Publications.

————. 1984. *Seminar on Dream Analysis.* Edited by William McGuire. Princeton: Princeton University Press.

————. 1990. *Collected Works.* Vol. 6. Translated by H. G. Baines. Revised by R. F. C. Hull. Princeton: Princeton University Press.

Karmay, Samten G., ed. 1972. *The Treasury of Good Sayings: A Tibetan History of Bon.* Translated by Samten G. Karmay. London: Oxford University Press.

Kinsley, David. 1988. *Hindu Godesses.* Berkeley: University of California Press.

Kluger, Rivkah S. 1950. "The Image of the Marriage between God and Israel as it occurs in the Prophets of the Old Testament, Especially Ezekiel." *Spring.*

————. 1967. *Satan in the Old Testament.* Evanston, Ill.: Northwestern University Press.

————. 1991. *The Archetypal Significance of Gilgamesh.* Einsiedeln, Switzerland: Daimon Verlag.

————. 1995. *Psyche in Scripture.* Toronto: Inner City Books.

Knapp, Bettina L. 1971. *Jean Racine: Mythos and Renewal in Modern Theater.* University: University of Alabama Press.

————. 1980. *Theatre and Alchemy.* Detroit: Wayne State University Press.

————. 1997. *Women in Myth.* Albany: State University of New York Press.

Kravitz, Nathaniel. 1972. *Three Thousand Years of Hebrew Literature.* Chicago: Swallow Press.

Krishnamoorthy, K. 1982. *Kalidasa.* Delhi: Motilal Banarsidass.

Lal, P. 1959. *Great Sanskrit Plays.* New York: New Directions.

Landa, Friar Diego de. 1978. *Yucatan Before and After the Conquest.* Translated by William Gates. New York: Dover Publications.

Lalou, Marcelle. 1957. *Les religions du Tibet.* Paris: Presses Universitaires de France.

Larrington, Carolyne, ed. 1992. *The Feminist Companion to Mythology.* New York: Pandora.

Lauter, Estelle, and Carol S. Rupprecht. 1985. *Feminist Archetypal Theory.* Knoxville: University of Tennesee Press.

Lee, Grace Farrell. 1987. *From Exile to Redemption.* Carbondale: Southern Illinois University Press.

Leonard, Linda. 1982. *The Wounded Woman: Healing the Father-Daughter Relationshbip.* Athens: Ohio University Press, Swallow Press Books.

Le Plongeon, Augustus. 1886. *Sacred Mysteries among the Mayas and the Quichés, etc.* New York: R. Macoy.

Lerner, Harriet G. 1988. *Women in Therapy.* New York: Harper and Row.

Lévi-Strauss, Claude. 1990. *The Raw and the Cooked.* Translated by John Weightman and Darren Weightman. Chicago: University of Chicago Press.

MacCana, Proinsias. 1970. *Celtic Mythology.* New York: Hamlyn Publishing Group.

MacDonald, D. 1931. *Tibetan Tales.* Vol. 42 of the London Folklore Society. London.

Mackenzie, Donald A. 1978. *Myths of Pre-Columbian America.* London: Gresham Publishing Company, 1924. Reprint, Boston: Longwood Press.

Majupuria, Indra. 1990. *Tibetan Women Then and Now.* Bangkok: Pratunam.

Markale, Jean. 1975. *Women of the Celts.* Translated from the French by A. Mygind, C. Hauch, and P. Henry. Rochester, Vt.: Inner Traditions International.

McConnell, Winder. 1984. *The Nibelungenlied.* Boston: Twayne Publishers, 1984.

Miller, Mary, and Karl Taube. 1993. *The Gods and Symbols of Ancient Mexico and the Maya.* London: Thames and Hudson.

Mitchell, G. F. 1967. "Prehistoric Ireland." In *The Course of Irish History,* edited by T. W. Moody and F. Martin. Cork: Mercier Press.

Moody, T. W., and F. Martin, eds. 1967. *The Course of Irish History.* Cork: Mercier Press.

Moore, John Rees. 1971. *Masks of Love and Death: Yeats as Dramatist.* Ithaca: Cornell University Press.

Moreau, Pierre. 1943a. *Racine.* Paris: Hatier.

———. 1943b. *Racine, L'homme et l'œuvre.* Paris: Boivin.

Morin, Edgar. 1973. *Le Paradigme perdu: la nature humaine.* Paris: Editions du Seuil.

———. 1970. *L'homme et la mort.* Paris: Editions du Seuil.

Morley, Sylvanus Griswold. 1946. *The Ancient Maya.* Stanford, Calif.: Stanford University Press.

Mowatt, D. G., and Hugh Sacker. 1967. *The Nibelungenlied: An Interpretive Commentary.* Toronto: University of Toronto Press.

Mueller, Werner A. 1966. *The Nibelungenlied Today.* New York: AMS Press.

Mukherjee, Bhudeb Rasa-Jala-Nidhi. 1938. *Ocean of Indian Chemistry and Alchemy.* Vol. 5. Calcutta: J. N. Dey.

Murdock, Maureen. 1988. *The Heroine's Journey.* New York: Doubleday.

Narasimhan, Chakravarthi V., trans. 1965. *The Mahabharata.* New York: Columbia University Press.

Nathan, Leonard E. 1965. *The Tragic Drama of William Butler Yeats.* New York: Columbia University Press.

Neeson, Eoin. 1990. *Irish Myths and Legends.* Dublin: Mercier Press.

Neumann, Erich. 1955. *The Great Mother.* New York: Pantheon.

———. 1959. *Art and the Creative Unconscious.* New York: Pantheon.

———. 1970. *The Origins and History of Consciousness.* New York: Putnam.

———. 1989. *The Place of Creation.* Princeton: Princeton University Press.

Ochs, Carol. 1977. *Behind the Sex of God.* Boston: Beacon Press.

O'Flaherty, Wendy Doniger. 1982. *Hindu Myths.* Harmondsworth, U.K.: Penguin Books.

Orel, Harold, ed. 1976. *Irish History and Culture.* Lawrence: University Press of Kansas.

Paglia, Camille. 1975. *Sexual Personae.* New York: Vintage Books.

Parrinder, Geoffrey, trans. 1975. *The Bhagavad Gita*. New York: Dutton, 1975.

Perera, Sylvia Brinton. 1981. *Descent to the Goddess*. Toronto: Inner City Books.

Pierce, Kenneth. 1984. *The View from the Top of the Temple*. Albuquerque: University of New Mexico Press.

Picard, Raymond. 1961. *La Carrière de Jean Racine*. Paris: Gallimard.

Piggott, Stuart. 1975. *The Druids*. London: Thames and Hudson.

Prabhavananda, Swami, and Frederick Manchester, trans. 1957. *The Upanishads*. New York: Mentor Books.

Pratt, Annis. 1981. *Archetypal Patterns in Women's Fiction*. Bloomington: Indiana University Press.

Racine, Jean. 1950. *Œuvres complètes*. Paris: Gallimard.

———. 1967. *The Complete Plays of Jean Racine*. Translated by Samuel Solomon. New York: Random House.

Raynaud, Georges. 1925. *Les dieux, les héros et les hommes de l'ancien Guatémala d'après le Livre du conseil (Popol Vuh)*. Paris: E. Leroux.

Read, John. 1937. *Prelude to Chemistry*. New York: Macmillan.

Rees, Alwyn, and Hugh Sacker. 1961. "On Irony and Symbolism in the *Nibelungenlied:* Two Preliminary Notes." *German Life and Letters*, n.s., 14:271–81.

Rees, Brinley. 1971. *Celtic Heritage*. New York: Thames and Hudson.

Reis, Patricia. 1991. *Through the Goddess*. New York: Continuum.

Rich, Adrienne. 1978. *Of Woman Born*. New York: W. W. Norton.

Richardson, Hugh. 1962. *A Short History of Tibet*. New York: E. P. Dutton.

———. 1984. *Tibet and its History*. Boulder, Colo.: Shambhala.

Rivet, Paul. 1962. *Maya Cities*. Translated by by Miriam Kochan and Lionel Kochan. New York: G. P. Putnam's Sons.

Rodas, N. Flavio; Corzo Olivio Rodas; and Lawrence F. Hawkins. 1940. *Chichicastenango: The Kiché Indians: Their History and Culture, Sacred Symbols of Their Dress and Textiles*. Guatemala: n.p.

Roys, Ralph L., trans. 1967. *The Book of Chilam Balam of Chumayel*. 1933. Reprint, Norman: University of Oklahoma Press.

Rugg, Carmen Neutze de. 1977. *Designs in Guatemalan Textiles*. Guatemala: Editorial Piedra Santa.

Saravia, E.Albertina. 1977. *Popol Vuh: Ancient Stories of the Quiché Indians of Guatemala*. Guatemala: Editorial Piedra Santa.

Saxo Grammaticus. 1979. *History of the Danish People*. Translated by P. Fisher and Ellis Davidson. Cambridge: Cambridge University Press.

Schele, Linda, and Mary Ellen Miller. 1986. *The Blood of Kings*. New York: George Braziller.

Schele, Linda, David Freidel, and Joy Parker. 1990. *A Forest of Kings*. New York: William Morrow.

Sharkey, John. 1975. *Celtic Mysteries*. London: Thames and Hudson.

Sharp, Daryl. 1987. *Personality Types*. Toronto: Inner City Books.

Shen, Tsung-Lien, and Shen-Chi Liu. 1953. *Tibet*. Stanford, Calif.: Stanford University Press.

Siegel, Morris. 1943. "The Creation Myth and Acculturation in Acatan, Guatemala." *JAF* 56:120–26.

Singer, Isaac Bashevis. 1964. *Short Friday and Other Stories*. New York: Farrar, Straus, & Giroux.

———. 1966. *In My Father's Court*. New York: Farrar, Straus & Giroux.

———. 1991. *The Collected Stories*. New York: Farrar, Straus, & Giroux.

Smith, Daniel H. 1968. *Selections from Vedic Hymns*. Berkeley, Calif.: McCutchan Publishing Corp.

Snellgrove, David, and Hugh Richardson. 1968. *A Cultural History of Tibet*. New York: Praeger.

Snyder, Henry L. 1976. "From the Beginnings to the End of the Middle Ages." In *Irish History and Culture*, by Harold Orel.. Lawrence: University Press of Kansas.

Sogyal Rinpoche. 1992. *The Tibetan Book of Living and Dying*. Edited by Patrick Gaffney and Andrew Harvey. San Francisco: HarperCollins.

Stein, Rolf A. 1956. *L'épopée tibétaine de Gésar*. Bibl. d. Et., t. 61. Paris: Annales du Musée Guimet.

———. 1959. *Recherches sur l'épopée et le barde au Tibet*. Paris: Presses Universitaires de France.

———. 1962. *La Civilisation Tibétaine*. Paris: Dunod.

Steinsaltz, Rabbi Adin. 1989. *The Talmud: The Steinsaltz Edition*. New York: Random House.

Stillman, John Maxson. 1960. *The Story of Alchemy and Early Chemistry*. 1924. Reprint, New York: Dover Publications.

Taylor, Richard. 1984. *A Reader's Guide to the Plays of W. B. Yeats*. New York: St. Martin's Press.

Tedlock, Dennis. 1986. "Creation in the *Popol Vuh*: A Hermeneutical Approach." In *Symbol and Meaning Beyond the Closed Community: Essays in Mesoamerican Ideas*, edited by Gary H. Gossen, 76–83. Albany: State University of New York Press.

———, trans. 1985. *Popol Vuh*. New York: Simon and Schuster.

Telushkin, Joseph. 1991. *Jewish Legacy*. New York: William Morrow.

Thompson, E. A. 1965. *The Early Germans*. Oxford: Clarendon Press.

Thompson, J. E. S. 1970a. *Maya History and Religion*. Norman: University of Oklahoma Press, 1970a.

———. 1970b. *The Rise and Fall of Maya Civilization*. Norman: University of Oklahoma Press.

———. 1985. *Popol Vuh: The Mayan Book of the Dawn of Life*. New York: Simon and Schuster.

Trungpa Rinpoche, Chögyam. 1981. Foreword to *The Superhuman Life of Gesar of Ling. La vie surhumaine de Gésar de Ling*, by Alexandra David-Neel and Lama Yongden. Translated by Violet Sydney. Boulder, Colo.: Prajna Press.

Turville-Petre, E. O. G. 1964. *Myth and Religion of the North*. Westport, Conn.: Greenwood Press.

Tucci, Giuseppe. 1967. *The Land of Snows*. Translated by J. E. Stapleton Driver.

———. 1980. *The Religions of Tibet*. Translated by Geoffrey Samuel. Berkeley: University of California Press.

Ulanov, A. B. 1981. *Receiving Woman*. Philadelphia: Westminster Press.

Upadhyaya, Bhagwat Saran. 1968. *India in Kalidasa*. Delhi: S. Chand.

Ure, Peter. 1946. *Towards a Mythology. Studies in the Poetry of W. B. Yeats*. Liverpool: University Press of Liverpool.

———. 1963. *Yeats the Playwright*. New York: Barnes and Noble.

Waddell, L. Austine. 1967. *The Buddhism of Tibet*. Reprint, Cambridge: W. Heffer and Sons.

Wailes, Stephen L. 1978. "The *Niebelungenlied* as Heroic Epic." In *Heroic Epic and Saga*, edited by J. Oinas. Bloomington: Indiana University Press.

Ware, James. 1966. *Alchemy, Medicine, Religion*. Cambridge: MIT Press.

Warner, Marina. 1976. *Alone of All Her Sex*. New York: Alfred A. Knopf.

Webster, Graham. 1986. *Celtic Religion in Roman Britain*. Totowa, N.J.: Barnes and Noble.

Whitmont, Edward C. 1984. *Return of the Goddess*, New York: Crossroad.

Woodman, Marion. 1982. *Addiction to Perfection*. Toronto: Inner City Books.

———. 1985. *The Pregnant Virgin*. Toronto: Inner City Books.

Yeats, W. B. 1938. *A Vision*. New York: Macmillan.

———. 1964. *Eleven Plays of William Butler Yeats*. Edited by A. Norman Jeffares. New York: Collier Books.

———. 1973. *Memoirs*. New York: Macmillan.

———. 1977. *Essays and Introductions*. New York: Collier Books.

Younger, Paul. N.d. *Introduction to Indian Religious Thought*. Philadelphia: Westminster Press.

Zimmer, Heinrich. 1974a. *Myths and Symbols in Indian Art and Civilization*. Princeton: Princeton University Press.

———. 1974b. *Philosophies of India*. Princeton: Princeton University Press.

Zink, Georges. 1950. *Les légendes héroïques de Dietrich et d'Ermrich dans les littératures germaniques*. Paris: IAC.

INDEX

261